Full Stack Development with Spring Boot and React

Third Edition

Build modern and scalable full stack applications using the power of Spring Boot and React

Juha Hinkula

BIRMINGHAM—MUMBAI

Full Stack Development with Spring Boot and React

Third Edition

Copyright © 2022 Packt Publishing

Group Product Manager: Pavan Ramchandani
Publishing Product Manager: Bhavya Rao
Senior Editor: Hayden Edwards
Content Development Editor: Abhishek Jadhav
Technical Editor: Simran Udasi
Copy Editor: Safis Editing
Project Coordinator: Rashika Ba
Proofreader: Safis Editing
Indexer: Hemangini Bari
Production Designer: Shyam Sundar Korumili
Marketing Coordinator: Anamika Singh

First published: June 2018
Second edition: May 2019
Third edition: May 2022

Production reference: 2300522

Published by Packt Publishing Ltd.
Livery Place
35 Livery Street
Birmingham
B3 2PB, UK.

ISBN 978-1-80181-678-6

www.packt.com

To my wife, Pirre, and daughter, Anni, for their support and the time that I was able to spend on this project. To all my motivated students, for inspiring me to continue the lifelong journey of learning.

– Juha Hinkula

Contributors

About the author

Juha Hinkula is a software development lecturer at Haaga-Helia University of Applied Sciences in Finland. He received an MSc degree in computer science from the University of Helsinki. He has over 18 years of industry experience in software development. Over the past few years, he has focused on modern full stack development. He is also a passionate mobile developer with Android-native technology and React Native.

About the reviewers

Kaidong Shen is a graduate student of information systems at Northeastern University. He used to be engaged in backend development in JD Retail Group and participated in building a backend service for an IoT platform.

Kolawole Mangabo is an expert full stack engineer who has designed, developed, and re-engineered products in foodtech and fintech with test-driven development and software quality assurance concepts. His other areas of expertise include Python, JavaScript, TypeScript, Django, Nodejs, React, AWS, PostgreSQL, Sentry, Docker, and CI/CD. He's currently a software engineer at Quatro and builds fintech products at Transfa.

Table of Contents

Part 2: Frontend Programming with React

6

Setting Up the Environment and Tools – Frontend

7
Getting Started with React

8
Consuming the REST API with React

9
Useful Third-Party Components for React

Part 3: Full Stack Development

10

Setting up the Frontend for Our Spring Boot RESTful Web Service

11

Adding CRUD Functionalities

12

Styling the Frontend with React MUI

13

Testing Your Frontend

Preface

Getting started with full stack development can be daunting. Even developers who are familiar with the best tools, such as Spring Boot and React, can struggle to nail the basics, let alone master the more advanced elements. If you're one of these developers, this comprehensive guide covers everything you need!

This updated edition of the Full Stack Development with Spring Boot and React book will take you from novice to proficient in this expansive domain. Taking a practical approach, this book will first walk you through the latest Spring Boot features for creating a robust backend, covering everything from setting up the environment and dependency injection to security and testing.

Once this has been covered, you'll advance to React frontend programming. If you've ever wondered about custom Hooks, third-party components, and MUI, this book will demystify all that and much more. You'll explore everything that goes into developing, testing, securing, and deploying your applications using all the latest tools from Spring Boot, React, and other cutting-edge technologies.

By the end of this book, you'll not only have learned the theory of building modern full stack applications but also have developed valuable skills that add value in any setting.

Who this book is for

This book is for Java developers who are familiar with Spring Boot but don't know where to start when it comes to building full stack applications. You'll also find this book useful if you're a frontend developer with knowledge of JavaScript basics, looking to learn full stack development, or a full stack developer experienced in other technology stacks, looking to learn a new one.

What this book covers

Chapter 1, Setting Up the Environment and Tools – Backend, explains how to install the software needed for backend development and how to create your first Spring Boot application.

Chapter 2, Understanding Dependency Injection, explains the basics of dependency injection.

Chapter 3, Using JPA to Create and Access a Database, introduces JPA and explains how to create and access databases with Spring Boot.

Chapter 4, Creating a RESTful Web Service with Spring Boot, explains how to create RESTful web services using Spring Data REST.

Chapter 5, Securing and Testing Your Backend, explains how to secure your backend using Spring Security and JWT.

Chapter 6, Setting Up the Environment and Tools – Frontend, explains how to install the software needed for frontend development.

Chapter 7, Getting Started with React, introduces the basics of the React library.

Chapter 8, Consuming the REST API with React, shows how to use REST APIs with React using the Fetch API.

Chapter 9, Useful Third-Party Components for React, demonstrates some useful components that we'll use in our frontend development.

Chapter 10, Setting up the Frontend for Our Spring Boot RESTful Web Service, explains how to set up the React app and Spring Boot backend for frontend development.

Chapter 11, Adding CRUD Functionalities, shows how to implement CRUD functionalities to the React frontend.

Chapter 12, Styling the Frontend with React MUI, shows how to polish the user interface using the React MUI component library.

Chapter 13, Testing Your Frontend, explains the basics of React frontend testing.

Chapter 14, Securing Your Application, explains how to secure the frontend using JWT.

Chapter 15, Deploying Your Application, demonstrates how to deploy an application to Heroku and how to use Docker containers.

Chapter 16, Best Practices, explains the basic technologies that are needed to become a full stack developer and covers some basic best practices for software development.

To get the most out of this book

You will need Spring Boot version 2.x in this book. There are some major changes in the upcoming Spring Boot version 3 that are mentioned in the book. All code examples are tested using Spring Boot 2.6 and React 18 on Windows. When installing any React libraries, you should check the latest installation command from their documentation and see whether there are any major changes related to the version used in this book.

Software/hardware covered in the book	Operating system requirements
Java version 8 or newer	Windows, macOS, or Linux
Spring Boot version 2.x	Windows, macOS, or Linux
MariaDB	Windows, macOS, or Linux
React	Windows, macOS, or Linux

If you are using the digital version of this book, we advise you to type the code yourself or access the code from the book's GitHub repository (a link is available in the next section). Doing so will help you avoid any potential errors related to the copying and pasting of code.

Download the example code files

You can download the example code files for this book from GitHub at `https://github.com/PacktPublishing/Full-Stack-Development-with-Spring-Boot-and-React`. If there's an update to the code, it will be updated in the GitHub repository.

We also have other code bundles from our rich catalog of books and videos available at `https://github.com/PacktPublishing/`. Check them out!

Code in Action

The *Code in Action* videos for this book can be viewed at `https://bit.ly/3t3Qe4r`.

Download the color images

We also provide a PDF file that has color images of the screenshots and diagrams used in this book. You can download it here: `https://static.packt-cdn.com/downloads/9781801816786_ColorImages.pdf`.

Conventions used

There are a number of text conventions used throughout this book.

`Code in text`: Indicates code words in text, database table names, folder names, filenames, file extensions, pathnames, dummy URLs, user input, and Twitter handles. Here is an example: "Import `Button` to the `AddCar.js` file."

A block of code is set as follows:

```
<dependency>
      <groupId>org.springframework.boot</groupId>
      <artifactId>spring-boot-starter-web</artifactId>
</dependency>
```

When we wish to draw your attention to a particular part of a code block, the relevant lines or items are set in bold:

```
public class Car {
    @Id
    @GeneratedValue(strategy=GenerationType.AUTO)
    private long id;
    private String brand, model, color, registerNumber;
    private int year, price;
}
```

Any command-line input or output is written as follows:

```
npm install component_name
```

Bold: Indicates a new term, an important word, or words that you see onscreen. For instance, words in menus or dialog boxes appear in **bold**. Here is an example: "You can select the **Run** menu and press **Run as | Java Application**."

> **Tips or Important Notes**
> Appear like this.

Get in touch

Feedback from our readers is always welcome.

General feedback: If you have questions about any aspect of this book, email us at customercare@packtpub.com and mention the book title in the subject of your message.

Errata: Although we have taken every care to ensure the accuracy of our content, mistakes do happen. If you have found a mistake in this book, we would be grateful if you would report this to us. Please visit www.packtpub.com/support/errata and fill in the form.

Piracy: If you come across any illegal copies of our works in any form on the internet, we would be grateful if you would provide us with the location address or website name. Please contact us at copyright@packt.com with a link to the material.

If you are interested in becoming an author: If there is a topic that you have expertise in and you are interested in either writing or contributing to a book, please visit authors.packtpub.com.

Share Your Thoughts

Once you've read *Full Stack Development with Spring Boot and React*, we'd love to hear your thoughts! Scan the QR code below to go straight to the Amazon review page for this book and share your feedback.

https://www.amazon.in/review/create-review/error?asin=1801816786

Your review is important to us and the tech community and will help us make sure we're delivering excellent quality content.

Part 1: Backend Programming with Spring Boot

Here, you will be familiarized with the basics of Spring Boot. This part provides the knowledge required to use databases and create RESTful web services.

We will cover the following chapters in this section:

- *Chapter 1, Setting Up the Environment and Tools – Backend*
- *Chapter 2, Understanding Dependency Injection*
- *Chapter 3, Using JPA to Create and Access a Database*
- *Chapter 4, Creating a RESTful Web Service with Spring Boot*
- *Chapter 5, Securing and Testing Your Backend*

1

Setting Up the Environment and Tools – Backend

In this book, we will learn about full stack development using Spring Boot in the backend and React in the frontend. The first half of this book focuses on backend development, and in the second half of the book, we will implement the frontend.

In this chapter, we will set up the environment and tools needed for backend programming with Spring Boot. Spring Boot is a modern Java-based backend framework that makes development faster than with traditional Java-based frameworks. With Spring Boot, you can make a standalone web application that has an embedded application server.

There are a lot of different **integrated development environment (IDE)** tools that you can use to develop Spring Boot applications. In this chapter, we will install Eclipse, which is an open source IDE for multiple programming languages. We will create our first Spring Boot project by using the Spring Initializr project starter page. The project is then imported into Eclipse and executed. Reading the console log is a crucial skill when developing Spring Boot applications, which we will also cover.

In this chapter, we will look into the following topics:

- Installing Eclipse
- Understanding Maven
- Using Spring Initializr
- Installing MariaDB

Technical requirements

The Java **software development kit (SDK)**, version 8 or higher, is necessary to use the Eclipse IDE. In this book, we are using the Windows operating system, but all tools are available for Linux and macOS as well.

Download the code for this chapter from GitHub, at `https://github.com/PacktPublishing/Full-Stack-Development-with-Spring-Boot-and-React/tree/main/Chapter01`.

Check out the following video to see the Code in Action: `https://bit.ly/3t32Fx6`

Installing Eclipse

Eclipse is an open source programming IDE developed by the Eclipse Foundation. An installation package or installer can be downloaded from `https://www.eclipse.org/downloads`. Eclipse is available for Windows, Linux, and macOS.

You can either download a ZIP package of Eclipse or an installer package that executes the installation wizard. In the installer, you should select **Eclipse IDE for Enterprise Java and Web Developers**, as shown in the following screenshot:

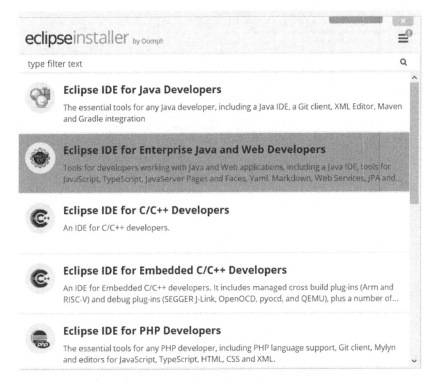

Figure 1.1 – Eclipse installer

If using the ZIP package, you just have to extract the package to your local disk, and it will contain an executable `eclipse.exe` file that you can run by double-clicking on the file. You should download the **Eclipse IDE for Enterprise Java and Web Developers** package.

Eclipse is an IDE for multiple programming languages, such as Java, C++, and Python. Eclipse contains different perspectives for your needs, which are a set of views and editors in the Eclipse workbench. The following screenshot shows common perspectives for Java development:

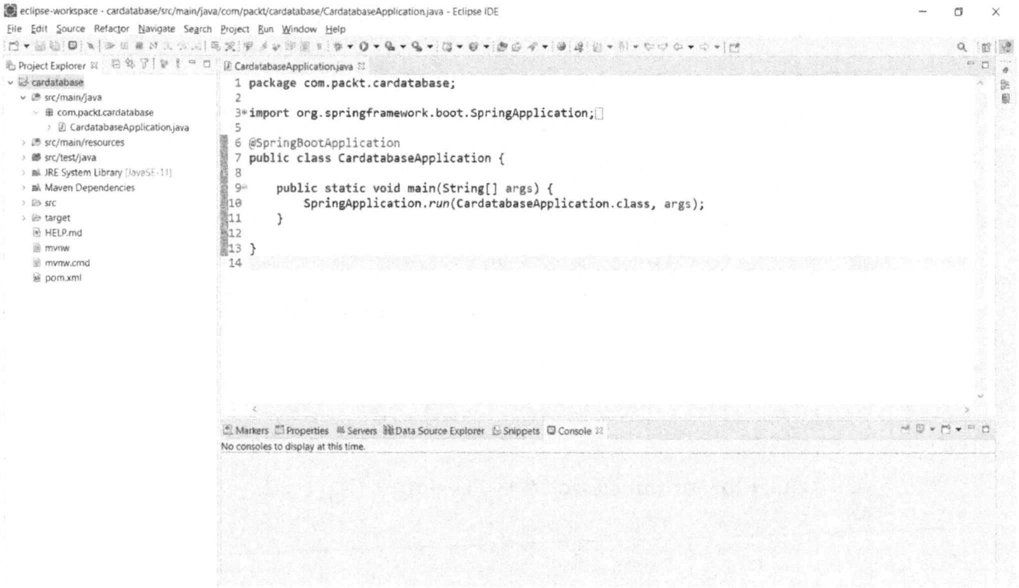

Figure 1.2 – Eclipse workbench

On the left-hand side, we have **Project Explorer**, where we can see our project structure and resources. **Project Explorer** is also used to open files by double-clicking on them. The files will be opened in the editor, which is located in the middle of the workbench. The **Console** view can be found in the lower section of the workbench. This view is really important because it shows application logging messages.

> **Important Note**
>
> You can get **Spring Tool Suite (STS)** for Eclipse if you want, but we are not going to use it in this book because the plain Eclipse installation is enough for our purposes. STS is a set of plugins that makes Spring application development simple, and you can find more information about it here: `https://spring.io/tools`.

Now that we have installed Eclipse, let's take a quick look at what Maven is and how it helps us.

Understanding Maven

Apache Maven is a software project management tool that makes the software development process simpler and also unifies the development process.

> **Important Note**
>
> You can also use another project management tool called **Gradle** with Spring Boot, but in this book, we will focus on using Maven.

The basis of Maven is the **Project Object Model** (**POM**). The POM is a pom.xml file that contains basic information about a project. There are also all the dependencies that Maven should download to be able to build a project.

Basic information about a particular project can be found at the beginning of the pom.xml file, which defines—for example—the version of the application, the packaging format, and so on. The minimum version of the pom.xml file should contain the following:

- project root
- modelVersion
- groupId—**Identifier** (**ID**) of the project group
- artifactId—ID of the project (artifact)
- version—Version of the project (artifact)

Dependencies are defined in the dependencies section, as shown in the following pom.xml code:

```
<?xml version="1.0" encoding="UTF-8"?>
<project xmlns="http://maven.apache.org/POM/4.0.0"
    xmlns:xsi="http://www.w3.org/2001/XMLSchema-instance"
    xsi:schemaLocation="http://maven.apache.org/POM/4.0.0
    https://maven.apache.org/xsd/maven-4.0.0.xsd">
    <modelVersion>4.0.0</modelVersion>
    <parent>
<groupId>org.springframework.boot</groupId>
        <artifactId>spring-boot-starter-parent
```

```
                    </artifactId>
          <version>2.5.2</version>
          <relativePath/> <!-- lookup parent from
                    repository -->
     </parent>
     <groupId>com.packt</groupId>
     <artifactId>cardatabase</artifactId>
     <version>0.0.1-SNAPSHOT</version>
     <name>cardatabase</name>
     <description>Demo project for Spring Boot
          </description>
     <properties>
  <java.version>11</java.version>
     </properties>
     <dependencies>
     <dependency>

          <groupId>org.springframework.boot</groupId>
               <artifactId>spring-boot-starter-web
                    </artifactId>
          </dependency>

          <dependency>
               <groupId>org.springframework.boot</groupId>
               <artifactId>spring-boot-devtools
                    </artifactId>
               <scope>runtime</scope>
               <optional>true</optional>
          </dependency>
          <dependency>
```

```
        <groupId>org.springframework.boot</groupId>
            <artifactId>spring-boot-starter-test
                </artifactId>
            <scope>test</scope>
        </dependency>
    </dependencies>

    <build>
        <plugins>
            <plugin>

                <groupId>org.springframework.boot</groupId>
                <artifactId>spring-boot-maven-plugin
                    </artifactId>
                </plugin>
            </plugins>
        </build>
    </project>
```

Maven is normally used from the command line, but Eclipse contains embedded Maven, and that handles all the Maven operations we need. Therefore, we are not focusing on Maven command-line usage here. The most important thing is to understand the structure of the pom.xml file and how to add new dependencies to it. We will learn how to add dependencies using Spring Initializr in the next section. Later in this book, we will also add new dependencies manually to the pom.xml file.

In the next section, we will create our first Spring Boot project and see how we can run it using the Eclipse IDE.

Using Spring Initializr

We will create our backend project using **Spring Initializr**, which is a web-based tool that's used to create **Spring Boot** projects. Then, we will learn how to run our Spring Boot project using the Eclipse IDE. At the end of this section, we will also look at how you can utilize Spring Boot logging.

Creating a project

To create our project using Spring Initalizr, complete the following steps:

1. Open Spring Initializr by navigating to `https://start.spring.io` using your web browser. You should then see the following page:

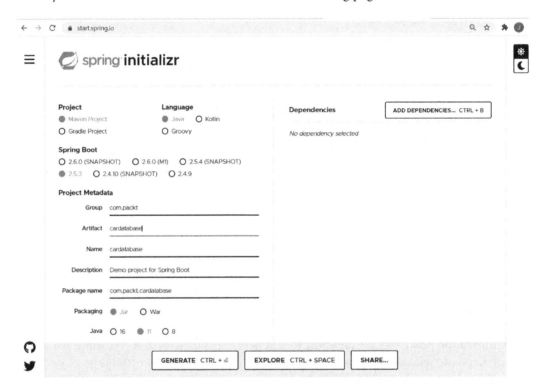

Figure 1.3 – Spring Initializr

2. We will generate a **Maven Project** with **Java** and the latest stable **Spring Boot** version. In the **Group** field, we will define our group ID (`com.packt`) that will also become a base package in our Java project. In the **Artifact** field, we will define an artifact ID (`cardatabase`) that will also be the name of our project in Eclipse.

> **Important Note**
>
> Select the correct Java version in Spring Initializr. In this book, we are using Java version 11. You should select the same version that you are using in your Eclipse IDE.
>
> In the upcoming Spring Boot 3 version, the Java baseline is Java 17. But in this book, we are using Spring Boot 2.

3. By clicking the **ADD DEPENDENCIES...** button, we will select the starters and dependencies that are needed in our project. Spring Boot provides starter packages that simplify your Maven configuration. Spring Boot starters are actually a set of dependencies that you can include in your project. You can add dependencies by clicking the **ADD DEPENDENCIES...** button in Spring Initializr. We will start our project by selecting two dependencies—**Spring Web** and **Spring Boot DevTools**. You can type the dependencies into the search field or select from a list that appears, as illustrated in the following screenshot:

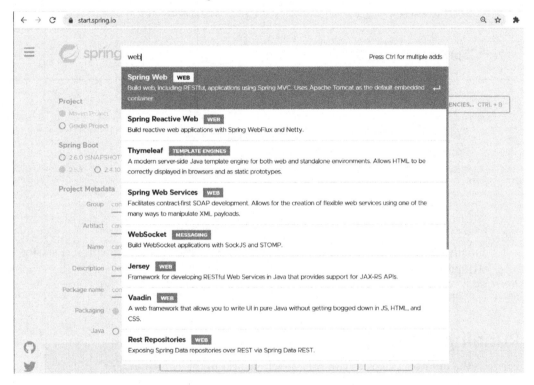

Figure 1.4 – Adding dependencies

The **Spring Boot DevTools** dependency provides us with the Spring Boot developer tools, which provide automatic restart functionality. It makes development much faster because the application is automatically restarted when changes have been saved. The web starter pack is a base for full stack development and provides an embedded Tomcat server. After you have added dependencies, your **Dependencies** section in Spring Initializr should look like this:

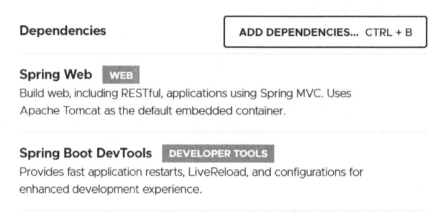

Figure 1.5 – Spring Initializr dependencies

4. Finally, you have to click on the **Generate** button, which generates a project starter ZIP package for us.

Next, we will learn how to run our project using the Eclipse IDE.

Running the project

Perform the following steps to run the Maven project in the Eclipse IDE:

1. Extract the project ZIP package that we created in the previous topic and open Eclipse.

2. We are going to import our project into the Eclipse IDE. To start the import process, select the **File | Import** menu and the import wizard will be opened. The following screenshot shows the first page of the wizard:

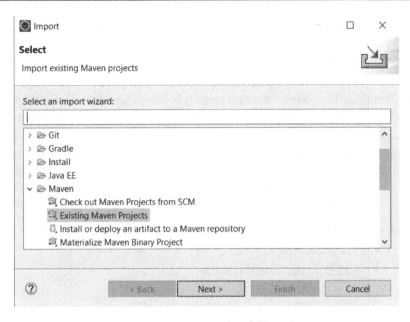

Figure 1.6 – Import wizard (Step 1)

3. In the first phase, you should select **Existing Maven Projects** from the list under the Maven folder, and then go to the next phase by pressing the **Next** > button. The following screenshot shows the second step of the import wizard:

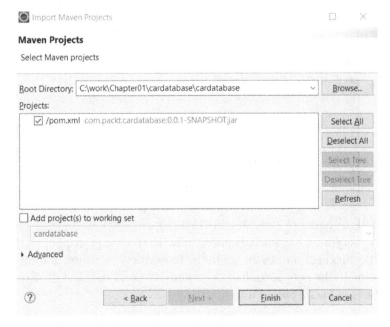

Figure 1.7 – Import wizard (Step 2)

4. In this phase, select the extracted project folder by pressing the **Browse...** button. Then, Eclipse will find the pom.xml file from the root of your project folder and show it inside the **Projects** section of the window.

5. Press the **Finish** button to finalize the import. If everything ran correctly, you should see the cardatabase project in the Eclipse IDE **Project Explorer**. It takes a while before the project is ready because all the dependencies will be downloaded by Maven after importing them. You can see the progress of the dependency download in the bottom-right corner of Eclipse. The following screenshot shows the Eclipse IDE **Project Explorer** after a successful import:

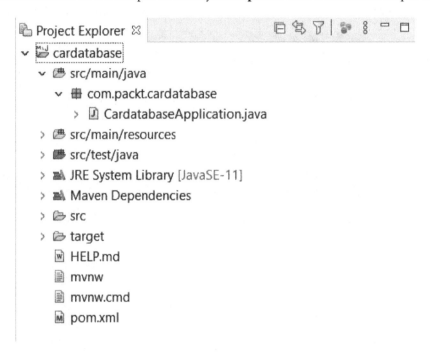

Figure 1.8 – Project Explorer

Project Explorer also shows the package structure of our project. In the beginning, there is only one package called com.packt.cardatabase. Under that package is our main application class, called CardatabaseApplication.java.

6. Now, we don't have any functionality in our application, but we can run it and see whether everything has started successfully. To run the project, open the main class by double-clicking on it, as shown in the following screenshot, and then press the **Run** button in the Eclipse toolbar. Alternatively, you can select the **Run** menu and press **Run as | Java Application**:

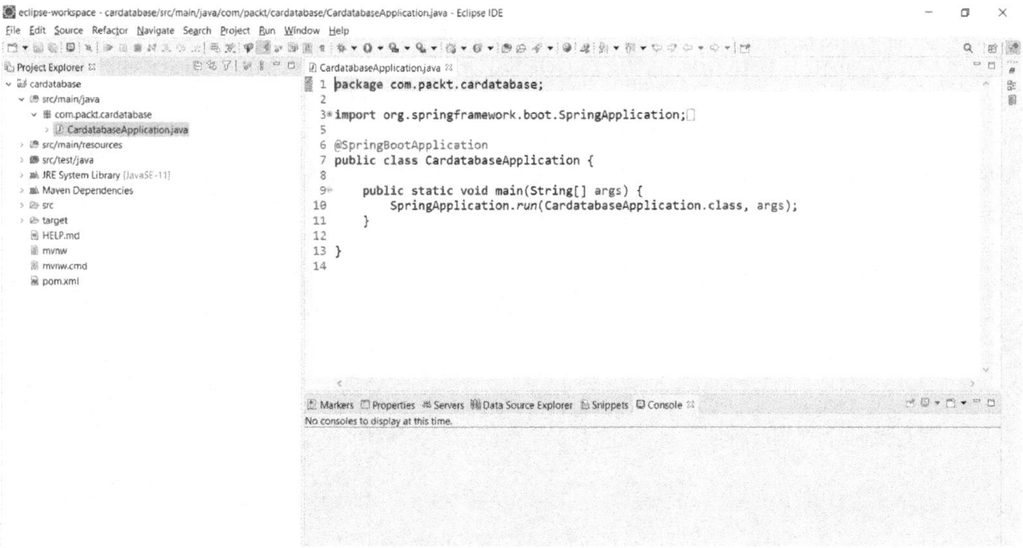

Figure 1.9 – Cardatabase project

You can see the **Console** view open in Eclipse, and that contains important information about the execution of the project. This is the view where all log texts and error messages appear, so it is really important to check the content of the view when something goes wrong.

Now, if the project was executed correctly, you should see the started CardatabaseApplication class in the text at the end of the console. The following screenshot shows the content of the Eclipse console after our Spring Boot project has been started:

Figure 1.10 – Eclipse console

In the root of our project, there is the pom.xml file, which is the Maven configuration file for our project. If you look at the dependencies inside the file, you can see that there are now dependencies that we selected on the Spring Initializr page. There is also a test dependency included automatically without any selection, as illustrated in the following code snippet:

```
<dependencies>
    <dependency>
        <groupId>org.springframework.boot</groupId>
        <artifactId>spring-boot-starter-web
        </artifactId>
    </dependency>

    <dependency>
        <groupId>org.springframework.boot</groupId>
        <artifactId>spring-boot-devtools</artifactId>
        <scope>runtime</scope>
        <optional>true</optional>
    </dependency>
    <dependency>
        <groupId>org.springframework.boot</groupId>
        <artifactId>spring-boot-starter-test
        </artifactId>
        <scope>test</scope>
    </dependency>
</dependencies>
```

In the following chapters, we are going to add more functionality to our application, and then we will add more dependencies manually to the pom.xml file.

Let's look at the Spring Boot main class more carefully. At the beginning of the class, there is the @SpringBootApplication annotation, which is actually a combination of multiple annotations, such as the following:

Annotation	Description
`@EnableAutoConfiguration`	This enables Spring Boot automatic configuration. Spring Boot will automatically configure your project based on dependencies. For example, if you have the `spring-boot-starter-web` dependency, Spring Boot assumes that you are developing a web application and configures your application accordingly.
`@ComponentScan`	This enables the Spring Boot component scan to find all the components of your application.
`@Configure`	This defines a class that can be used as a source of bean definitions.

Table 1.1 – SpringBootApplication annotations

The following code snippet shows the Spring Boot application's `main` class:

```
package com.packt.cardatabase;

import org.springframework.boot.SpringApplication;
import org.springframework.boot.autoconfigure.
SpringBootApplication;

@SpringBootApplication
public class CardatabaseApplication {
    public static void main(String[] args) {
        SpringApplication.run
                (CardatabaseApplication.class, args);
    }
}
```

The execution of the application starts from the `main` method, as in standard Java applications.

> **Important Note**
> It is recommended that you locate the main application class in the root package above other classes. A common reason for an application not working correctly is due to Spring Boot being unable to find some critical classes.

Spring Boot development tools

Spring Boot development tools make the application development process simpler. The most important feature of the development tools is automatic restart whenever files on `classpath` are modified. Projects will include the developer tools if the following dependency is added to the Maven `pom.xml` file:

```
<dependency>
    <groupId>org.springframework.boot</groupId>
    <artifactId>spring-boot-devtools</artifactId>
    <scope>runtime</scope>
    <optional>true</optional>
</dependency>
```

Development tools are disabled when you create a fully-packed production version of your application. The application is automatically restarted when you make changes to your project's `classpath` files. You can test that by adding one comment line to your `main` class, as follows:

```
package com.packt.cardatabase;


import org.springframework.boot.SpringApplication;
import org.springframework.boot.autoconfigure.
SpringBootApplication;


@SpringBootApplication
public class CardatabaseApplication {
    public static void main(String[] args) {
        // After adding this comment the application is
restarted
        SpringApplication.run
                (CardatabaseApplication.class, args);
    }
}
```

After saving the file, you can see in the console that the application has restarted.

Logs and problem solving

Logging can be used to monitor your application flow, and it is a good way to capture unexpected errors in your program code. Spring Boot starter packages provide a logback that we can use for logging without any configuration. The following sample code shows how you can use logging:

```
package com.packt.cardatabase;

import org.slf4j.Logger;
import org.slf4j.LoggerFactory;
import org.springframework.boot.SpringApplication;
import org.springframework.boot.autoconfigure.
SpringBootApplication;

@SpringBootApplication
public class CardatabaseApplication {
    private static final Logger logger =
            LoggerFactory.getLogger
                    (CardatabaseApplication.class);

    public static void main(String[] args) {
        SpringApplication.run
                    (CardatabaseApplication.class, args);
        logger.info("Application started");
    }

}
```

The `logger.info` method prints a logging message in the console. Logging messages can be seen in the console after you run a project, as shown in the following screenshot:

```
Markers  Properties  Servers  Data Source Explorer  Snippets  Console
CardatabaseApplication [Java Application]
2021-06-02 10:55:42.986  INFO 25060 --- [ restartedMain] w.s.c.ServletWebServerApplicationContext : Root WebApplicationContext: initializ
2021-06-02 10:55:43.063  INFO 25060 --- [ restartedMain] o.s.b.d.a.OptionalLiveReloadServer       : LiveReload server is running on port
2021-06-02 10:55:43.069  INFO 25060 --- [ restartedMain] o.s.b.w.embedded.tomcat.TomcatWebServer  : Tomcat started on port(s): 8080 (http
2021-06-02 10:55:43.070  INFO 25060 --- [ restartedMain] c.p.cardatabase.CardatabaseApplication   : Started CardatabaseApplication in 0.3
2021-06-02 10:55:43.071  INFO 25060 --- [ restartedMain] o.s.b.a.ApplicationAvailabilityBean      : Application availability state Livene
2021-06-02 10:55:43.072  INFO 25060 --- [ restartedMain] .ConditionEvaluationDeltaLoggingListener : Condition evaluation unchanged
2021-06-02 10:55:43.072  INFO 25060 --- [ restartedMain] o.s.b.a.ApplicationAvailabilityBean      : Application availability state Readin
2021-06-02 10:55:43.072  INFO 25060 --- [ restartedMain] c.p.cardatabase.CardatabaseApplication   : Application started
```

Figure 1.11 – Logging message

There are seven different levels of logging: TRACE, DEBUG, INFO, WARN, ERROR, FATAL, and OFF. You can configure the level of logging in your Spring Boot application. properties file. The file can be found in the resources folder inside your project, as illustrated in the following screenshot:

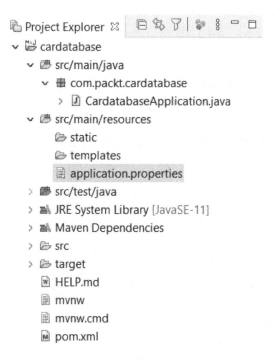

Figure 1.12 – Application properties file

If we set the logging level to DEBUG, we can see log messages from levels that are log level DEBUG or higher (that is DEBUG, INFO, WARN, and ERROR). In the following example, we set the log level for the root, but you can also set it at the package level:

```
logging.level.root=DEBUG
```

Now, when you run the project, you can't see the TRACE messages anymore. That might be a good setting for a development version of your application. The default logging level is INFO if you don't define anything else.

There is one common failure that you might encounter when running a Spring Boot application. Spring Boot uses Apache Tomcat (http://tomcat.apache.org/) as an application server by default. As a default, Tomcat is running on port 8080. You can change the port in the application.properties file. The following setting will start Tomcat on port 8081:

```
server.port=8081
```

If the port is occupied, the application won't start, and you will see the following message in the console:

```
***************************
APPLICATION FAILED TO START
***************************

Description:

Web server failed to start. Port 8080 was already in use.

Action:

Identify and stop the process that's listening on port 8080 or configure this application to listen on another port.
```

Figure 1.13 – Port already in use

If this happens, you will have to stop the process that is listening on port 8080 or use another port in your Spring Boot application.

In the next section, we will install a MariaDB database to use as a database in our backend.

Installing MariaDB

In *Chapter 3, Using JPA to Create and Access a Database*, we are going to use MariaDB, so you will need to install it locally on your computer. MariaDB is a widely used open source relational database. MariaDB is available for Windows and Linux, and you can download the latest stable community version from `https://mariadb.com/downloads/`. MariaDB is developed under a **GNU's Not UNIX (GNU) General Public License version 2 (GPLv2)** license. The following steps guides you to install MariaDB:

1. For Windows, there is the **Microsoft Installer (MSI)** installer, which we will use here. Download the installer and execute it. Install all features from the installation wizard, as illustrated in the following screenshot:

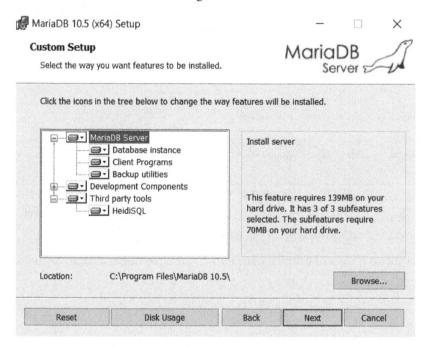

Figure 1.14 – MariaDB installation (Step 1)

2. In the next step, you should give the password for the root user. This password is needed in the next chapter when we'll connect our application to the database. The process is illustrated in the following screenshot:

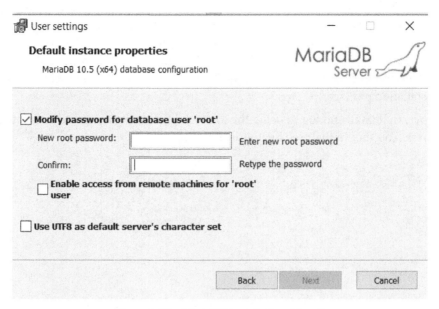

Figure 1.15 – MariaDB installation (Step 2)

3. In the next phase, we can use the default settings, as illustrated in the following screenshot:

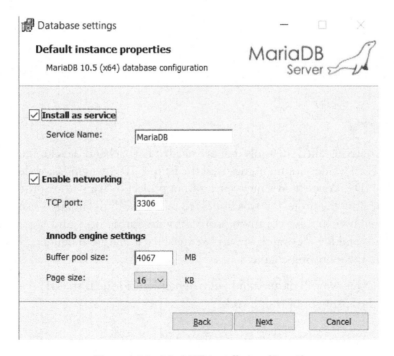

Figure 1.16 – MariaDB installation (Step 3)

4. Now, the installation will start, and MariaDB will be installed on your local computer. The installation wizard will install **HeidiSQL** for us. This is a graphical easy-to-use database client. We will use this to add a new database and make queries to our database. You can also use the Command Prompt included in the installation package.

5. Open HeidiSQL and log in using the password that you gave in the installation phase. You should then see the following screen:

Figure 1.18 – HeidiSQL

We now have everything needed to start the implementation of the backend.

Summary

In this chapter, we installed the tools that are needed for backend development with Spring Boot. For Java development, we used the Eclipse IDE, which is a widely used programming IDE. We created a new Spring Boot project by using the Spring Initializr page. After creating the project, it was imported to Eclipse and—finally—executed. We also covered how to solve common problems with Spring Boot and how to find important error and log messages. Finally, we installed a MariaDB database that we are going to use in the following chapters.

In the next chapter, we will understand what **dependency injection** (**DI**) is and how it can be used with the Spring Boot framework.

Questions

1. What is Spring Boot?

2. What is the Eclipse IDE?

3. What is Maven?

4. How do we create a Spring Boot project?

5. How do we run a Spring Boot project?

6. How do we use logging with Spring Boot?

7. How do we find error and log messages in Eclipse?

Further reading

Packt Publishing has other great resources for learning about Spring Boot, as listed here:

- *Learning Spring Boot 2.0 - Second Edition* by *Greg L. Turnquist* (`https://www.packtpub.com/product/learning-spring-boot-2-0-second-edition/9781786463784`)

- *Spring 5.0 Projects* by *Nilang Patel* (`https://www.packtpub.com/product/spring-5-0-projects/9781788390415`)

2
Understanding Dependency Injection

In this chapter, we will learn what **Dependency Injection** (**DI**) is and how we can use it with the Spring Boot framework. The Spring Boot framework provides DI; therefore, it is good to understand the basics. DI reduces component dependencies and makes your code easier to test and maintain.

In this chapter, we will look into the following:

- Introducing DI
- Using DI with Spring Boot

Technical requirements

Java SDK version 8 or higher is necessary to use Eclipse IDE. In this book, we are using Windows, but all the tools are available for Linux and macOS as well.

All of the code for this chapter can be found at the following GitHub link: `https://github.com/PacktPublishing/Full-Stack-Development-with-Spring-Boot-and-React/tree/main/Chapter02`.

Introducing DI

DI is a software development technique where we can create objects that depend on other objects. DI helps with interaction between classes but at the same time keeps the classes independent.

There are three types of classes in DI:

- A **service** is a class that can be used (this is the dependency).
- The **client** is a class that uses the dependency.
- The **injector** passes the dependency (the service) to the dependent class (the client).

The three types of classes in DI are shown in the following diagram:

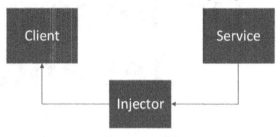

Figure 2.1 – DI

DI makes classes loosely coupled. This means that the creation of client dependencies is separated from the client's behavior, which makes unit testing easier.

Let's take a look at a simplified example of DI using Java code. In the following code, we don't have DI, because the client `Car` class is creating an object of the service class:

```java
public class Car {
    private Owner owner;

    public Car() {
        owner = new Owner();
    }
}
```

In the following code, the service object is not directly created in the client class. It is passed as a parameter in the class constructor:

```java
public class Car {
    private Owner owner;
```

```
public Car(Owner owner)   {
   this.owner = owner;
  }
}
```

The service class can also be an abstract class; we can then use any implementation of that in our client class and use mocks when testing.

There are different types of DI; let's take a look at two of them here:

- **Constructor injection**: Dependencies are passed to a client class constructor. An example of the constructor injection was already shown in the preceding `Car` example code.

- **Setter injection**: Dependencies are provided through setters. The following example code shows an example of the setter injection:

```
public class Car {
   private Owner owner;

   public void setOwner(Owner owner) {
      this.owner = owner;
   }
 }
```

Here, the dependency is now passed in the setter as an argument.

The DI reduces dependencies in your code and makes your code more reusable. It also improves the testability of your code. Now, we have learned the basics of DI; next, we will look at how DI is used in Spring Boot.

Using DI in Spring Boot

Spring Boot scans your application classes and registers classes with certain annotations (`@Service`, `@Repository`, and `@Controller`) as Spring beans. These beans can then be injected using an `@Autowired` annotation:

```
public class Car {
   @Autowired
   private Owner owner;
   ...
}
```

A fairly common situation is where we need database access for some operations, and, in Spring Boot, we use repository classes for that. In this situation, we can inject the repository class and start to use its methods:

```
public class Car {
  @Autowired
  private CarRepository carRepository;
  // Fetch all cars from db carRepositoty.findAll();
  ...
}
```

Java (javax.annotation) also provides an @Resource annotation that can be used to inject resources. You can define the name or type of the injected bean when using the @Resource annotation. For example, the following code shows some use cases. Imagine that we have a resource defined as follows:

```
@Configuration
public class ConfigFileResource
  @Bean(name="configFile")
  public File configFile() {
    File configFile = new File("configFile.xml");
    return configFile;
  }
}
```

We can then inject the bean by using an @Resource annotation:

```
// By bean name
@Resource(name="configFile")
private ConfigFile cFile


OR


// Without name
@Resource
private ConfigFile cFile
```

We have now gone through the basics of DI in Spring Boot. We will put this into practice in the following chapters.

Summary

In this chapter, we learned what DI is. We also learned how to use DI in the Spring Boot framework, which we are using in our backend.

In the next chapter, we will look at how we can use the **Java Persistent API (JPA)** with Spring Boot and how to set up a MariaDB database. We will also learn about the creation of CRUD repositories and the one-to-many connection between database tables.

Questions

1. What is DI?
2. How does the `@Autowired` annotation work in Spring Boot?
3. How do you inject resources in Spring Boot?

Further reading

Packt has other great resources for learning about Spring Boot:

- *Learning Spring Boot 2.0 (Second Edition)* by Greg L. Turnquist (`https://www.packtpub.com/product/learning-spring-boot-2-0-second-edition/9781786463784`)

- *Spring 5.0 Projects* by Nilang Patel (`https://www.packtpub.com/product/spring-5-0-projects/9781788390415`)

3
Using JPA to Create and Access a Database

This chapter covers how to use **Java Persistent API (JPA)** with Spring Boot and how to define a database by using entity classes. In the first phase, we will be using the H2 in-memory database for development and demonstration purposes. H2 is an in-memory SQL database that is good for fast development or demonstration purposes. In the second phase, we will move from H2 to use **MariaDB**. This chapter also describes the creation of CRUD repositories and a one-to-many connection between database tables.

In this chapter, we will cover the following topics:

- Basics of ORM, JPA, and Hibernate
- Creating the entity classes
- Creating CRUD repositories
- Adding relationships between tables
- Setting up the MariaDB database

Technical requirements

Java SDK version 8 or higher is necessary to use Spring Boot (`http://www.oracle.com/technetwork/java/javase/downloads/index.html`). The Spring Boot application we created in previous chapters is required.

A MariaDB installation is necessary to create the database application (`https://downloads.mariadb.org/`).

The code for this chapter can be found at the following GitHub link: `https://github.com/PacktPublishing/Full-Stack-Development-with-Spring-Boot-and-React/tree/main/Chapter03`.

Check out the following video to see the Code in Action: `https://bit.ly/3lVCuVe`

Basics of ORM, JPA, and Hibernate

Object Relational Mapping (**ORM**) is a technique that allows you to fetch from and manipulate a database by using an object-oriented programming paradigm. ORM is really good for programmers because it relies on object-oriented concepts rather than database structures. It also makes development much faster and reduces the amount of source code. ORM is mostly independent of databases, and developers don't have to worry about vendor-specific SQL statements.

Java Persistent API (**JPA**) provides object-relational mapping for Java developers. The JPA entity is a Java class that presents the structure of a database table. The fields of an entity class present the columns of the database tables.

Hibernate is the most popular Java-based JPA implementation and is used in Spring Boot by default. Hibernate is a mature product and is widely used in large-scale applications.

Next, we will start to implement our first entity class using the H2 database.

Creating the entity classes

An **entity class** is a simple Java class that is annotated with JPA's @Entity annotation. Entity classes use the standard JavaBean naming convention and have proper getter and setter methods. The class fields have private visibility.

JPA creates a database table called by the name of the class when the application is initialized. If you want to use some other name for the database table, you can use the @Table annotation in your entity class.

At the beginning of this chapter, we will use the H2 database (https://www. h2database.com/), which is embedded in our in-memory database. To be able to use JPA and the H2 database, we have to add the following dependencies to the pom.xml file:

```
<dependency>
    <groupId>org.springframework.boot</groupId>
    <artifactId>spring-boot-starter-data-jpa</artifactId>
</dependency>
<dependency>
    <groupId>com.h2database</groupId>
    <artifactId>h2</artifactId>
    <scope>runtime</scope>
</dependency>
```

Let's look at the following steps to create entity classes:

1. To create an entity class in Spring Boot, we must create a package for entities. The package should be created under the root package. To start this, activate the root package in Eclipse's **Project Explorer** and right-click to make a context menu appear.

2.   From this menu, select **New | Package**. The following screenshot shows how to create a package for entity classes:

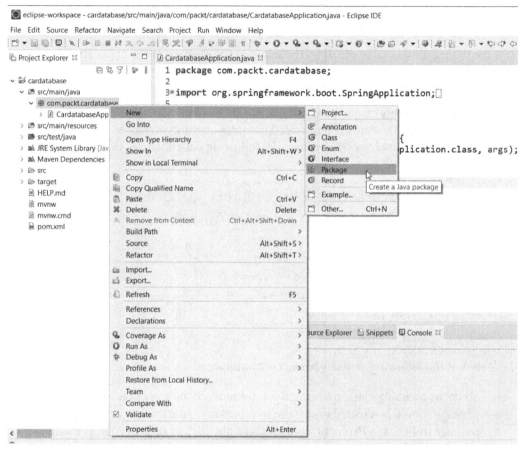

Figure 3.1 – New package

3.   We will name our package `com.packt.cardatabase.domain`:

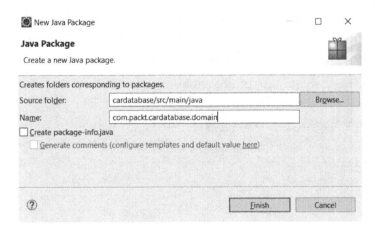

Figure 3.2 – New Java Package

4. Next, we will create our entity class. Activate a new `com.packt.cardatabase.domain` package, right-click it, and select **New | Class** from the menu.

5. Because we are going to create a car database, the name of the entity class will be `Car`. Type `Car` in the **Name** field and then press the **Finish** button, as shown in the following screenshot:

Figure 3.3 – New Java Class

6. Open the Car class file in the editor by double-clicking it in the project explorer. First, we must annotate the class with the @Entity annotation. The @Entity annotation is imported from the javax.persistence package:

```
package com.packt.cardatabase.domain;

import javax.persistence.Entity;

@Entity
public class Car {

}
```

> **Tip**
> You can use the Ctrl + Shift + O shortcut in Eclipse IDE to import missing packages automatically.

> **Important Note**
> This book is based on Spring Boot 2 and the upcoming Spring Boot 3 is using Jakarta EE instead of Java EE. Therefore, you need to replace all javax imports with jakarta if you are using Spring Boot 3.
>
> For example, javax.persistence.Entity is replaced with jakarta.persistence.Entity

7. Next, we must add some fields to our class. The entity class fields are mapped to database table columns. The entity class must also contain a unique ID that is used as a primary key in the database:

```
package com.packt.cardatabase.domain;

import javax.persistence.Entity;
import javax.persistence.GeneratedValue;
import javax.persistence.GenerationType;
import javax.persistence.Id;

@Entity
public class Car {
    @Id
    @GeneratedValue(strategy=GenerationType.AUTO)
    private long id;
```

```
    private String brand, model, color,
            registerNumber;
    private int year, price;
}
```

> **Tip**
> You can use the *Ctrl + Shift + O* shortcut in the Eclipse IDE to import missing packages automatically.

The primary key is defined by using the `@Id` annotation. The `@GeneratedValue` annotation defines that the ID is automatically generated by the database. We can also define our key generation strategy; the `AUTO` type means that the JPA provider selects the best strategy for a particular database and that it is also the default generation type. As well as this, you can create a composite primary key by annotating multiple attributes with the `@Id` annotation.

The database columns are named according to class field naming conventions by default. If you want to use some other naming convention, you can use the `@Column` annotation. With the `@Column` annotation, you can define the column's length and whether the column is `nullable`. The following code shows an example of using the `@Column` annotation. With this definition, the column's name in the database is `explanation`, the length of the column is `512`, and it is not `nullable`:

```
@Column(name="explanation", nullable=false, length=512)
private String description
```

8. Finally, we must add getters, setters, and constructors with attributes to the entity class. We don't need an ID field in our constructor due to automatic ID generation. The source code of the `Car` entity class constructors is as follows:

> **Tip**
> Eclipse provides the automatic addition of getters, setters, and constructors. Activate your cursor inside the class and right-click. From the menu, select **Source | Generate Getters and Setters...** or **Source | Generate Constructor using fields...**.

```
package com.packt.cardatabase.domain;


import javax.persistence.Entity;
import javax.persistence.GeneratedValue;
import javax.persistence.GenerationType;
```

```
import javax.persistence.Id;

@Entity
public class Car {
    @Id
    @GeneratedValue(strategy=GenerationType.AUTO)
    private long id;
    private String brand, model, color,
        registerNumber;
    private int year, price;


    public Car() {}


    public Car(String brand, String model, String
        color,
            String registerNumber, int year, int
                price) {
        super();
        this.brand = brand;
        this.model = model;
        this.color = color;
        this.registerNumber = registerNumber;
        this.year = year;
        this.price = price;
    }
}
```

The following is the source code for the Car entity class's getters and setters:

```
public long getId() {
    return id;
}


public void setId(long id) {
    this.id = id;
}


public String getBrand() {
    return brand;
```

```
        }

    public void setBrand(String brand) {
        this.brand = brand;
    }

    public String getModel() {
        return model;
    }

    public void setModel(String model) {
        this.model = model;
    }
    // Rest of the setters and getters. See the whole
source    code from GitHub
```

9. We also have to add new properties to the `application.properties` file.
    This allows us to log the SQL statements to the console. Since Spring Boot version
    2.3.0, we also have to define the data source URL. Open the `application.`
    `properties` file and add the following two lines to the file:

    ```
    spring.datasource.url=jdbc:h2:mem:testdb
    spring.jpa.show-sql=true
    ```

    > **Important Note**
    >
    > When you are editing the `application.properties` file, you have to
    > make sure that there are no extra spaces at the end of the lines. Otherwise, the
    > settings won't work. This might happen often when you copy/paste settings.

10. Now, the `car` table is created in the database when we run the application. At this
    point, we can see the table creation statements in the console when running
    the application:

```
Markers  Properties  Servers  Data Source Explorer  Snippets  Console
CardatabaseApplication [Java Application]
2021-07-02 13:45:39.781  INFO 18388 --- [ restartedMain] o.hibernate.annotations.common.Version    : HCANN000001: Hibernate Commons Annota
2021-07-02 13:45:39.893  INFO 18388 --- [ restartedMain] org.hibernate.dialect.Dialect             : HHH000400: Using dialect: org.hiberna
Hibernate: drop table if exists car CASCADE
Hibernate: drop sequence if exists hibernate_sequence
Hibernate: create sequence hibernate_sequence start with 1 increment by 1
Hibernate: create table car (id bigint not null, brand varchar(255), color varchar(255), model varchar(255), price integer not null, regis
2021-07-02 13:45:40.345  INFO 18388 --- [ restartedMain] o.h.e.t.j.p.i.JtaPlatformInitiator        : HHH000490: Using JtaPlatform implemen
2021-07-02 13:45:40.351  INFO 18388 --- [ restartedMain] j.LocalContainerEntityManagerFactoryBean  : Initialized JPA EntityManagerFactory
2021-07-02 13:45:40.394  WARN 18388 --- [ restartedMain] JpaBaseConfiguration$JpaWebConfiguration  : spring.jpa.open-in-view is enabled by
```

Figure 3.4 – Car table SQL statements

> **Important Note**
>
> If `spring.datasource.url` is not defined in the `application.properties` file, Spring Boot creates a random data source URL that can be seen in the console when you run the application; for example, `H2 console available at '/h2-console'. Database available at 'jdbc:h2:mem:`**b92ad05e-8af4-4c33-b22d-ccbf9ffe491e**`'`.

11. The H2 database provides a web-based console that can be used to explore a database and execute SQL statements. To enable the console, we have to add the following lines to the `application.properties` file. The first setting enables the H2 console, while the second defines the path of the H2 console:

```
spring.h2.console.enabled=true
spring.h2.console.path=/h2-console
```

12. You can access the H2 console by navigating to `localhost:8080/h2-console` using your web browser. Use `jdbc:h2:mem:testdb` as **JDBC URL** and leave the **Password** field empty in the **Login** window. Press the **Connect** button to log into the console, as shown in the following screenshot:

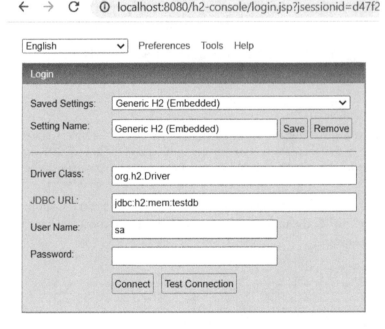

Figure 3.5 – H2 console login

> **Tip**
>
> You can also change the H2 database username and password by using the
> following settings in the `application.properties` file: `spring.`
> `datasource.username` and `spring.datasource.password`.

Now, you can see our `CAR` table in the database. You may notice that the register number
has an underscore between the words. The reason for the underscore is the camel case
naming of the attribute (`registerNumber`):

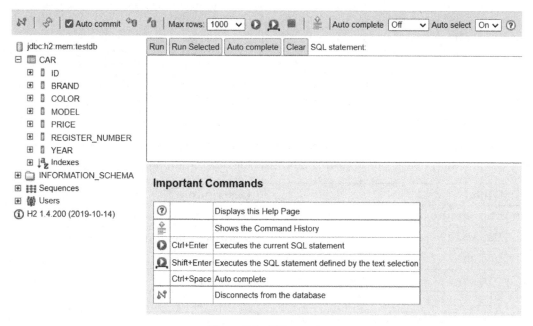

Figure 3.6 – H2 console

With that, we have created our first entity class and learned how JPA generates a database
table from the entity class. Next, we will create a repository class that provides CRUD
operations.

Creating CRUD repositories

The Spring Boot Data JPA provides a `CrudRepository` interface for **Create**, **Read**,
Update, and **Delete** (**CRUD**) operations. It provides CRUD functionalities to our
entity class.

Let's create our repository in the domain package, as follows:

1. Create a new class called CarRepository in the com.packt.cardatabase.
   domain package and modify the file according to the following code snippet:

```
package com.packt.cardatabase.domain;
import org.springframework.data.repository
.CrudRepository;

public interface CarRepository extends
CrudRepository<Car, Long> {
}
```

CarRepository now extends the Spring Boot JPA CrudRepository interface.
The <Car, Long> type arguments define that this is the repository for the Car
entity class and that the type of the ID field is Long.

The CrudRepository interface provides multiple CRUD methods that we can
now start to use. The following table lists the most commonly used methods:

Method	Description
long count()	Returns the number of entities
Iterable<T> findAll()	Returns all items of a given type
Optional<T> findById(ID Id)	Returns one item by ID
void delete(T entity)	Deletes an entity
void deleteAll()	Deletes all the entities in the repository
<S extends T> save(S entity)	Saves an entity
List<S> saveAll(Iterable<S> entities)	Saves multiple entities

Figure 3.7 – CRUD methods

If the method returns only one item, Optional<T> is returned instead of T. The
Optional class was introduced in Java 8 SE and is a type of single-value container
that either contains a value or doesn't. If there is value, the isPresent() method
returns true; otherwise, it returns false. If there is a value, you can get it by using
the get() method. By using Optional, we can prevent null pointer exceptions.

2. After adding the `CarRepository` class, your project structure should look as follows:

Figure 3.8 – Project structure

3. Now, we are ready to add some demonstration data to our H2 database. For that, we will use the Spring Boot `CommandLineRunner` interface. The `CommandLineRunner` interface allows us to execute additional code before the application has fully started. Therefore, it is a good point to add demo data to your database. Your Spring Boot application's `main` class implements the `CommandLineRunner` interface. Therefore, we should implement the `run` method, as shown in the following `CardatabaseApplication.java` code:

```
package com.packt.cardatabase;


import org.springframework.boot.CommandLineRunner;
import org.springframework.boot.SpringApplication;
```

```
import org.springframework.boot.autoconfigure.
SpringBootApplication;


@SpringBootApplication
public class CardatabaseApplication implements
CommandLineRunner {
    public static void main(String[] args) {
        SpringApplication.run
            (CardatabaseApplication.class, args);
    }


    @Override
    public void run(String... args) throws Exception {
        // Place your code here
    }
}
```

4. Next, we have to inject our car repository into the main class to be able to save
    new car objects to the database. An @Autowired annotation is used to enable
    dependency injection. This allows us to pass dependencies into an object. We will
    also add a logger to our main class:

```
package com.packt.cardatabase;


import org.slf4j.Logger;
import org.slf4j.LoggerFactory;
import org.springframework.beans.factory.annotation
.Autowired;
import org.springframework.boot.CommandLineRunner;
import org.springframework.boot.SpringApplication;
import org.springframework.boot.autoconfigure.
SpringBootApplication;


import com.packt.cardatabase.domain.Car;
import com.packt.cardatabase.domain.CarRepository;


@SpringBootApplication
public class CardatabaseApplication implements
```

```
CommandLineRunner {
    private static final Logger logger =
        LoggerFactory.getLogger(CardatabaseAp
            plication.class);


    @Autowired
    private CarRepository repository;

    public static void main(String[] args) {
        SpringApplication.run
            (CardatabaseApplication.class, args);
    }


    @Override
    public void run(String... args) throws Exception {
      // Place your code here
    }
}
```

5. Once we have injected the repository class, we can use the CRUD methods it provides in the `run` method. The following sample code shows how to insert a few cars into the database using the `save` method. We will also use the repository's `findAll()` method to fetch all the cars from the database and print them to the console using the logger:

```
// CardataseApplication.java run method
@Override
public void run(String... args) throws Exception {
    repository.save(new Car("Ford", "Mustang", "Red",
        "ADF-1121", 2021, 59000));
    repository.save(new  Car("Nissan", "Leaf",
"White",
        "SSJ-3002", 2019, 29000));
    repository.save(new Car("Toyota", "Prius",
        "Silver",
        "KKO-0212", 2020, 39000));

    // Fetch all cars and log to console
```

```
for (Car car : repository.findAll()) {
    logger.info(car.getBrand() + " " + car
        .getModel());
}
}
```

The `insert` statements and cars we logged can be seen in the Eclipse console once the application has been executed:

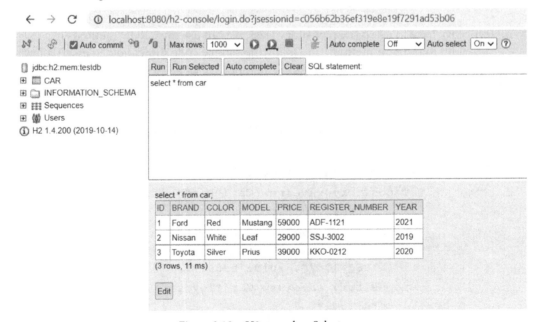

Figure 3.9 – Insert statements

You can now use the H2 console to fetch cars from the database, as shown in the following screenshot:

Figure 3.10 – H2 console – Select cars

6. You can define your queries in the Spring Data repositories. The query must start with a prefix; for example, `findBy`. After the prefix, you must define the entity class fields that are used in the query. The following is some sample code for three simple queries:

```
package com.packt.cardatabase.domain;

import java.util.List;
import org.springframework.data.repository.
CrudRepository;

public interface CarRepository extends CrudRepository
    <Car, Long> {
    // Fetch cars by brand
    List<Car> findByBrand(String brand);

    // Fetch cars by color
    List<Car> findByColor(String color);

    // Fetch cars by year
    List<Car> findByYear(int year);
}
```

There can be multiple fields after the `By` keyword, concatenated with the `And` and `or` keywords:

```
package com.packt.cardatabase.domain;

import java.util.List;
import org.springframework.data.repository.
CrudRepository;

public interface CarRepository extends CrudRepository
    <Car, Long> {
    // Fetch cars by brand and model
    List<Car> findByBrandAndModel(String brand, String
        model);

    // Fetch cars by brand or color
```

```
    List<Car> findByBrandOrColor(String brand, String
    color);
}
```

Queries can be sorted by using the `OrderBy` keyword in the query method:

```
package com.packt.cardatabase.domain;

import java.util.List;
import org.springframework.data.repository.
CrudRepository;
public interface CarRepository extends CrudRepository
    <Car, Long> {
    // Fetch cars by brand and sort by year
    List<Car> findByBrandOrderByYearAsc(String brand);
}
```

7. You can also create queries by using SQL statements via the `@Query` annotation. The following example shows the usage of a SQL query in `CrudRepository`:

```
package com.packt.cardatabase.domain;

import java.util.List;
import org.springframework.data.jpa.repository.Query;
import org.springframework.data.repository.
CrudRepository;

public interface CarRepository extends CrudRepository
    <Car, Long> {
    // Fetch cars by brand using SQL
    @Query("select c from Car c where c.brand = ?1")
    List<Car> findByBrand(String brand);
}
```

With the `@Query` annotation, you can use more advanced expressions, such as `like`. The following example shows the usage of the `like` query in `CrudRepository`:

```java
package com.packt.cardatabase.domain;


import java.util.List;
import org.springframework.data.jpa.repository.Query;
import org.springframework.data.repository.
CrudRepository;


public interface CarRepository extends CrudRepository
    <Car, Long> {
    // Fetch cars by brand using SQL
    @Query("select c from Car c where c.brand like
        %?1")
    List<Car> findByBrandEndsWith(String brand);
}
```

Spring Data JPA also provides `PagingAndSortingRepository`, which extends `CrudRepository`. This offers methods to fetch entities using pagination and sorting. This is a good option if you are dealing with larger amounts of data because you don't have to return everything from a large result set. You can also sort your data into some meaningful order. `PagingAndSortingRepository` can be created in a similar way to how we created `CrudRepository`:

```java
package com.packt.cardatabase.domain;


import org.springframework.data.repository.
PagingAndSortingRepository;


public interface CarRepository extends
    PagingAndSortingRepository <Car, Long> {
}
```

In this case, you now have the two new additional methods that the repository provides:

Method	Description
Iterable<T> findAll(Sort sort)	Returns all entities sorted by the given options
Page<T> findAll(Pageable pageable)	Returns all entities according to the given paging options

Figure 3.11 – PagingAndSortingRepository methods

At this point, we have completed our first database table and we are ready to add relationships between the database tables.

Adding relationships between tables

Next, we create a new table called owner that has a one-to-many relationship with the car table. In this case, a one-to-many relationship means that the owner can own multiple cars, but a car can only have one owner. The following **Unified Modeling Language (UML)** diagram shows the relationship between the tables:

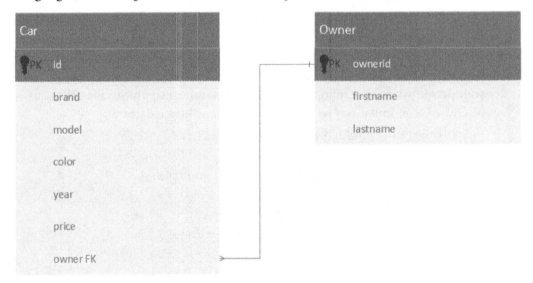

Figure 3.12 – OneToMany relationship

The following are the steps to create a new table:

1. First, we must create the Owner entity and repository in the com.packt. cardatabase.domain package. The Owner entity and repository are created in a similar way to the Car class.

The following is the source code of the Owner entity class:

```java
// Owner.java
package com.packt.cardatabase.domain;

import javax.persistence.Entity;
import javax.persistence.GeneratedValue;
import javax.persistence.GenerationType;
import javax.persistence.Id;

@Entity
public class Owner {
    @Id
    @GeneratedValue(strategy=GenerationType.AUTO)
    private long ownerid;
    private String firstname, lastname;

    public Owner() {}

    public Owner(String firstname, String lastname) {
        super();
        this.firstname = firstname;
        this.lastname = lastname;
    }

    public long getOwnerid() {
        return ownerid;
    }

    public void setOwnerid(long ownerid) {
        this.ownerid = ownerid;
    }

    public String getFirstname() {
        return firstname;
    }
```

```java
        public void setFirstname(String firstname) {
            this.firstname = firstname;
        }


        public String getLastname() {
            return lastname;
        }


        public void setLastname(String lastname) {
            this.lastname = lastname;
        }

}
```

The following is the source code for `OwnerRepository`:

```java
// OwnerRepository.java
package com.packt.cardatabase.domain;


import org.springframework.data.repository.
CrudRepository;


public interface OwnerRepository extends
    CrudRepository<Owner, Long> {

}
```

2. Now is a good time to check that everything is working. Run the project and check
    that both database tables have been created and that there are no errors in the
    console. The following screenshot shows the console messages when the tables
    are created:

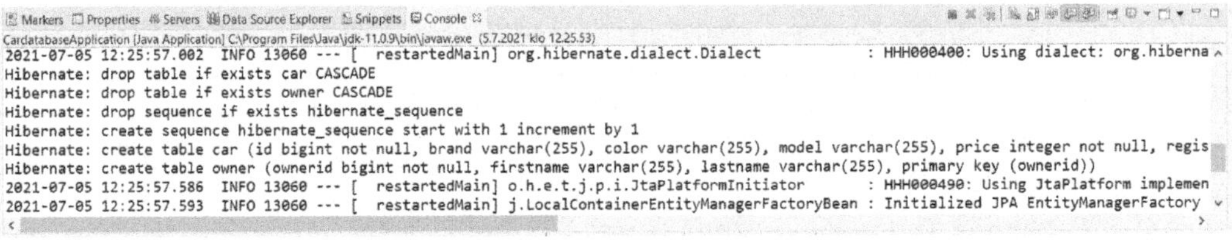

Figure 3.13 – The car and owner tables

Now, our domain package contains two entity classes and repositories:

Figure 3.14 – Project Explorer

3. The one-to-many relationship can be added by using the `@ManyToOne` and `@OneToMany` annotations. In the car entity class, which contains a foreign key, you must define the relationship with the `@ManyToOne` annotation. You should also add the getter and setter for the owner field. It is recommended that you use `FetchType.LAZY` for all associations. For the toMany relationships, that is the default value, but for the toOne relationships, you should define it. `FetchType` defines the strategy for fetching data from the database. The value can be either `EAGER` or `LAZY`. In our case, the lazy strategy means that when the owner is fetched from the database, all the cars associated with the owner will be fetched when needed. Eager means that the cars will be fetched immediately by the owner. The following source code shows how to define a one-to-many relationship in the `Car` class:

```
// Car.java
@ManyToOne(fetch=FetchType.LAZY)
@JoinColumn(name="owner")
```

```
private Owner owner;

//Getter and setter
public Owner getOwner() {
    return owner;
}

public void setOwner(Owner owner) {
    this.owner = owner;
}
```

4. In the owner entity site, the relationship is defined with the @OneToMany annotation. The type of field is List<Car> because the owner may have multiple cars. Now, you can add the getter and setter for this, as follows:

```
// Owner.java
@OneToMany(cascade=CascadeType.ALL, mappedBy="owner")
private List<Car> cars;

public List<Car> getCars() {
    return cars;
}

public void setCars(List<Car> cars) {
    this.cars = cars;
}
```

The @OneToMany annotation has two attributes that we are using. The cascade attribute defines how cascading affects the entities in the case of deletions or updates. The ALL attribute setting means that all operations are cascaded. For example, if the owner is deleted, the cars that are linked to that owner are deleted as well. The mappedBy="owner" attribute setting tells us that the Car class has the owner field, which is the foreign key for this relationship.

When you run the project, by looking in the console, you will see that the relationship has been created:

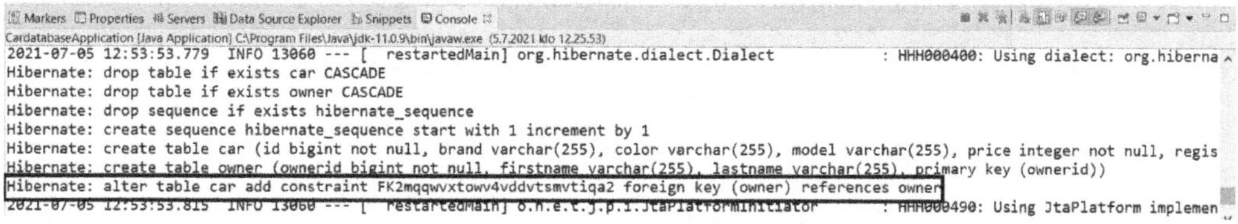

Figure 3.15 – Console

5. Now, we can add some owners to the database with `CommandLineRunner`. Let's also modify the `Car` entity class constructor and add an `owner` object there:

```
// Car.java constructor
public Car(String brand, String model, String color,
    String registerNumber, int year, int price, Owner
        owner) {
    super();
    this.brand = brand;
    this.model = model;
    this.color = color;
    this.registerNumber = registerNumber;
    this.year = year;
    this.price = price;
    this.owner = owner;
}
```

6. First, we will create two owner objects and save these to the database using the repository's `saveAll` method, which we can use to save multiple entities at once. To save the owners, we have to inject `OwnerRepository` into the main class. Then, we must connect the owners to the cars by using the `Car` constructor. First, let's modify the `CardatabaseApplication` class by adding the following imports:

```
// CardatabaseApplication.java
import com.packt.cardatabase.domain.Owner;
import com.packt.cardatabase.domain.OwnerRepository;
```

Now, let's inject `OwnerRepository` into the `CardatabaseApplication` class:

```
@Autowired
private OwnerRepository orepository;
```

At this point, we must modify the run method to save owners and link owners and cars:

```
@Override
public void run(String... args) throws Exception {
    // Add owner objects and save these to db
    Owner owner1 = new Owner("John" , "Johnson");
    Owner owner2 = new  Owner("Mary" , "Robinson");
    orepository.saveAll(Arrays.asList(owner1,
        owner2));

    // Add car object and link to owners and save
        these to db
    Car car1 = new Car("Ford", "Mustang", "Red",
      "ADF-1121", 2021, 59000, owner1);
    Car car2 = new Car("Nissan", "Leaf", "White",
      "SSJ-3002", 2019, 29000, owner2);
    Car car3 = new Car("Toyota", "Prius", "Silver",
      "KKO-0212", 2020, 39000, owner2);
    repository.saveAll(Arrays.asList(car1, car2,
        car3));

    for (Car car : repository.findAll()) {
        logger.info(car.getBrand() + " " +
            car.getModel());
    }
}
```

Now, if you run the application and fetch cars from the database, you will see that the owners are now linked to the cars:

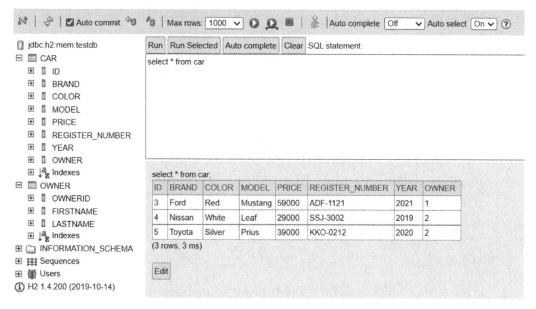

Figure 3.16 – OneToMany relationship

If you want to create a many-to-many relationship instead, which means, in practice, that an owner can have multiple cars and a car can have multiple owners, you should use the @ManyToMany annotation. In our example application, we will use a one-to-many relationship. The code that you have completed here will be needed in the next chapter.

Next, you will learn how to change the relationship to many-to-many. In a many-to-many relationship, it is recommended that you use `Set` instead of `List` with Hibernate:

1. In the `Car` entity class's many-to-many relationship, define the getters and setters in the following way:

```java
// Car.java
@ManyToMany(mappedBy="cars")
private Set<Owner> owners = new HashSet<Owner>();

public Set<Owner> getOwners() {
    return owners;
}

public void setOwners(Set<Owner> owners) {
    this.owners = owners;
}
```

2. In the `Owner` entity class, the many-to-many relationship is defined as follows:

```java
// Owner.java
@ManyToMany(cascade=CascadeType.PERSIST)
@JoinTable(name="car_owner",
    joinColumns = { @JoinColumn(name="ownerid") },
    inverseJoinColumns = { @JoinColumn(name="id") })
private Set<Car> cars = new HashSet<Car>();

public Set<Car> getCars() {
    return cars;
}

public void setCars(Set<Car> cars) {
    this.cars = cars;
}
```

3. Now, if you run the application, there will be a new join table called `car_owner` that is created between the car and owner tables. The join table is a special kind of table that manages the many-to-many relationship between two tables. The join table is defined by using the `@JoinTable` annotation. With this annotation, we can set the name of the join table and join columns. The following screenshot shows the database structure when using a many-to-many relationship:

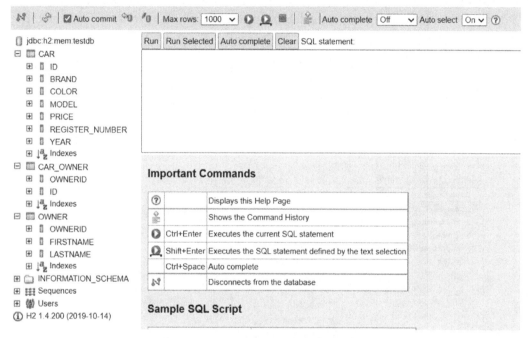

Figure 3.17 – Many-to-many relationship

Now, the database UML diagram looks as follows:

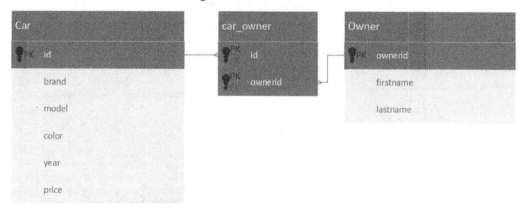

Figure 3.18 – ManyToMany relationship

Now that we have used an in-memory H2 database, we are going to use a MariaDB database instead.

Setting up a MariaDB database

Now, we will switch our database from H2 to MariaDB. The database tables are still created automatically by JPA. However, before we run our application, we have to create a database for it. In this section, we will be using the one-to-many relationship from the previous section.

The database can be created by using HeidiSQL. Open HeidiSQL and follow these steps:

1. Right-click inside the database list.

2. Then, select **Create new** | **Database**:

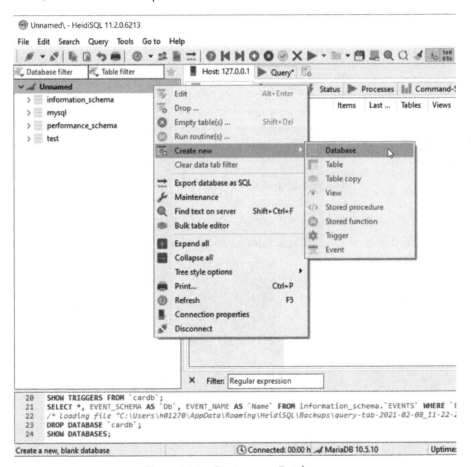

Figure 3.19 – Create new – Database

3. Let's name our database `cardb`. After clicking **OK**, you should see the new `cardb` database in the database list:

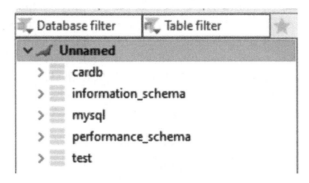

Figure 3.20 – The cardb database

4. In Spring Boot, add a MariaDB Java client dependency to the `pom.xml` file and remove the H2 dependency since we don't need it anymore:

```
<dependency>
    <groupId>org.mariadb.jdbc</groupId>
    <artifactId>mariadb-java-client</artifactId>
</dependency>
```

5. In the `application.properties` file, you must define the database connection. First, you must define the database's URL, username, password (defined in *Chapter 1, Setting Up the Environment and Tools – Backend*), and database driver class:

```
spring.datasource.url=jdbc:mariadb://localhost:3306/cardb
spring.datasource.username=root
spring.datasource.password=YOUR_PASSWORD
spring.datasource.driver-class-name=org.mariadb.jdbc.
Driver
```

6. The `spring.jpa.generate-ddl` setting defines whether JPA should initialize the database (true/false). The `spring.jpa.hibernate.ddl-auto` setting defines the behavior of the database initialization. The possible values are `none`, `validate`, `update`, `create`, and `create-drop`. The default value depends on your database. If you are using an embedded database such as H2, the default value is `create-drop`, otherwise, the default value is `none`. `create-drop` means that the database is created when an application starts and it is dropped when the application is stopped. The `create` value only creates the database when the application is started. The `update` value creates the database and updates the schema if it has changed:

```
spring.datasource.url=jdbc:mariadb:
//localhost:3306/cardb
spring.datasource.username=root
spring.datasource.password=YOUR_PASSWORD
spring.datasource.driver-class-name=
    org.mariadb.jdbc.Driver
spring.jpa.generate-ddl=true
spring.jpa.hibernate.ddl-auto=create-drop
```

7. Check that the MariaDB database server is running and run your Spring Boot application. After running the application, you should see the tables in MariaDB. You might have to refresh the database tree in HeidiSQL first by pressing the *F5* key. The following screenshot shows the HeidiSQL user interface once the database has been created. You can also run SQL queries in HeidiSQL, as shown in the following screenshot:

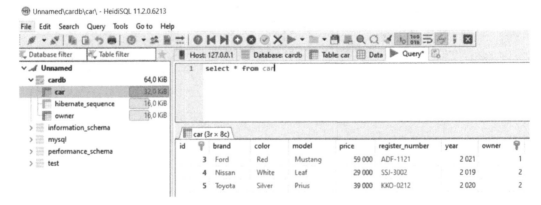

Figure 3.21 – MariaDB cardb

Now, your application is ready to use with MariaDB.

Summary

In this chapter, we used JPA to create our Spring Boot application database. First, we created entity classes, which are mapped to database tables. Then, we created `CrudRepository` for our entity class, which provides CRUD operations for the entity. After that, we managed to add some demo data to our database by using `CommandLineRunner`. We also created one-to-many relationships between two entities. At the beginning of this chapter, we used the H2 in-memory database, while at the end, we switched the database to MariaDB.

In the next chapter, we will create a RESTful web service for our backend. We will also look at testing the RESTful web service with the curl command-line tool, and also by using Postman GUI.

Questions

Answer the following questions to test your knowledge of this chapter:

1. What are ORM, JPA, and Hibernate?
2. How can you create an entity class?
3. How can you create `CrudRepository`?
4. What does `CrudRepository` provide for your application?
5. How can you create a one-to-many relationship between tables?
6. How can you add demo data to a database with Spring Boot?
7. How can you access the H2 console?
8. How can you connect your Spring Boot application to MariaDB?

Further reading

Packt has other great resources for Spring Boot:

- *Learning Spring Boot 2.0 – Second Edition* by *Greg L. Turnquist* (`https://www.packtpub.com/application-development/learning-spring-boot-20-second-edition`).

- *Master Hibernate and JPA with Spring Boot in 100 steps* (`https://www.packtpub.com/product/master-hibernate-and-jpa-with-spring-boot-in-100-steps-video/9781788995320`).

4

Creating a RESTful Web Service with Spring Boot

In this chapter, we will first create a **RESTful web service** using the controller class. After that, we will demonstrate how to use **Spring Data REST** to create a RESTful web service that also provides all CRUD functionalities automatically. After you have created a RESTful API for your application, you can implement the frontend using a JavaScript library such as React. We will be using the database application that we created in the previous chapter as a starting point.

Web services are applications that communicate over the internet using the HTTP protocol. There are many different types of web service architectures, but the principal idea across all designs is the same. In this book, we are creating a RESTful web service from what is nowadays a really popular design.

In this chapter, we will cover the following topics:

- Basics of a RESTful web service
- Creating a RESTful web service with Spring Boot
- Using Spring Data REST

Technical requirements

The Spring Boot application created in the previous chapters is required. Postman, cURL, or another suitable tool for transferring data using various HTTP methods is also necessary.

The following GitHub link will also be required: `https://github.com/PacktPublishing/Full-Stack-Development-with-Spring-Boot-and-React/tree/main/Chapter04`.

Check out the following video to see the Code in Action: `https://bit.ly/3PP2SOn`

Basics of REST

Representational State Transfer (**REST**) is an architectural style for creating web services. REST is not a standard, but it defines a set of constraints defined by Roy Fielding. The six constraints are as follows:

- **Stateless**: The server doesn't hold any information about the client state.
- **Client**: The client and server act independently. The server does not send any information without a request from the client.
- **Cacheable**: Many clients often request the same resources; therefore, it is useful to cache responses in order to improve performance.
- **Uniform interface**: Requests from different clients look the same. Clients may include, for example, a browser, a Java application, and a mobile application.
- **Layered system**: REST allows us to use a layered system architecture.
- **Code on demand**: This is an optional constraint.

The uniform interface is an important constraint, and it means that every REST architecture should have the following elements:

- **Identification of resources**: There are resources with their unique identifiers, for example, URIs in web-based REST services. REST resources should expose easily understood directory structure URIs. Therefore, a good resource naming strategy is very important.
- **Resource manipulation through representation**: When making a request to a resource, the server responds with a representation of the resource. Typically, the format of the representation is JSON or XML.

- **Self-descriptive messages**: Messages should have sufficient information that the server knows how to process them.

- **Hypermedia as the Engine of Application State (HATEOAS)**: Responses can contain links to other areas of service.

The RESTful web service that we are going to develop in the following topics follows the REST architectural principles above.

Creating a RESTful web service

In Spring Boot, all HTTP requests are handled by controller classes. To be able to create a RESTful web service, first, we have to create a controller class. We will create our own Java package for our controller:

1. Activate the root package in the Eclipse Project Explorer and right-click. Select **New | Package** from the menu. We will name our new package `com.packt.cardatabase.web`:

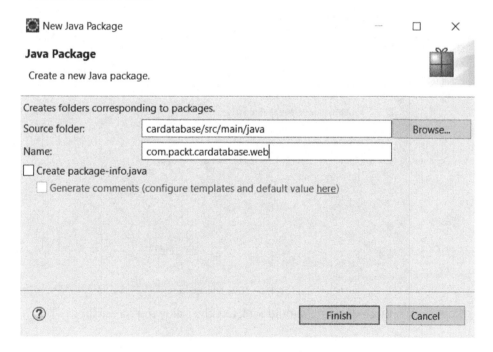

Figure 4.1 – New Java package

2. Next, we will create a new `controller` class in a new web package. Activate the `com.packt.cardatabase.web` package in the Eclipse Project Explorer. Right-click and select **New | Class** from the menu; we will name our class `CarController`:

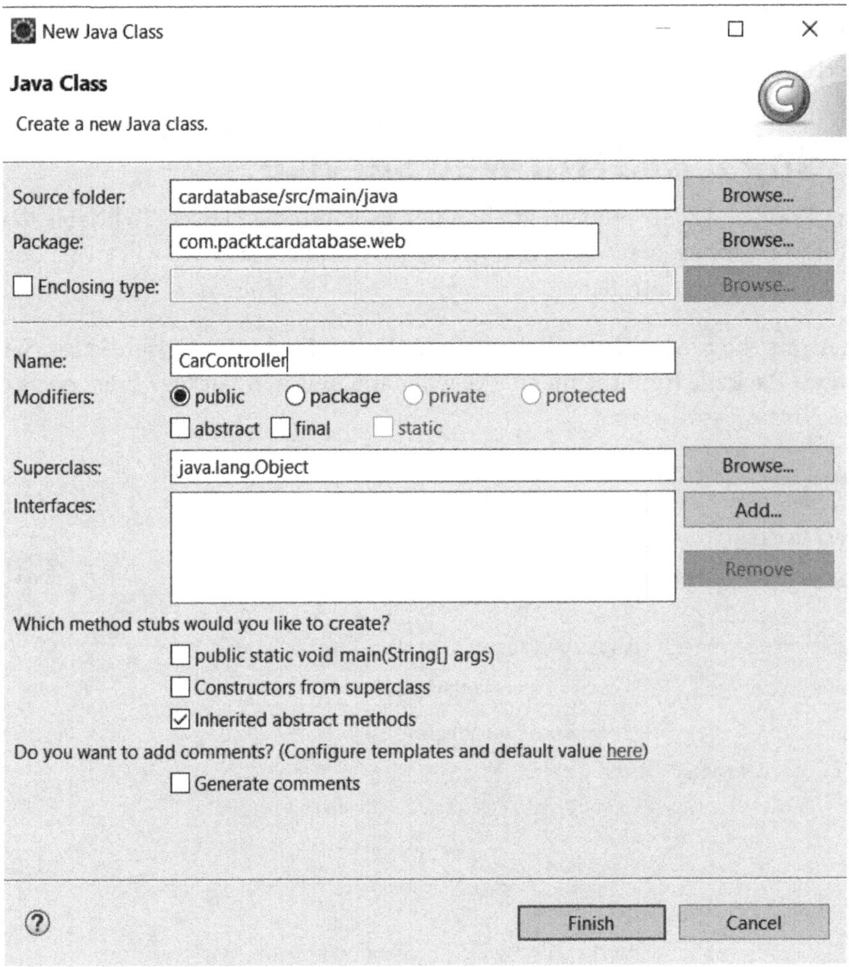

Figure 4.2 – New Java class

3. Now, your project structure should look like the following screenshot:

Figure 4.3 – Project structure

Important Note

If you create classes in the wrong package accidentally, you can drag and drop the files between packages in the Eclipse Project Explorer. Sometimes, the Eclipse Project Explorer view might not be rendered correctly when you make some changes. Refreshing Project Explorer helps (activate Project Explorer and press *F5*).

---

4. Open your controller class in the editor window and add the @RestController annotation before the class definition. Refer to the following source code. The @RestController annotation identifies that this class will be the controller for the RESTful web service:

```
package com.packt.cardatabase.web;
```

```
import org.springframework.web.bind.annotation.
RestController;

@RestController
public class CarController {
}
```

5. Next, we add a new method inside our controller class. The method is annotated with the @RequestMapping annotation, which defines the endpoint that the method is mapped to. In the following code snippet, you can see the sample source code. In this example, when a user navigates to the /cars endpoint, the getCars() method is executed:

```
package com.packt.cardatabase.web;

import    org.springframework.web.bind.annotation.
RequestMapping;
import org.springframework.web.bind.annotation.
RestController;

@RestController
public class CarController {
        @RequestMapping("/cars")
        public Iterable<Car> getCars() {
            // Fetch and return cars
        }
}
```

The getCars() method returns all the car objects, which are then marshaled to JSON objects by the **Jackson** library (https://github.com/FasterXML/jackson).

By default, @RequestMapping handles all the HTTP method (GET, PUT, POST, and so on) requests. You can define which method is accepted using the following @RequestMapping(value="/cars", method=GET) parameter. Now, this method handles only GET requests from the /cars endpoint. You can also use the @GetMapping annotation instead and then only the GET requests are mapped to the getCars() method. There are other annotations for the different HTTP methods, such as @GetMapping, @PostMapping, @DeleteMapping, and so on.

6. To be able to return cars from the database, we have to inject `CarRepository` into the controller. Then, we can use the `findAll()` method that the repository provides to fetch all cars. Due to the `@RestController` annotation, the data is now serialized to JSON format in the response. The following source code shows the controller code:

```java
package com.packt.cardatabase.web;

import org.springframework.beans.factory.annotation.Autowired;
import org.springframework.web.bind.annotation.RequestMapping;
import org.springframework.web.bind.annotation.RestController;

import com.packt.cardatabase.domain.Car;
import com.packt.cardatabase.domain.CarRepository;

@RestController
public class CarController {
    @Autowired
    private CarRepository repository;

    @RequestMapping("/cars")
    public Iterable<Car> getCars() {
        return repository.findAll();
    }
}
```

7. Now, we are ready to run our application and navigate to `localhost:8080/cars`. We can see that there is something wrong, and the application seems to be in an infinite loop. This happens on account of our one-to-many relationship between the car and owner tables. So, what happens in practice? First, the car is serialized, and it contains an owner who is then serialized, and that, in turn, contains cars that are then serialized and so on. To avoid this, we can use different solutions. One way is to use the `@JsonIgnore` annotation to the `cars` field in the `Owner` class, which ignores the `cars` field in the serialization process. We will also use the `@JsonIgnoreProperties` annotation to ignore fields that are generated by Hibernate:

```java
// Owner.java
import com.fasterxml.jackson.annotation.JsonIgnore;
import com.fasterxml.jackson.annotation.
JsonIgnoreProperties;

@Entity
@JsonIgnoreProperties({"hibernateLazyInitializer",
    "handler"})
public class Owner {
    @Id
    @GeneratedValue(strategy=GenerationType.AUTO)
    private long ownerid;
    private String firstname, lastname;

    public Owner() {}

    public Owner(String firstname, String lastname) {
        super();
        this.firstname = firstname;
        this.lastname = lastname;
    }

    @JsonIgnore
    @OneToMany(cascade=CascadeType.ALL, mappedBy=
        "owner")
    private List<Car> cars;
```

8. Now, when you run the application and navigate to `localhost:8080/cars`, everything should go as expected and you will get all the cars from the database in JSON format, as shown in the following screenshot:

```
←  →  C    ⓘ localhost:8080/cars
1    // 20210706124616
2    // http://localhost:8080/cars
3
4  ▾ [
5  ▾    {
6          "id": 3,
7          "brand": "Ford",
8          "model": "Mustang",
9          "color": "Red",
10         "registerNumber": "ADF-1121",
11         "year": 2021,
12         "price": 59000,
13 ▾       "owner": {
14            "ownerid": 1,
15            "firstname": "John",
16            "lastname": "Johnson"
17         }
18      },
19 ▾    {
20         "id": 4,
21         "brand": "Nissan",
22         "model": "Leaf",
23         "color": "White",
24         "registerNumber": "SSJ-3002",
25         "year": 2019,
```

Figure 4.4 – GET request to http://localhost:8080/cars

Important Note

Your output might differ from the screenshot due to using a different browser. In this book, we are using the Chrome browser and the JSON Viewer extension, which makes JSON output more readable. JSON Viewer can be downloaded from the Chrome Web Store for free.

We have written our first RESTful web service, which returns all the cars. Spring Boot provides a much more powerful way of creating RESTful web services and we go through this in the next topic.

Using Spring Data REST

Spring Data REST (`https://spring.io/projects/spring-data-rest`) is part of the Spring Data project. It offers an easy and fast way to implement RESTful web services with Spring. To start using Spring Data REST, you have to add the following dependency to the `pom.xml` file:

```
<dependency>
  <groupId>org.springframework.boot</groupId>
  <artifactId>spring-boot-starter-data-rest</artifactId>
</dependency>
```

By default, Spring Data REST finds all public repositories from the application and creates RESTful web services for your entities automatically. In our case, we have two repositories: `CarRepository` and `OwnerRepository`, therefore Spring Data REST creates RESTful web services automatically for those repositories.

You can define the endpoint of service in your `application.properties` file as follows:

```
spring.data.rest.basePath=/api
```

Now, you can access the RESTful web service from the `localhost:8080/api` endpoint. By calling the root endpoint of the service, it returns the resources that are available. Spring Data REST returns JSON data in the **Hypertext Application Language (HAL)** format. The HAL format provides a set of conventions for expressing hyperlinks in JSON and it makes your RESTful web service easier to use for frontend developers:

```
     ←  →  C    ⓘ localhost:8080/api

1      // 20210706130242
2      // http://localhost:8080/api
3
4  ▾   {
5  ▾     "_links": {
6  ▾       "cars": {
7            "href": "http://localhost:8080/api/cars"
8          },
9  ▾       "owners": {
10           "href": "http://localhost:8080/api/owners"
11         },
12 ▾       "profile": {
13           "href": "http://localhost:8080/api/profile"
14         }
15       }
16     }
```

Figure 4.5 – Spring Boot Data REST resources

We can see that there are links to the car and owner entity services. The Spring Data REST service path name is derived from the entity class name. The name will then be pluralized and uncapitalized. For example, the entity Car service path name will be cars. The profile link is generated by Spring Data REST and contains application-specific metadata. If you want to use different path naming, you can use the @RepositoryRestResouce annotation in your repository class as shown in the next example:

```
package com.packt.cardatabase.domain;


import org.springframework.data.repository.CrudRepository;
import org.springframework.data.rest.core.annotation.
RepositoryRestResource;


@RepositoryRestResource(path="vehicles")
public interface CarRepository extends CrudRepository<Car,
    Long> {

}
```

Now, if you call the endpoint `localhost:8080/api`, you can see that endpoint is changed from `/cars` to `/vehicles`.

```
←  →  C    ⓘ  localhost:8080/api

1     // 20210707132317
2     // http://localhost:8080/api
3
4  ▾  {
5  ▾    "_links": {
6  ▾      "owners": {
7          "href": "http://localhost:8080/api/owners"
8        },
9  ▾      "cars": {
10         "href": "http://localhost:8080/api/vehicles"
11       },
12 ▾      "profile": {
13         "href": "http://localhost:8080/api/profile"
14       }
15     }
16   }
```

Figure 4.6 – Spring Boot Data REST resources

You can remove the different naming and we will continue with the default endpoint name, `/cars`.

Now, we'll start to examine different services more carefully. There are multiple tools available for testing and consuming RESTful web services. In this book, we are using the **Postman** (`https://www.postman.com/downloads/`) desktop app, but you can use tools that you are familiar with, such as **cURL**. Postman can be acquired as a desktop application or as a browser plugin. cURL is also available for Windows 10 by using Windows Ubuntu Bash.

If you make a request to the `/cars` endpoint, `http://localhost:8080/api/cars`, using the `GET` method (note, you can use a web browser for `GET` requests), you will get a list of all the cars, as shown in the following screenshot:

```
1      // 20210706130838
2      // http://localhost:8080/api/cars
3
4    ▾ {
5    ▾    "_embedded": {
6    ▾      "cars": [
7    ▾        {
8             "brand": "Ford",
9             "model": "Mustang",
10            "color": "Red",
11            "registerNumber": "ADF-1121",
12            "year": 2021,
13            "price": 59000,
14   ▾        "_links": {
15   ▾          "self": {
16               "href": "http://localhost:8080/api/cars/3"
17             },
18   ▾          "car": {
19               "href": "http://localhost:8080/api/cars/3"
20             },
21   ▾          "owner": {
22               "href": "http://localhost:8080/api/cars/3/owner"
23             }
24           }
25         },
26   ▾      {
27            "brand": "Nissan",
28            "model": "Leaf",
29            "color": "White",
```

Figure 4.7 – Fetch cars

In the JSON response, you can see that there is an array of cars, and each car contains car-specific data. All the cars also have the _links attribute, which is a collection of links, and with these links, you can access the car itself or get the owner of the car. To access one specific car, the path will be http://localhost:8080/api/cars/{id}.

The GET request to `http://localhost:8080/api/cars/3/owner` returns the owner of the car with `id` 3. The response now contains owner data, a link to the owner, and links to other cars of the owner:

```
                localhost:8080/api/cars/3/owner
1       // 20210706131159
2       // http://localhost:8080/api/cars/3/owner
3
4     ▾ {
5           "firstname": "John",
6           "lastname": "Johnson",
7     ▾     "_links": {
8     ▾         "self": {
9                   "href": "http://localhost:8080/api/owners/1"
10              },
11    ▾         "owner": {
12                  "href": "http://localhost:8080/api/owners/1"
13              },
14    ▾         "cars": {
15                  "href": "http://localhost:8080/api/owners/1/cars"
16              }
17          }
18      }
```

Figure 4.8 – Car owner

The Spring Data REST service provides all CRUD operations. The following table shows which HTTP methods you can use for different CRUD operations:

HTTP Method	CRUD
GET	Read
POST	Create
PUT/PATCH	Update
DELETE	Delete

Figure 4.9 – Spring Data REST operations

Next, we will look at how to delete a car from the database by using our RESTful web service. In a delete operation, you have to use the DELETE method and the link to the car that will be deleted (`http://localhost:8080/api/cars/{id}`).

The following screenshot shows how you can delete one car with id 3 by using the Postman desktop app (note, you have to check some car id from your database and use that instead). In Postman, you have to select the correct HTTP method from the drop-down list, enter the request URL, and then click the **Send** button:

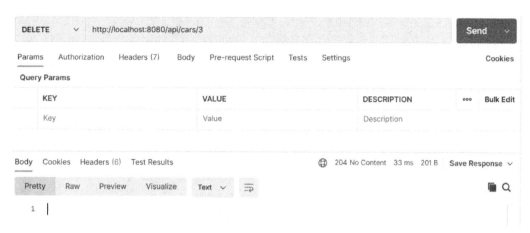

Figure 4.10 – DELETE request to delete car

If everything went correctly, you will see the response status **204 No Content** in Postman. After the successful delete request, you will also see that there are now two cars left in the database if you make a GET request to the http://localhost:8080/api/cars/ endpoint. If you got the **404 Not Found** status in the response, check that you are using a car ID that exists in the database.

When we want to add a new car to the database, we have to use the POST method, and the request URL is http://localhost:8080/api/cars. The header must contain the Content-Type field with the value application/json, and the new car object will be embedded in the request body in JSON format. Here is one car example:

```
{
  "brand":"Toyota",
  "model":"Corolla",
  "color":"silver",
  "registerNumber":"BBA-3122",
  "year":2021,
  "price":32000
}
```

If you click the **Body** tab and select **raw** in Postman, you can type a new car JSON string to the **Body** tab as shown in the following screenshot:

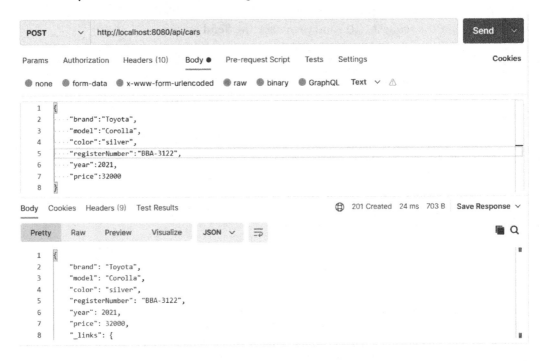

Figure 4.11 – POST request to add a new car

You also have to set a header by clicking the **Headers** tab in Postman, as shown in the following screenshot:

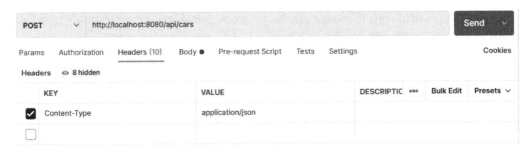

Figure 4.12 – POST request headers

The response will send a newly created car object back and the status of the response will be 201 Created if everything went correctly. Now, if you again make a GET request to the http://localhost:8080/api/cars path, you will see that the new car exists in the database:

```
57              "href": "http://localhost:8080/api/cars/5"
58            },
59 ▾        "owner": {
60              "href": "http://localhost:8080/api/cars/5/owner"
61          }
62        }
63      },
64 ▾    {
65        "brand": "Toyota",
66        "model": "Corolla",
67        "color": "silver",
68        "registerNumber": "BBA-3122",
69        "year": 2021,
70        "price": 32000,
71 ▾      "_links": {
72 ▾        "self": {
73              "href": "http://localhost:8080/api/cars/6"
74            },
75 ▾        "car": {
76              "href": "http://localhost:8080/api/cars/6"
77            },
78 ▾        "owner": {
79              "href": "http://localhost:8080/api/cars/6/owner"
80          }
81        }
82      }
83    ]
84  },
```

Figure 4.13 – New car added

To update entities, we can use the PATCH method and the link to the car that we want to update (`http://localhost:8080/api/cars/{id}`). The header must contain the Content-Type field with the value application/json, and the car object with edited data will be given inside the request body. If you are using PATCH, you have to send only fields that are updated. If you are using PUT, you have to include all fields in the request body.

Let's edit the car that we created in the previous example, and we will change the color to white. The Postman request is shown in the following screenshot (note, we set the header as in the POST example and use the car id in the URL):

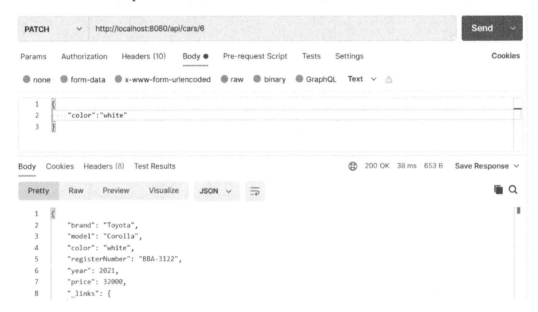

Figure 4.14 – PATCH request to update existing car

If update succeeded, the response status is **200 OK**. If you now fetch the updated car by using the GET request, you will see that the color
is updated.

```
← → C  ⓘ localhost:8080/api/cars/6

1    // 20210708113916
2    // http://localhost:8080/api/cars/6
3
4  ▾ {
5      "brand": "Toyota",
6      "model": "Corolla",
7      "color": "white",
8      "registerNumber": "BBA-3122",
9      "year": 2021,
10     "price": 32000,
11 ▾   "_links": {
12 ▾     "self": {
13         "href": "http://localhost:8080/api/cars/6"
14       },
15 ▾     "car": {
16         "href": "http://localhost:8080/api/cars/6"
17       },
18 ▾     "owner": {
19         "href": "http://localhost:8080/api/cars/6/owner"
20       }
21     }
22   }
```

Figure 4.15 – Updated car

Next, we will add an owner to the new car that we just created. We can use the PUT method and the `http://localhost:8080/api/cars/{id}/owner` path. In this example, the ID of the new car is 6, therefore the link is `http://localhost:8080/api/cars/6/owner`. The content of the body is now linked to an owner, for example, `http://localhost:8080/api/owners/1`.

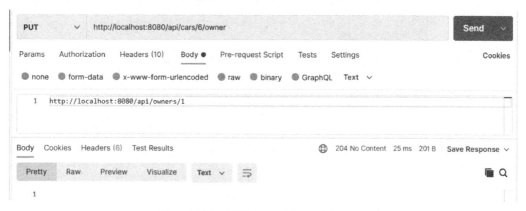

Figure 4.16 – PUT request to update owner

The Content-Type value of the headers should be text/uri-list in this case.

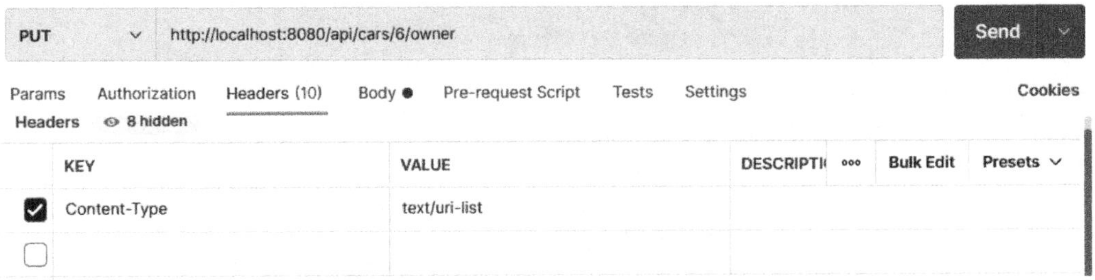

Figure 4.17 – PUT request headers

Finally, you can make a GET request for the car's owner and you should see that now the owner is linked to the car as shown in the following screenshot:

Figure 4.18 – Car owner

In the previous chapter, we created queries to our repository. These queries can also be included in our service. To include queries, you have to add the @RepositoryRestResource annotation to the repository class. Query parameters are annotated with the @Param annotation. The following source code shows CarRepository with these annotations:

```java
package com.packt.cardatabase.domain;


import java.util.List;


import org.springframework.data.repository.CrudRepository;
import org.springframework.data.repository.query.Param;
import org.springframework.data.rest.core.annotation.
RepositoryRestResource;


@RepositoryRestResource
public interface CarRepository extends CrudRepository<Car,
    Long> {
    // Fetch cars by brand
    List<Car> findByBrand(@Param("brand") String brand);


    // Fetch cars by color
    List<Car> findByColor(@Param("color") String color);
}
```

Now, when you make a GET request to the `http://localhost:8080/api/cars` path, you can see that there is a new endpoint called `/search`. Calling the `http://localhost:8080/api/cars/search` path returns the following response:

```
                    ←  →  C    ① localhost:8080/api/cars/search

1       // 20210707151938
2       // http://localhost:8080/api/cars/search
3
4   ▾   {
5   ▾     "_links": {
6   ▾       "findByBrand": {
7             "href": "http://localhost:8080/api/cars/search/findByBrand{?brand}",
8             "templated": true
9           },
10  ▾       "findByColor": {
11            "href": "http://localhost:8080/api/cars/search/findByColor{?color}",
12            "templated": true
13          },
14  ▾       "self": {
15            "href": "http://localhost:8080/api/cars/search"
16          }
17        }
18      }
```

Figure 4.19 – REST queries

From the response, you can see that both queries are now available in our service. The following URL demonstrates how to fetch cars by brand: `http://localhost:8080/api/cars/search/findByBrand?brand=Ford`.

The following screenshot is the output of the preceding URL:

```
←  →  C    ⓘ  localhost:8080/api/cars/search/findByBrand?brand=Ford

1    // 20210707152435
2    // http://localhost:8080/api/cars/search/findByBrand?brand=Ford
3
4  ▾  {
5  ▾    "_embedded": {
6  ▾      "cars": [
7  ▾        {
8            "brand": "Ford",
9            "model": "Mustang",
10           "color": "Red",
11           "registerNumber": "ADF-1121",
12           "year": 2021,
13           "price": 59000,
14  ▾        "_links": {
15  ▾          "self": {
16              "href": "http://localhost:8080/api/cars/3"
17             },
18  ▾          "car": {
19              "href": "http://localhost:8080/api/cars/3"
20             },
21  ▾          "owner": {
22              "href": "http://localhost:8080/api/cars/3/owner"
23             }
```

Figure 4.20 – REST query response

We have now created the RESTful API to our backend, and we will consume that later with our React frontend.

Summary

In this chapter, we created a RESTful web service with Spring Boot. First, we created a controller and one method that returns all cars in JSON format. Next, we used Spring Data REST to get a fully functional web service with all CRUD functionalities. We covered different types of requests that are needed to use CRUD functionalities of the service that we created. Finally, we also included our queries to RESTful web service.

In the next chapter, we will secure our backend using Spring Security.

Questions

1. What is REST?

2. How can you create a RESTful web service with Spring Boot?

3. How can you fetch items using our RESTful web service?

4. How can you delete items using our RESTful web service?

5. How can you add items using our RESTful web service?

6. How can you update items using our RESTful web service?

7. How can you use queries with our RESTful web service?

Further reading

Packt has other great resources available for learning about Spring Boot RESTful web services:

- *Learning Spring Boot 2.0 – Second Edition*, by *Greg L. Turnquist* (`https://www.packtpub.com/application-development/learning-spring-boot-20-second-edition`)

- *Building a RESTful Web Service with Spring*, by *Ludovic Dewailly* (`https://www.packtpub.com/web-development/building-restful-web-service-spring`)

- *Modern API Development with Spring and Spring Boot*, by *Sourabh Sharma* (`https://www.packtpub.com/product/modern-api-development-with-spring-and-spring-boot`)

5
Securing and Testing Your Backend

This chapter explains how to secure and test your Spring Boot backend. Securing your backend is a crucial part of code development. In the testing part of this chapter, we will create some unit tests in relation to our backend—these will make your backend code easier to maintain. We will use the database application that we created in the previous chapter as a starting point.

In this chapter, we will cover the following topics:

- Understanding Spring Security
- Securing your backend with a **JSON Web Token** (**JWT**)
- Testing in Spring Boot
- Creating unit tests

Technical requirements

The Spring Boot application that we created in the previous chapters is required.

The following GitHub link will also be required: `https://github.com/PacktPublishing/Full-Stack-Development-with-Spring-Boot-and-React/tree/main/Chapter05`.

Check out the following video to see the Code in Action: `https://bit.ly/3Gv9wVD`

Understanding Spring Security

Spring Security (`https://spring.io/projects/spring-security`) provides security services for Java-based web applications. The Spring Security project was started in 2003 and was previously named *Acegi Security System for Spring*.

By default, Spring Security enables the following features:

- An `AuthenticationManager` bean with an in-memory single user. The username is `user`, and the password is printed to the console output.

- Ignored paths for common static resource locations, such as `/css` and `/images`. **HyperText Transfer Protocol (HTTP)** basic security for all other endpoints.

- Security events published to Spring's `ApplicationEventPublisher` interface.

- Common low-level features are on by default (**HTTP Strict Transport Security (HSTS)**, **cross-site scripting (XSS)**, **cross-site request forgery (CSRF)**, and so forth).

- Default autogenerated login page.

You can include Spring Security in your application by adding the following dependencies to the `pom.xml` file. The first dependency is for the application and the second is for testing:

```
<dependency>
  <groupId>org.springframework.boot</groupId>
  <artifactId>spring-boot-starter-security</artifactId>
</dependency>
<dependency>
  <groupId>org.springframework.security</groupId>
  <artifactId>spring-security-test</artifactId>
  <scope>test</scope>
</dependency>
```

When you start your application, you can see from the console that Spring Security has created an in-memory user with a username of `user`. The user's password can be seen in the console output, as illustrated here:

```
Console ☒
CardatabaseApplication [Java Application]
Hibernate: create table car (id bigint not null, brand varchar(255), color varch
Hibernate: create table owner (ownerid bigint not null, firstname varchar(255),
Hibernate: alter table car add constraint FK2mqqwvxtowv4vddvtsmvtiqa2 foreign ke
2021-07-08 12:46:23.057  INFO 20844 --- [  restartedMain] o.h.e.t.j.p.i.JtaPlatf
2021-07-08 12:46:23.064  INFO 20844 --- [  restartedMain] j.LocalContainerEntity
2021-07-08 12:46:23.491  WARN 20844 --- [  restartedMain] JpaBaseConfiguration$J
2021-07-08 12:46:24.398  INFO 20844 --- [  restartedMain] .s.s.UserDetailsServic

Using generated security password: 7113c80f-fa23-486b-a30e-5373b1174097

2021-07-08 12:46:24.598  INFO 20844 --- [  restartedMain] o.s.s.web.DefaultSecur
2021-07-08 12:46:24.690  INFO 20844 --- [  restartedMain] o.s.b.d.a.OptionalLive
2021-07-08 12:46:24.720  INFO 20844 --- [  restartedMain] o.s.b.w.embedded.tomca
```

Figure 5.1 – Spring Security enabled

If there is no password in the console, try to restart your project by pressing the red
Terminate button in the console and rerun your project.

Now, if you make a GET request to your **application programming interface (API)**
root endpoint, you will see that it is now secured. Open your web browser and navigate
to http://localhost:8080/api. Now, you will see that you are redirected to the
Spring Security default login page, as illustrated in the following screenshot:

Figure 5.2 – Secured REpresentational State Transfer (REST) API

To be able to make a successful GET request, we have to authenticate. Type user into the **Username** field and copy the generated password from the console to the **Password** field. With authentication, we can see that the response contains our API resources, as illustrated in the following screenshot:

```
← → C    ⓘ localhost:8080/api            ⚿  ☆

▼ {
    ▼ "_links": {
        ▼ "owners": {
              "href": "http://localhost:8080/api/owners"
          },
        ▼ "cars": {
              "href": "http://localhost:8080/api/cars"
          },
        ▼ "profile": {
              "href": "http://localhost:8080/api/profile"
          }
      }
  }
```

Figure 5.3 – Basic authentication

To configure how Spring Security behaves, we have to add a new configuration class that extends WebSecurityConfigurerAdapter. Create a new class called SecurityConfig in your application root package (com.packt.cardatabase). The following source code shows the structure of the security configuration class. The @Configuration and @EnableWebSecurity annotations switch off the default web security configuration, and we can define our own configuration in this class. Inside the configure(HttpSecurity http) method, we can define which endpoints in our application are secure and which are not. We don't actually need this method yet because we can use the default settings where all the endpoints are secured:

```
package com.packt.cardatabase;


import org.springframework.context.annotation.
Configuration;
import org.springframework.security.config.annotation.
web.builders.HttpSecurity;
```

```
import org.springframework.security.config.
annotation.web.configuration.EnableWebSecurity;
import org.springframework.security.config.annotation.
web.configuration.WebSecurityConfigurerAdapter;

@Configuration
@EnableWebSecurity
public class SecurityConfig extends
    WebSecurityConfigurerAdapter {
    @Override
    protected void configure(HttpSecurity http) throws
        Exception {
    }
}
```

We can also add in-memory users to our application by adding the userDetailsService() method to our SecurityConfig class. The following source code of the method will create an in-memory user with a username of user and a password of password:

```
// SecurityConfig.java
@Bean
@Override
public UserDetailsService userDetailsService() {
    UserDetails user =
        User.withDefaultPasswordEncoder()
        .username("user")
        .password("password")
        .roles("USER")
        .build();

        return new InMemoryUserDetailsManager(user);
}
```

The use of in-memory users is fine in the development phase, but the real application should save users in the database.

> **Important Note**
>
> The `withDefaultPasswordEncoder()` method should only be used for demonstration purposes and it is not safe for production.

To save users to the database, you have to create a user entity class and repository. Passwords shouldn't be saved to the database in plaintext format. Spring Security provides multiple hashing algorithms, such as `bcrypt`, that you can use to hash passwords. The following steps show you how to implement this:

1. Create a new class called `User` in the `com.packt.cardatabase.domain` package. Activate the domain package and right-click it. Select **New | Class** from the menu and name the new class `User`. After that, your project structure should look like this:

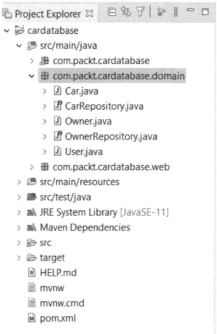

Figure 5.4 – Project structure

2. Annotate the `User` class with the `@Entity` annotation. Add the **identifier** (**ID**), username, password, and role class fields. Finally, add the constructors, getters, and setters. We will set all the fields to be `nullable`, and specify that the username must be unique by using the `@Column` annotation. Refer to the following `User.java` source code of the fields and constructors:

```
package com.packt.cardatabase.domain;
```

```
import javax.persistence.Column;
import javax.persistence.Entity;
import javax.persistence.GeneratedValue;
import javax.persistence.GenerationType;
import javax.persistence.Id;

@Entity
public class User {
    @Id
    @GeneratedValue(strategy=GenerationType.IDENTITY)
    @Column(nullable=false, updatable=false)
    private Long id;

    @Column(nullable=false, unique=true)
    private String username;

    @Column(nullable=false)
    private String password;

    @Column(nullable=false)
    private String role;

    public User() {}

    public User(String username, String password,
        String role) {
        super();
        this.username = username;
        this.password = password;
        this.role = role;
    }
```

Here is the rest of the User.java source code with the getters and setters:

```
    public Long getId() {
        return id;
    }
```

```java
    public void setId(Long id) {
        this.id = id;
    }

    public String getUsername() {
        return username;
    }

    public void setUsername(String username) {
        this.username = username;
    }

    public String getPassword() {
        return password;
    }

    public void setPassword(String password) {
        this.password = password;
    }

    public String getRole() {
        return role;
    }

    public void setRole(String role) {
        this.role = role;
    }
}
```

3. Create a new class called UserRepository in the domain package. Activate the domain package and right-click it. Select **New | Class** from the menu and name the new class UserRepository.

4. The source code of the repository class is similar to what we made in the previous chapter, but there is one query method, `findByUsername`, that we need for the steps that follow. That is used to find `user` from the database in the authentication process. The method returns `Optional` to avoid a null exception. Refer to the following `UserRepository` source code:

```
package com.packt.cardatabase.domain;

import java.util.Optional;
import org.springframework.data.repository.
CrudRepository;

public interface UserRepository extends CrudRepository
    <User, Long> {
    Optional<User> findByUsername(String username);
}
```

5. Next, we will create a class that implements the `UserDetailsService` interface that's provided by Spring Security. Spring Security uses this for user authentication and authorization. Create a new `service` package in the root package. Activate the root package and right-click it. Select **New** | **Package** from the menu and name the new package `service`, as illustrated in the following screenshot:

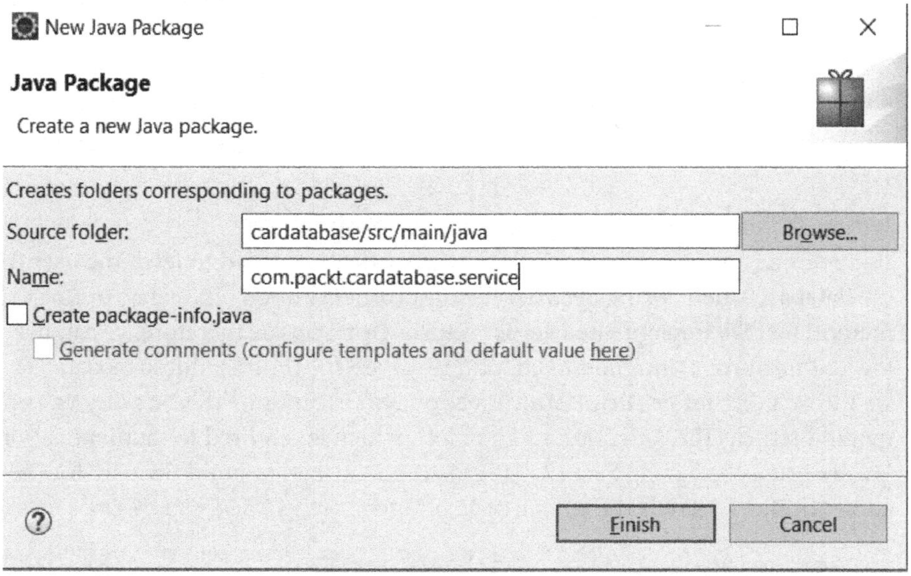

Figure 5.5 – The service package

6. Create a new class called `UserDetailsServiceImpl` in the `service` package
    we just created. Now, your project structure should look like this:

Figure 5.6 – Project structure

7. We have to inject the `UserRepository` class into the
    `UserDetailsServiceImpl` class because that is needed to fetch the user from
    the database when Spring Security handles authentication. The `findByUsername`
    method that we implemented earlier returns `Optional`, therefore we can use
    the `isPresent()` method to check if `user` exists. If `user` doesn't exist,
    we throw a `UsernameNotFoundException` exception. The `loadByUsername`
    method returns the `UserDetails` object, which is required for authentication.
    We are using the Spring Security `UserBuilder` class to build the user for the
    authentication. Here is the source code of `UserDetailsServiceImpl.java`:

```
package com.packt.cardatabase.service;
```

```java
import java.util.Optional;
import org.springframework.beans.factory.annotation.
Autowired;
import org.springframework.security.core.userdetails.
User.UserBuilder;
import org.springframework.security.core.userdetails.
UserDetails;
import org.springframework.security.core.userdetails.
UserDetailsService;
import org.springframework.security.core.userdetails.
UsernameNotFoundException;
import org.springframework.stereotype.Service;
import com.packt.cardatabase.domain.User;


import com.packt.cardatabase.domain.UserRepository;


@Service
public class UserDetailsServiceImpl implements
    UserDetailsService {
    @Autowired
    private UserRepository repository;

    @Override
    public UserDetails loadUserByUsername(String
        username)
      throws UsernameNotFoundException {
      Optional<User> user =
        repository.findByUsername(username);
      UserBuilder builder = null;
      if (user.isPresent()) {
        User currentUser = user.get();
        builder =
          org.springframework.security.core.userdetails.
          User.withUsername(username);
        builder.password(currentUser.getPassword());
        builder.roles(currentUser.getRole());
```

```
    } else {
        throw new UsernameNotFoundException("User not
            found.");
    }


    return builder.build();
    }
}
```

8. In our security configuration class, we have to define that Spring Security
    should use users from the database instead of in-memory users. Delete the
    `userDetailsService()` method from the `SecurityConfig` class to disable
    in-memory users. Add a new `configureGlobal` method to enable users from
    the database. We should never save the password as plain text to the database.
    Therefore, we will define a password hashing algorithm in the `configureGlobal`
    method. In this example, we are using the `bcrypt` algorithm. This can be
    easily implemented with the Spring Security `BCryptPasswordEncoder`
    class that encodes a hashed password in the authentication process. Here is the
    `SecurityConfig.java` source code. Now, the password must be hashed using
    BCrypt before it's saved to the database:

```
package com.packt.cardatabase;


import org.springframework.beans.factory.annotation.
Autowired;
import org.springframework.context.annotation.
Configuration;
import org.springframework.security.config.annotation.
authentication.builders.AuthenticationManagerBuilder;
import org.springframework.security.config.annotation.
web.configuration.EnableWebSecurity;
import org.springframework.security.config.annotation
.web.configuration.WebSecurityConfigurerAdapter;
import org.springframework.security.crypto.bcrypt.
BCryptPasswordEncoder;


import com.packt.cardatabase.service.
UserDetailsServiceImpl;
```

```java
@Configuration
@EnableWebSecurity
public class SecurityConfig extends
    WebSecurityConfigurerAdapter {
  @Autowired
  private UserDetailsServiceImpl userDetailsService;


  @Autowired
  public void configureGlobal
      (AuthenticationManagerBuilder auth)
    throws Exception {
      auth.userDetailsService(userDetailsService)
        .passwordEncoder(new BCryptPasswordEncoder());
    }
}
```

9. Finally, we can save a couple of test users to the database using the
    CommandLineRunner interface. Open the CardatabaseApplication.
    java file and add the following code at the beginning of the class to inject
    UserRepository into the main class:

```java
@Autowired
private UserRepository urepository;
```

10. Let's save two users to the database with bcrypt hashed passwords. In the
    following code snippet, we save two users with bcrypt hashed passwords. You can
    find bcrypt calculators or generators from the internet if you type plain text
    password and get hashed password, and you should use these here:

```java
@Override
public void run(String... args) throws Exception {
    // Add owner objects and save to db
    Owner owner1 = new Owner("John", "Johnson");
    Owner owner2 = new Owner("Mary", "Robinson");
    orepository.saveAll(Arrays.asList(owner1,
        owner2));


    // Add car object and link to owners and save to
```

```
        db
    Car car1 = new Car("Ford", "Mustang", "Red",
       "ADF-1121", 2021, 59000, owner1);
    Car car2 = new Car("Nissan", "Leaf", "White",
       "SSJ-3002", 2019, 29000, owner2);
    Car car3 = new Car("Toyota", "Prius", "Silver",
       "KKO-0212", 2020, 39000, owner2);
    repository.saveAll(Arrays.asList(car1, car2,
       car3));


    for (Car car : repository.findAll()) {
        logger.info(car.getBrand() + " " +
           car.getModel());
    }


    // Username: user, password: user
    urepository.save(new User("user",
"$2a$10$NVM0n8ElaRgg7zWO1CxUdei7vWoPg91Lz2aYavh9.
f9q0e4bRadue","USER"));


    // Username: admin, password: admin
    urepository.save(new User("admin",
"$2a$10$8cjz47bjbR4Mn8GMg9IZx.vyjhLXR/SKKMSZ9.
mP9vpMu0ssKi8GW", "ADMIN"));
    }
```

> **Important Note**
>
> **BCrypt** is a strong hashing function that was designed by Niels Provos and David Mazières. Here is an example of a BCrypt hash that is generated from the admin string:
>
> $2a$10$8cjz47bjbR4Mn8GMg9IZx.vyjhLXR/SKKMSZ9.
> mP9vpMu0ssKi8GW
>
> $2a represents the algorithm version and $10 represents the strength of the algorithm. The default strength of Spring Security's BcryptPasswordEncoder class is 10. BCrypt generates a random salt in hashing, therefore the hashed result is always different.

After running your application, you will see that there is now a `user` table in the database and that two user records are saved with hashed passwords, as illustrated in the following screenshot:

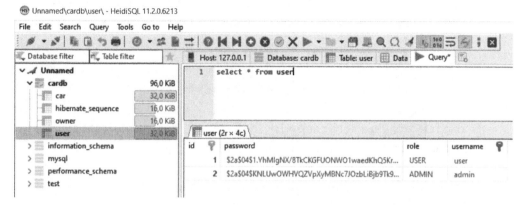

Figure 5.7 – Users

11. Now, you will get a `401 Unauthorized` error if you try to send a `GET` request to the `http://localhost:8080/api` path without authentication. You should authenticate to be able to send a successful request. The difference, when compared with the previous example, is that we are using the users from the database to authenticate.

You can see a `GET` request to the `/api` endpoint using the `admin` user in the following screenshot. We can also use Postman and basic authentication:

Figure 5.8 – GET request authentication

12. Now, you can see that we get users by calling the `/users` endpoint in our RESTful web service, and that is something we want to avoid. As mentioned earlier, Spring Data REST generates a RESTful web service from all public repositories by default. We can use the `exported` flag of the `@RepositoryRestResource` annotation and set it to `false`, and then the following repository is not exposed as a REST resource:

```
package com.packt.cardatabase.domain;

import org.springframework.data.repository.
CrudRepository;
import org.springframework.data.rest.core.annotation.
RepositoryRestResource;

@RepositoryRestResource(exported = false)
public interface UserRepository extends CrudRepository
    <User, Long> {

}
```

Now, if you make a GET request to the `/users` endpoint, you will see that `/users` endpoint is not visible anymore, as shown in the following screenshot:

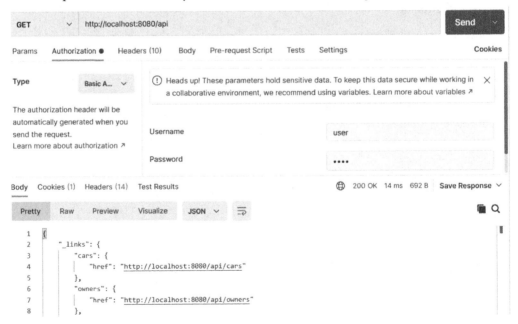

Figure 5.9 – GET request

Next, we will start to implement authentication using a JWT.

Securing your backend using a JWT

In the previous section, we covered how to use basic authentication with a RESTful web service. This method cannot be used when we develop our own frontend with React, so we are going to use JWT authentication instead. A JWT is a compact way to implement authentication in modern web applications. A JWT is really small in size and can therefore be sent in the **Uniform Resource Locator** (**URL**), in the POST parameter, or inside the header. It also contains all the necessary information pertaining to the user.

A JWT contains three different parts, separated by dots: *xxxxx.yyyyy.zzzzz*. These parts are broken up as follows:

- The first part (*xxxxx*) is the header that defines the type of the token and the hashing algorithm.

- The second part (*yyyyy*) is the payload that, typically, in the case of authentication, contains user information.

- The third part (*zzzzz*) is the signature that is used to verify that the token hasn't been changed along the way.

Here is an example of a JWT:

```
eyJhbGciOiJIUzI1NiJ9.eyJzdWIiOiJKb2UifD.ipevRNuRP6Hf1G8cFKnmUPtypruR
C4fc1DWtoLL62SY¶
```

Figure 5.10 – JWT

The following diagram shows a simplified representation of the JWT authentication process:

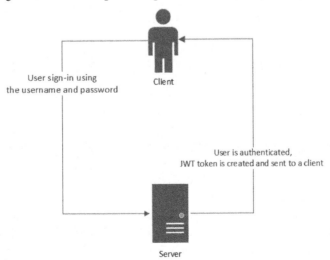

Figure 5.11 – JWT authentication process

After successful authentication, the requests sent by the client should always contain the JWT that was received in the authentication.

We will use the Java `jjwt` library (`https://github.com/jwtk/jjwt`), which is the JWT library for Java and Android. Therefore, we have to add the following dependency to the `pom.xml` file. The `jjwt` library is used for creating and parsing JWTs:

```
<dependency>
    <groupId>io.jsonwebtoken</groupId>
    <artifactId>jjwt-api</artifactId>
    <version>0.11.2</version>
</dependency>
<dependency>
    <groupId>io.jsonwebtoken</groupId>
    <artifactId>jjwt-impl</artifactId>
    <version>0.11.2</version>
    <scope>runtime</scope>
</dependency>
<dependency>
    <groupId>io.jsonwebtoken</groupId>
    <artifactId>jjwt-jackson</artifactId>
    <version>0.11.2</version>
    <scope>runtime</scope>
</dependency>
```

The following steps demonstrate how to enable JWT authentication in our backend. We will start with the login functionality:

1. First, we will create a class that generates and verifies a signed JWT. Create a new class called `JwtService` in the `com.packt.cardatabase.service` package. At the beginning of the class, we will define a few constants: `EXPIRATIONTIME` defines the expiration time of the token in **milliseconds (ms)**, `PREFIX` defines the prefix of the token, and the `Bearer` schema is typically used. A secret key is created using the `jjwt` library's `secretKeyFor` method, and this can be used for the demonstration. In a production environment, you should read your secret key from the application configuration. The `getToken` method generates and returns the token. The `getAuthUser` method gets the token from the response `Authorization` header. Then, we use the `parserBuilder` method provided by the `jjwt` library to create a `JwtParserBuilder` instance. The `setSigningKey` method is used to specify a secret key for the token verification.

Finally, we use the get Subject method to get the username. The whole JwtService source code can be seen here:

```
package com.packt.cardatabase.service;


import io.jsonwebtoken.Jwts;
import io.jsonwebtoken.SignatureAlgorithm;
import io.jsonwebtoken.security.Keys;
import java.security.Key;
import org.springframework.http.HttpHeaders;
import org.springframework.stereotype.Component;
import javax.servlet.http.HttpServletRequest;
import java.util.Date;


@Component
public class JwtService {
  static final long EXPIRATIONTIME = 86400000; // 1
    day in ms
  static final String PREFIX = "Bearer";
  // Generate secret key. Only for the demonstration
  // You should read it from the application
    configuration
  static final Key key =   Keys.secretKeyFor
    (SignatureAlgorithm.HS256);


  // Generate signed JWT token
  public String getToken(String username) {
    String token = Jwts.builder()
    .setSubject(username)
    .setExpiration(new Date(System.currentTimeMillis()
       + EXPIRATIONTIME))
    .signWith(key)
    .compact();

    return token;
  }
```

```
// Get a token from request Authorization header,
// verify a token and get username
public String getAuthUser(HttpServletRequest
    request) {
  String token = request.getHeader
    (HttpHeaders.AUTHORIZATION);

  if (token != null) {
    String user = Jwts.parserBuilder()
    .setSigningKey(key)
    .build()
    .parseClaimsJws(token.replace(PREFIX, ""))
    .getBody()
    .getSubject();

    if (user != null)
      return user;
  }
  return null;
  }
}
```

2. Next, we will add a new simple **Plain Old Java Object (POJO)** class to keep
   credentials for authentication. Create a new class called `AccountCredentials`
   in the `com.packt.cardatabase.domain` package. The class has two fields:
   `username` and `password`. Here is the source code of the class. This class doesn't
   have the `@Entity` annotation because we don't have to save credentials to
   the database:

```
package com.packt.cardatabase.domain;

public class AccountCredentials {
    private String username;
    private String password;

    public String getUsername() {
        return username;
    }
```

```
    public void setUsername(String username) {
        this.username = username;
    }

    public String getPassword() {
        return password;
    }

    public void setPassword(String password) {
        this.password = password;
    }
}
```

3. Now, we will implement the `controller` class for login. Login is done by calling the `/login` endpoint using the `POST` method and sending the username and password inside the request body. Create a class called `LoginController` inside the `com.packt.cardatabase.web` package. We have to inject a `JwtService` instance into the controller class because that is used to generate a signed JWT in the case of a successful login. The code is illustrated in the following snippet:

```
package com.packt.cardatabase.web;

import org.springframework.beans.factory.annotation
.Autowired;
import org.springframework.http.HttpHeaders;
import org.springframework.http.MediaType;
import org.springframework.http.ResponseEntity;
import org.springframework.security.authentication.
AuthenticationManager;
import org.springframework.security.authentication.
UsernamePasswordAuthenticationToken;
import org.springframework.security.core.
Authentication;
import org.springframework.web.bind.annotation.
RequestBody;
import org.springframework.web.bind.annotation.
RequestMapping;
```

```
import org.springframework.web.bind.annotation.
RequestMethod;
import org.springframework.web.bind.annotation.
RestController;

import com.packt.cardatabase.domain.
AccountCredentials;
import com.packt.cardatabase.service.JwtService;

@RestController
public class LoginController {
  @Autowired
  private JwtService jwtService;

  @Autowired
  AuthenticationManager authenticationManager;

  @RequestMapping(value="/login", method=RequestMethod
    .POST)
  public ResponseEntity<?> getToken(@RequestBody
    AccountCredentials credentials) {
    // Generate token and send it in the response
      Authorization
    // header
  }
}
```

4. Next, we will implement the getToken method that handles the login functionality, as follows:

```
// LoginController.java
@RequestMapping(value="/login", method=RequestMethod
    .POST)
public ResponseEntity<?> getToken(@RequestBody
    AccountCredentials credentials) {
  UsernamePasswordAuthenticationToken creds =
  new UsernamePasswordAuthenticationToken(
```

```
    credentials.getUsername(),
    credentials.getPassword());


  Authentication auth =
      authenticationManager.authenticate(creds);


  // Generate token
  String jwts = jwtService.getToken(auth.getName());


  // Build response with the generated token
  return ResponseEntity.ok()
  .header(HttpHeaders.AUTHORIZATION, "Bearer " + jwts)
  .header(HttpHeaders.ACCESS_CONTROL_EXPOSE_HEADERS,
      "Authorization")
  .build();
}
```

5. We have also injected `AuthenticationManager` into the `LoginController` class, therefore we have to add the following code to the `SecurityConfig` class:

```
package com.packt.cardatabase;


import org.springframework.beans.factory.annotation
    .Autowired;
import org.springframework.context.annotation.Bean;
import org.springframework.context.annotation.
Configuration;
import org.springframework.security.authentication.
AuthenticationManager;
import org.springframework.security.config.annotation.
authentication.builders.AuthenticationManagerBuilder;
import org.springframework.security.config.annotation.
web.configuration.EnableWebSecurity;
import org.springframework.security.config.annotation.
web.configuration.WebSecurityConfigurerAdapter;
import org.springframework.security.crypto.bcrypt.
BCryptPasswordEncoder;
```

```
import com.packt.cardatabase.service.
UserDetailsServiceImpl;

@Configuration
@EnableWebSecurity
public class SecurityConfig extends
WebSecurityConfigurerAdapter {
    @Autowired
    private UserDetailsServiceImpl userDetailsService;

    @Autowired
    public void configureGlobal
    (AuthenticationManagerBuilder auth)
    throws Exception {
        auth.userDetailsService(userDetailsService)
            .passwordEncoder(new BcryptPassword
            Encoder());
    }

    @Bean
    public AuthenticationManager
        getAuthenticationManager() throws
Exception {
    return authenticationManager();
        }
}
```

6. In this phase, we have to configure Spring Security functionality. Spring Security's `configure` method defines which paths are secured and which are not secured. Add the following `configure` method to the `SecurityConfig` class. There, we define that the POST method request to the `/login` endpoint is allowed without authentication and that requests to all other endpoints require authentication. We will also define that Spring Security will never create a session, and therefore we can also disable `csrf`:

```
// SecurityConfig.java
@Override
protected void configure(HttpSecurity http) throws
```

```
Exception {
    http.csrf().disable()
    .sessionManagement()
    .sessionCreationPolicy(SessionCreationPolicy.
        STATELESS).and()
    .authorizeRequests()
    // POST request to /login endpoint is not secured
    .antMatchers(HttpMethod.POST, "/login").
        permitAll()
    // All other requests are secured
    .anyRequest().authenticated();
}
```

7. Finally, we are ready to test our login functionality. Open Postman and make a POST request to the `http://localhost:8080/login` URL. Define a valid user inside the request body—for example, `{"username":"user", "password":"user"}`—and set the `Content-Type` header to `application/json`. Now, you should see an `Authorization` header in the response that contains the signed JWT, like the one shown in the following screenshot:

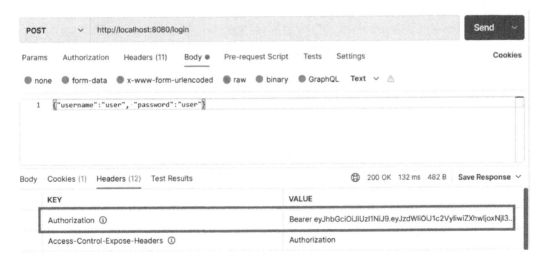

Figure 5.12 – Login request

You can also test login using the wrong password, and see that the response doesn't contain the `Authorization` header.

We have now finalized the login step, and we will move on to handing authentication in the rest of the incoming requests. In the authentication process, we are using filters that allow us to perform some operations before a request goes to the controller or before a response is sent to a client. The following steps demonstrate the rest of the authentication process:

1. We will use a filter class to authenticate all other incoming requests. Create a new class called `AuthenticationFilter` in the root package. The `AuthenticationFilter` class extends Spring Security's `OncePerRequestFilter` interface that provides a `doFilterInternal` method where we implement our authentication. We have to inject a `JwtService` instance into the filter class because that is needed to verify a token from the request. The code is illustrated in the following snippet:

```java
// Imports


@Component
public class AuthenticationFilter extends
    OncePerRequestFilter {
  @Autowired
  private JwtService jwtService;


  @Override
  protected void doFilterInternal(HttpServletRequest
    request,
                    HttpServletResponse response,
                    FilterChain filterChain)
                    throws ServletException,
                    java.io.IOException {
    // Get token from the Authorization header
    String jws = request.getHeader
      (HttpHeaders.AUTHORIZATION);
    if (jws != null) {
      // Verify token and get user
      String user = jwtService.getAuthUser(request);
      // Authenticate
```

```
      Authentication authentication =
          new UsernamePasswordAuthenticationToken(user,
              null,
              java.util.Collections.emptyList());

          SecurityContextHolder.getContext()
              .setAuthentication(authentication);
      }

      filterChain.doFilter(request, response);
   }
}
```

2. Next, we have to add our filter class to the Spring Security configuration. Open the `SecurityConfig` class and inject the `AuthenticationFilter` class that we just implemented, as follows:

```
@Autowired
private AuthenticationFilter authenticationFilter;
```

3. Then, modify the `configure` method in the `SecurityConfig` class and add the following lines of code:

```
@Override
protected void configure(HttpSecurity http) throws
Exception {
  http.csrf().disable()
   .sessionManagement()
   .sessionCreationPolicy(SessionCreationPolicy.
STATELESS).and()
   .authorizeRequests()
   .antMatchers(HttpMethod.POST, "/login").permitAll()
   .anyRequest().authenticated().and()
   .addFilterBefore(authenticationFilter,
     UsernamePasswordAuthenticationFilter.class);
}
```

Now, we are ready to test the whole workflow. After we run the application, we can first log in by calling the /login endpoint with the POST method and, in the case of a successful login, we will receive a JWT in the Authorization header. Remember to add a valid user inside the body and set the Content-Type header to application/json. The following screenshot illustrates the process:

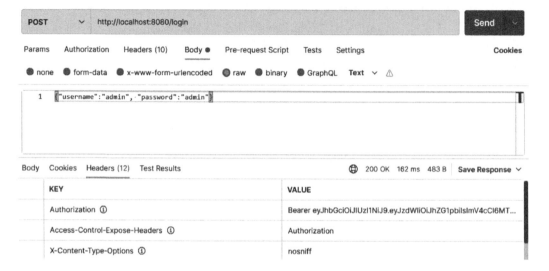

Figure 5.13 – Login request

4. Following a successful login, we can call the other RESTful service endpoints by sending the JWT that was received from the login in the Authorization header. Copy the token from the login response (without the Bearer prefix) and add the Authorization header with the token in the VALUE column. Refer to the example in the following screenshot:

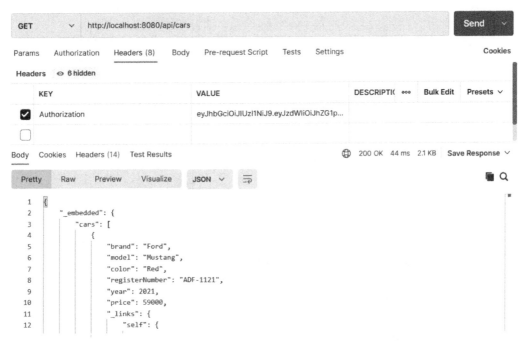

Figure 5.14 – Authenticated GET request

5. We should also handle exceptions in the authentication. Now, if you try to log in using the wrong password, you get a 403 Forbidden status without any further clarification. Spring Security provides an AuthenticationEntryPoint interface that can be used to handle exceptions. Create a new class named AuthEntryPoint in the root package that implements AuthenticationEntryPoint.

We implement the commence method that gets an exception as a parameter. In the case of an exception, we set the response status to 401 Unauthorized and write an exception message to the response body. The code is illustrated in the following snippet:

```
package com.packt.cardatabase;

import java.io.IOException;
import java.io.PrintWriter;

import javax.servlet.ServletException;
import javax.servlet.http.HttpServletRequest;
import javax.servlet.http.HttpServletResponse;

import org.springframework.http.MediaType;
```

```
import org.springframework.security.core.
AuthenticationException;
import org.springframework.security.web.
AuthenticationEntryPoint;
import org.springframework.stereotype.Component;

@Component
public class AuthEntryPoint implements
    AuthenticationEntryPoint {
  @Override
  public void commence(
    HttpServletRequest request,
    HttpServletResponse response,
    AuthenticationException authException) throws
    IOException, ServletException {

    response.setStatus
        (HttpServletResponse.SC_UNAUTHORIZED);
    response.setContentType
        (MediaType.APPLICATION_JSON_VALUE);
    PrintWriter writer = response.getWriter();
    writer.println("Error: " + authException.
        getMessage());
  }
}
```

6. Then, we have to configure Spring Security for the exception handling. Inject our
    AuthEntryPoint class into the SecurityConfig class, as follows:

```
// SecurityConfig.java
@Autowired
private AuthEntryPoint exceptionHandler;
```

Then, modify the configure method, as follows:

```
// SecurityConfig.java
@Override
protected void configure(HttpSecurity http) throws
    Exception {
```

```
http.csrf().disable()
  .sessionManagement()
  .sessionCreationPolicy
      (SessionCreationPolicy.STATELESS).and()
  .authorizeRequests()
  .antMatchers(HttpMethod.POST, "/login").permitAll()
  .anyRequest().authenticated().and()
  .exceptionHandling()
  .authenticationEntryPoint(exceptionHandler).and()
  .addFilterBefore(authenticationFilter,
    UsernamePasswordAuthenticationFilter.class);
}
```

7. Now, if you send a login POST request with the wrong credentials, you will get
    a 401 Unauthorized status in the response and an error message in the body,
    as shown in the following screenshot:

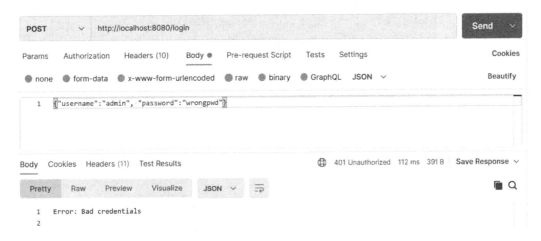

Figure 5.15 – Bad credentials

We will also add a **cross-origin resource sharing (CORS)** filter to our security
configuration class. This is needed for the frontend, which is sending requests from
the other origin. The CORS filter intercepts requests, and if these are identified
as cross-origin, it adds proper headers to the request. For that, we will use Spring
Security's CorsConfigurationSource interface. In this example, we will allow
all origins' HTTP methods and headers. You can define a list of permissible origins,
methods, and headers here if you require a more finely graded definition.

8. Add the following imports and methods to your `SecurityConfig` class to enable the CORS filter:

```java
// SecurityConfig.java

// Add the following imports
import java.util.Arrays;

import org.springframework.web.cors.CorsConfiguration;
import org.springframework.web.cors.
CorsConfigurationSource;
import org.springframework.web.cors.
UrlBasedCorsConfigurationSource;

// Add Global CORS filter inside the class
@Bean
CorsConfigurationSource corsConfigurationSource() {
  UrlBasedCorsConfigurationSource source =
    new UrlBasedCorsConfigurationSource();
  CorsConfiguration config = new CorsConfiguration();
  config.setAllowedOrigins(Arrays.asList("*"));
  config.setAllowedMethods(Arrays.asList("*"));
  config.setAllowedHeaders(Arrays.asList("*"));
  config.setAllowCredentials(false);
  config.applyPermitDefaultValues();

  source.registerCorsConfiguration("/**", config);
  return source;
}
```

9. If you want to explicitly define the origins, you can set this in the following way:

```java
// localhost:3000 is allowed
config.setAllowedOrigins(Arrays.asList
    ("http://localhost:3000"));
```

We also have to add the `cors()` function to the `configure` method, as shown in the following code snippet:

```java
// SecurityConfig.java
@Override
protected void configure(HttpSecurity http) throws
    Exception {
  http.csrf().disable().cors().and()
   .sessionManagement()
   .sessionCreationPolicy(SessionCreationPolicy.
      STATELESS).and()
   .authorizeRequests()
   .antMatchers(HttpMethod.POST, "/login").permitAll()
   .anyRequest().authenticated().and()
   .exceptionHandling()
   .authenticationEntryPoint(exceptionHandler).and()
   .addFilterBefore(authenticationFilter,
      UsernamePasswordAuthenticationFilter.class);
}
```

Now, all the functionalities that are required have been implemented in our backend. Next, we will continue with backend unit testing.

Testing in Spring Boot

The Spring Boot test starter package is added to the `pom.xml` file by Spring Initializr when we create our project. This is added automatically without any selection in the **Spring Initializr** page. The code can be seen in the following snippet:

```xml
<dependency>
        <groupId>org.springframework.boot</groupId>
        <artifactId>spring-boot-starter-test</artifactId>
        <scope>test</scope>
</dependency>
```

The Spring Boot test starter provides lots of handy libraries for testing, such as JUnit, Mockito, and AssertJ. In this book, we are using the JUnit 5 version (JUnit Jupiter). If you take a look, your project structure already has its own package created for test classes, as we can see in the following screenshot:

Figure 5.16 – Test classes

By default, Spring Boot uses an in-memory database for testing. We are now using MariaDB, but H2 can also be used for testing if we add the following dependency to the pom.xml file. The scope defines that the H2 database will only be used for running tests; otherwise, the application will use the MariaDB database:

```
<dependency>
    <groupId>com.h2database</groupId>
    <artifactId>h2</artifactId>
    <scope>test</scope>
</dependency>
```

If you also want to use the default database for testing, you can use the @AutoConfigureTestDatabase annotation.

Creating unit tests

For unit testing, we are using JUnit, which is a popular Java-based unit testing library. The following source code shows an example skeleton of the Spring Boot test class. The @SpringBootTest annotation specifies that the class is a regular test class that runs Spring Boot-based tests. The @Test annotation before the method specifies to JUnit that the method can be run as a test case:

```
@SpringBootTest
public class MyTestsClass {
```

```
@Test
public void testMethod() {
    // Test case code
}
}
```

First, we will create our first test case that will test the major functionality of our application before we create any formal test cases. Proceed as follows:

1. Open the `CardatabaseApplicationTest` test class that has already been made for your application. There is one test method called `contextLoads` here, and this is where we will add the test. The following test checks that the instance of the controller was created and injected successfully:

```
package com.packt.cardatabase;

import static org.assertj.core.api.Assertions.assertThat;
import org.junit.jupiter.api.Test;
import org.springframework.beans.factory.annotation.
Autowired;
import org.springframework.boot.test.context.
SpringBootTest;
import com.packt.cardatabase.web.CarController;

@SpringBootTest
class CardatabaseApplicationTests {
    @Autowired
    private CarController controller;

    @Test
    void contextLoads() {
        assertThat(controller).isNotNull();
    }
}
```

2. To run tests in Eclipse, activate the test class in **Project Explorer** and right-click. Select **Run As | JUnit test** from the menu. You should now see the **JUnit** tab in the lower part of the Eclipse workbench. The test results are shown in this tab and the test case has been passed, as illustrated in the following screenshot:

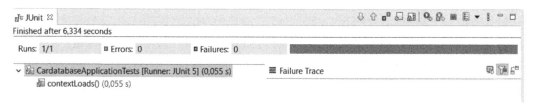

Figure 5.17 – JUnit test run

You can use @DisplayName annotation to give a more descriptive name to your test case. The name defined in the @DisplayName annotation is shown in the JUnit test runner. The code is illustrated in the following snippet:

```
@Test
@DisplayName("First example test case")
void contextLoads() {
    assertThat(controller).isNotNull();
}
```

3. Next, we will create unit tests for our owner repository to test **create, read, update, and delete (CRUD)** operations. Create a new class called OwnerRepositoryTest in the root test package. Instead of the @SpringBootTest annotation, @DataJpaTest can be used if the test is focused on **Java Persistence API (JPA)** components. When using this annotation, the H2 Hibernate database and Spring Data are configured automatically for testing. **Structured Query Language (SQL)** logging is also turned on. The code is illustrated in the following snippet:

```
package com.packt.cardatabase;

import static org.assertj.core.api.Assertions.assertThat;
import org.junit.jupiter.api.Test;
import org.springframework.beans.factory.annotation.
Autowired;
import org.springframework.boot.test.autoconfigure.
orm.jpa.DataJpaTest;
```

```
import com.packt.cardatabase.domain.Owner;
import com.packt.cardatabase.domain.OwnerRepository;


@DataJpaTest
public class OwnerRepositoryTest {
    @Autowired
    private OwnerRepository repository;


}
```

4. We will add our first test case to test the addition of a new owner to the database. A new owner object is created and saved to the database with the save method. Then, we check that the owner can be found. Add the following query to your OwnerRepository.java file. We will use this query in our test case:

```
Optional<Owner> findByFirstname(String firstName);
```

5. The following source code shows the test case method. Add the following method code to your OwnerRepositoryTest class:

```
@Test
void saveOwner() {
    repository.save(new Owner("Lucy", "Smith"));
    assertThat(repository.findByFirstname
        ("Lucy").isPresent())
      .isTrue();
}
```

6. The second test case will test the deletion of owner from the database. A new owner object is created and saved to the database. Then, all owners are deleted from the database, and finally, the count() method should return zero. The following source code shows the test case method. Add the following method code to your OwnerRepositoryTest class:

```
@Test
void deleteOwners() {
    repository.save(new Owner("Lisa", "Morrison"));
    repository.deleteAll();
    assertThat(repository.count()).isEqualTo(0);
}
```

7. Run the test cases and check the Eclipse **JUnit** tab to find out whether the tests passed. The following screenshot shows that they have indeed passed:

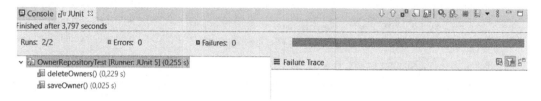

Figure 5.18 – Repository test cases

8. Next, we will demonstrate how to test your RESTful web service JWT authentication functionality. To test the controllers or any endpoint that is exposed, we can use a `MockMvc` object. By using the `MockMvc` object, the server is not started, but the tests are performed in the layer where Spring handles HTTP requests, and therefore it mocks the real situation. `MockMvc` provides the `perform` method to send these requests. To test authentication, we have to add credentials to the request body. Finally, we check that the response status is `OK`. The code is illustrated in the following snippet:

```
package com.packt.cardatabase;


import static org.springframework.test.web.servlet.
request.MockMvcRequestBuilders.post;
import static org.springframework.test.web.
servlet.result.MockMvcResultHandlers.print;
import static org.springframework.test.web.
servlet.result.MockMvcResultMatchers.status;


import org.junit.jupiter.api.Test;
import org.springframework.beans.factory.annotation.
Autowired;
import org.springframework.boot.test.autoconfigure.
web.servlet.AutoConfigureMockMvc;
import org.springframework.boot.test.context.
SpringBootTest;
import org.springframework.http.HttpHeaders;
import org.springframework.test.web.servlet.MockMvc;


@SpringBootTest
```

```
@AutoConfigureMockMvc
public class CarRestTest {
  @Autowired
  private MockMvc mockMvc;

  @Test
  public void testAuthentication() throws Exception {
    // Testing authentication with correct credentials
  this.mockMvc.
    perform(post("/login").
    content("{\"username\":\"admin\",\"password\":\
        "admin\"}").
    header(HttpHeaders.CONTENT_TYPE,
        "application/json")).
    andDo(print()).andExpect(status().isOk());
  }
}
```

Now, when we run the authentication tests, we will see that the test passed, as the following screenshot confirms:

Figure 5.19 – Login test

At this point, we have covered the basics of testing in the Spring Boot application, and you have gained the knowledge that's required to implement more test cases for your application.

Summary

In this chapter, we focused on securing and testing the Spring Boot backend. First, securing was done with Spring Security. The frontend will be developed with React in upcoming chapters; therefore, we implemented JWT authentication, which is a lightweight authentication method suitable for our needs.

We also covered the basics of testing a Spring Boot application. We used JUnit for unit testing and implemented test cases for JPA and RESTful web service authentication.

In the next chapter, we will set up the environment and tools related to frontend development.

Questions

1.   What is Spring Security?

2.   How can you secure your backend with Spring Boot?

3.   What is a JWT?

4.   How can you secure your backend with a JWT?

5.   How can you create unit tests with Spring Boot?

6.   How can you run and check the results of unit tests?

Further reading

Packt has other great resources available for you to learn about Spring Security and testing. These are listed here:

-   *Spring Security – Third Edition. Mick Knutson, Robert Winch*, and *Peter Mularien*. (`https://www.packtpub.com/application-development/spring-security-third-edition`)

-   *Mastering Software Testing with JUnit 5. Boni García.* (`https://www.packtpub.com/web-development/mastering-software-testing-junit-5`)

Part 2: Frontend Programming with React

Here, you will be familiarized with the basics of React. This part teaches you how to consume a RESTful web service with React and test the frontend.

We will cover the following chapters in this section:

- *Chapter 6, Setting Up the Environment and Tools – Frontend*
- *Chapter 7, Getting Started with React*
- *Chapter 8, Consuming the REST API with React*
- *Chapter 9, Useful Third-Party Components for React*

6
Setting Up the Environment and Tools – Frontend

This chapter describes the development environment and tools that are needed for React and are required so that you can start frontend development. In this chapter, we will create a simple starter React app by using the `create-react-app` starter kit, which is developed by Facebook.

In this chapter, we will cover the following topics:

- Installing Node.js
- Installing Visual Studio Code
- Visual Studio Code extensions
- Creating and running a React.js app using `create-react-app`
- Modifying the React app

Technical requirements

In this book, we are using the Windows OS, but all the tools we use are available for Linux and macOS as well.

The following GitHub link will also be required: `https://github.com/PacktPublishing/Full-Stack-Development-with-Spring-Boot-and-React/tree/main/Chapter06`.

Installing Node.js

Node.js is an open source, JavaScript-based server-side environment. Node.js is available for multiple operating systems, such as Windows, macOS, and Linux, and is required to develop React apps.

The Node.js installation package can be found at `https://nodejs.org/en/download/`. Download the latest **Long-Term Support** (**LTS**) version for your operating system. In this book, we are using the Windows 10 operating system, and you can get the Node.js MSI installer for it, which makes installation really straightforward.

When you execute the installer, you will go through the installation wizard, and you can do so using the default settings:

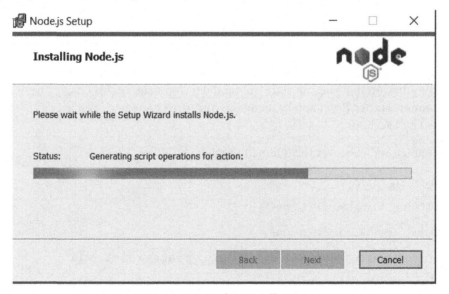

Figure 6.1 – Node.js installation

Once the installation is complete, we can check that everything proceeded correctly. Open PowerShell, or whatever terminal you are using, and type the following commands:

```
node -v
npm -v
```

These commands should show you the installed versions of Node.js and npm:

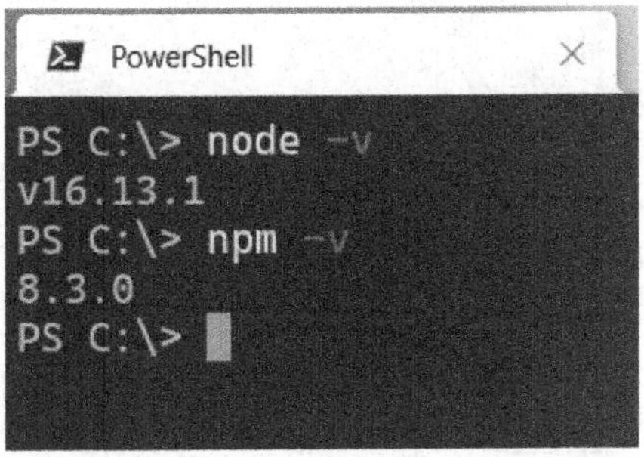

Figure 6.2 – Node.js and npm versions

npm comes with the Node.js installation and is a package manager for JavaScript. We will use this a lot in the following chapters when we install different node modules on our React app. There is also another package manager called **Yarn** that you can use as well.

Now, we have installed Node.js, and next, we will install a code editor that helps us to start coding.

Installing VS Code

Visual Studio Code (**VS Code**) is an open source code editor for multiple programming languages. VS Code was developed by Microsoft. There are a lot of different code editors available, such as Atom and Brackets, and you can use something other than VS Code if you are familiar with it. VS Code is available for Windows, macOS, and Linux, and you can download it from `https://code.visualstudio.com/`.

Installation for Windows is done with the MSI installer, and you can execute the installation with default settings. The following screenshot shows the workbench of VS Code. On the left-hand side is the activity bar, which you can use to navigate between different views. Next to the activity bar is a sidebar that contains different views, such as the project file explorer.

The editor takes up the rest of the workbench:

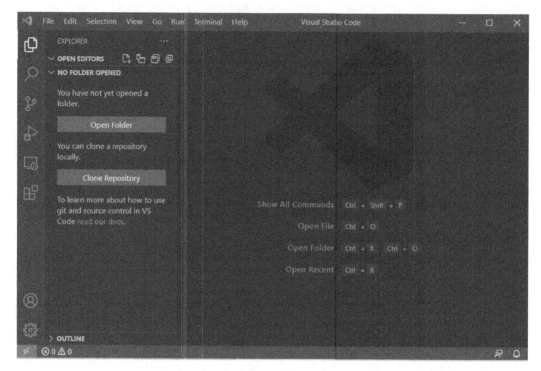

Figure 6.3 – VS Code workbench

VS Code provides an integrated terminal that you can use to create and run React apps. The terminal can be found in the **View | Integrated terminal** menu. You will use this in later chapters when we create more React apps.

VS Code extension

There are a lot of extensions available for different programming languages and frameworks. If you open **Extensions** from the activity bar, you can search for different extensions. One really useful extension for React development is React.js code snippets, which we recommend installing. It has multiple code snippets available for React.js apps, which makes your development process faster. We will show you how to use that extension later.

The following screenshot shows the React.js code snippets installation page:

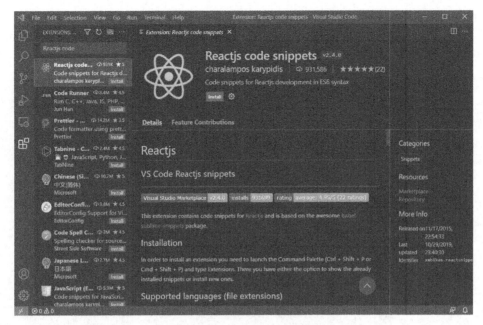

Figure 6.4 – React code snippets

The **ESLint extension** helps you find typos and syntax errors quickly and makes formatting the source code easier:

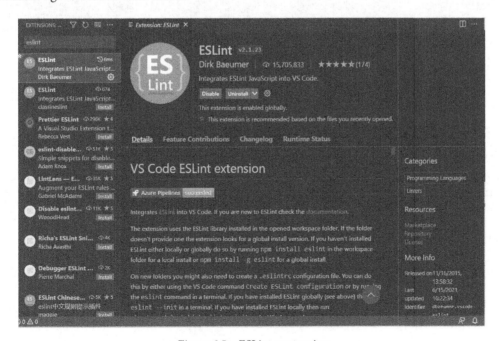

Figure 6.5 – ESLint enxtension

Prettier is a code formatter. With the Prettier extension, you can get automatic code formatting. You can also set this from the VS Code settings so that you can format code automatically after saving your code:

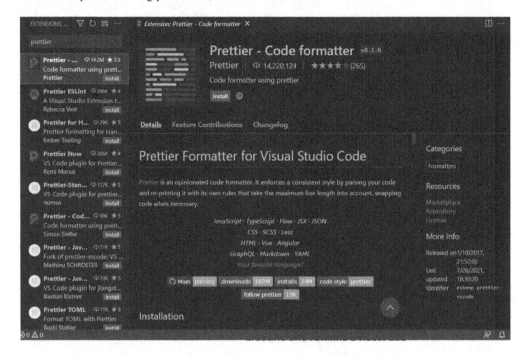

Figure 6.6 – Prettier extension

These are just a few examples of the great extensions you can get for VS Code. Next, we will create our first React app and learn how to run and modify it.

Creating and running a React app

Now that we have Node.js and the code editor installed, we are ready to create our first React.js app. We are using Facebook's `create-react-app` (`https://github.com/facebook/create-react-app`) kit for this. Here are the steps you need to follow in order to make your first app:

1. Open PowerShell or a terminal that you use and type the following command:

```
npx create-react-app myapp
```

This command creates a React app named `myapp`. The npm package runner is `npx` and, when you're using it, you don't have to install the package before running it:

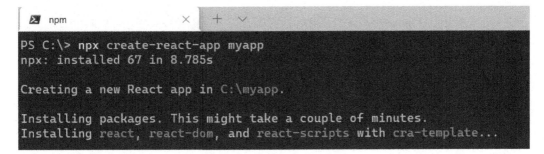

Figure 6.7 – create-react-app

2. Once the app has been created, move it into your app folder:

```
cd myapp
```

3. Then, we can run the app with the following command. This command runs the app in the 3000 localhost port and opens the app in a browser:

```
npm start
```

4. Now, your app is running, and you should see the following page in your browser. The npm start command starts the app in development mode:

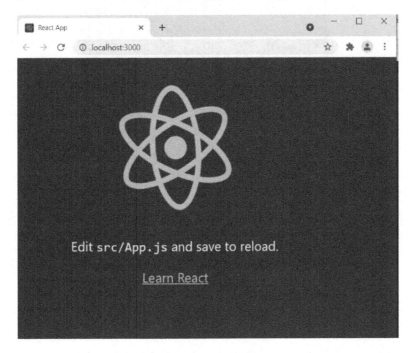

Figure 6.8 – React app

You can stop the development server by pressing *Ctrl + C* in PowerShell. To build a minified version of your app for production, you can use the `npm run build` command, which builds your app in the build folder.

Modifying a React app

Now, we learn how to modify our React app that we created using `create-react-app`. We will use VS Code, which we installed earlier:

1. Open your React app folder with VS Code by selecting **File | Open folder**.
    You should see the app's structure in the file explorer. The most important folder in this phase is the `src` folder, which contains the JavaScript source code:

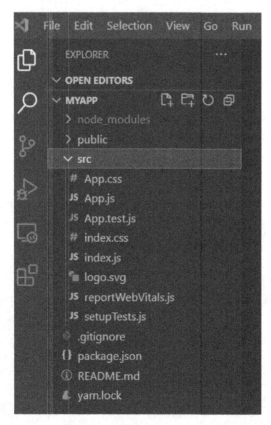

Figure 6.9 – Project structure

Important Note

You can also open VS Code by typing the code . command into the terminal.
This command opens VS Code and the folder where you are located.

---

2.   Open the App.js file from the src folder in the code editor. Modify the text inside
the link element to Hello React (an <a> element) and save the file. You don't
need to know anything else about this file at the moment. We will go deeper into
this topic in *Chapter 7, Getting Started with React*:

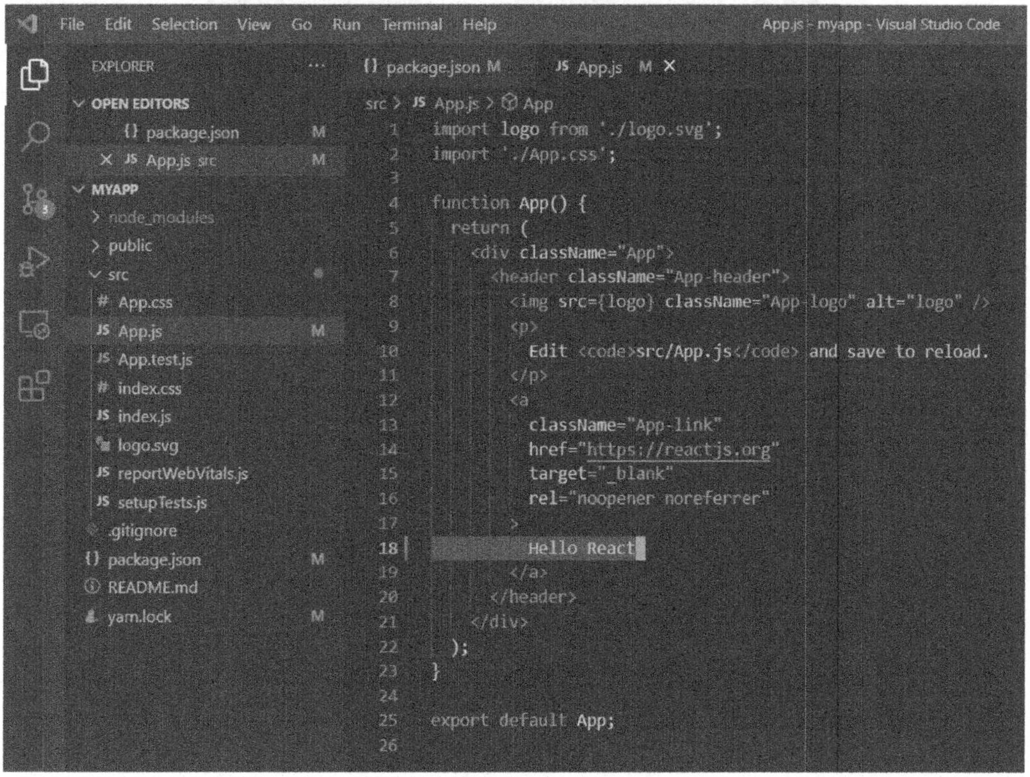

Figure 6.10 – App.js code

3. Now, if you look at the browser, you should immediately see that the link text is changed. The browser is refreshed automatically when you modify and save JavaScript files in your React project:

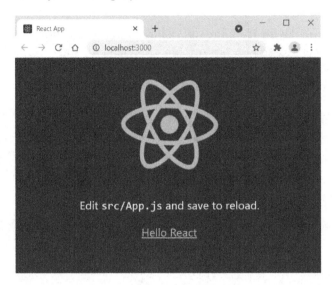

Figure 6.11 – Modified React app

To debug React apps, we should also install React Developer Tools, which is available for Chrome, Firefox, and Edge browsers. Chrome plugins can be installed from the Chrome web store (`https://chrome.google.com/webstore/category/extensions`), while Firefox add-ons can be installed from the Firefox add-ons site (`https://addons.mozilla.org`). After you have installed React Developer Tools, you should see a new **Components** tab in your browser's developer tools once you navigate to your React app.

You can open the developer tools by pressing the *Ctrl + Shift + I* (or *F12*) in the Chrome browser. The following screenshot shows the developer tools in the Chrome browser:

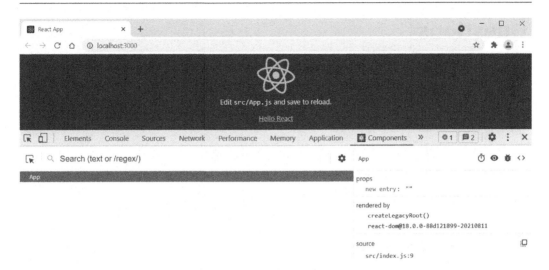

Figure 6.12 – React Developer Tools

The browser's developer tools are really important tools, and it is good to open them during development so that you can see errors and warnings immediately.

Summary

In this chapter, we installed everything that is needed to embark on our frontend development with React.js. First, we installed Node.js and the VS Code editor. Then, we used the `create-react-app` starter kit to create our first React.js app. Finally, we ran the app and demonstrated how to modify it. This is just an overview of the app's structure and modification, and we will continue this in the following chapters.

In the next chapter, we will familiarize ourselves with the basics of React programming. In JavaScript, we will be using ES6 syntax because it provides several features that make coding cleaner.

Questions

1. What are Node.js and npm?

2. How do you install Node.js?

3. What is VS Code?

4. How do you install VS Code?

5. How do you create a React.js app with `create-react-app`?

6. How do you run a React.js app?

7. How do you make basic modifications to your app?

Further reading

Packt has other great resources available for learning about React. These are as follows:

- *React 17 Design Patterns and Best Practices, Carlos Santana Roldán* (`https://subscription.packtpub.com/book/web_development/9781800560444`)

- *React Projects, Roy Derks* (`https://subscription.packtpub.com/book/programming/9781789954937`)

7
Getting Started with React

This chapter describes the basics of React programming. We will cover the skills that are required to create basic functionalities for the React frontend. In JavaScript, we use the **ECMAScript 2015 (ES6)** syntax because it provides many features that make coding cleaner.

In this chapter, we will look at the following topics:

- How to create React components
- Useful ES6 features
- **JavaScript XML (JSX)** and styling
- **Properties (props)** and state
- Stateless components
- Conditional rendering
- React hooks
- Custom hooks

- The Context **application programming interface (API)**

- Handling lists with React

- Handling events with React

- Handling forms with React

Technical requirements

In this book, we will be using the Windows **operating system (OS)**, but all of the tools can be used with Linux and macOS as well. For our work with React hooks, React version 16.8 or higher will be required.

You can find more resources at the GitHub link at `https://github.com/ PacktPublishing/Full-Stack-Development-with-Spring-Boot-and- React/tree/main/Chapter07`.

How to create React components

According to Meta Platforms, Inc., React is a JavaScript library for **user interfaces (UIs)**. Since version 15, React has been developed under the **Massachusetts Institute of Technology (MIT)** license. React is component-based, and the components are independent and reusable. The components are the basic building blocks of React. When you start to develop a UI with React, it is good to start by creating mock interfaces. That way, it will be easy to identify what kinds of components you have to create and how they interact.

From the following screenshot of the mock UI, we can see how the UI can be split into components. In this case, there will be an application root component, a search bar component, a table component, and a table row component:

Id	Description	Date	Priority
1	React exam	1.2.2022	High
2	Swimming	7.6.2022	Medium
3	Coffee with Mike	3.4.2022	Low
4	Movie night	5.2.2022	High

(Figure showing Root component containing Search component with Search field and SEARCH button, and Table component containing the above table with Table row component highlighting row 1)

Figure 7.1 – React components

The components can then be arranged in a tree hierarchy, as shown in the following screenshot. The root component has two child components: the search component and the table component. The table component has one child component: the table row component. The important thing to understand with React is that the data flow is going from a parent component to a child component. We will learn later how data can be passed from a parent component to a child component using props:

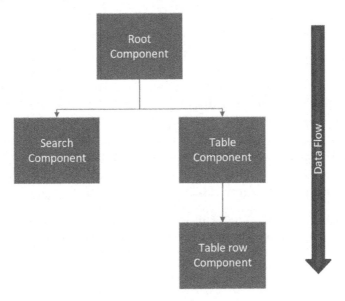

Figure 7.2 – Component tree

React uses the **virtual Document Object Model** (**VDOM**) for selective re-rendering of the UI, which makes it more cost-effective. The VDOM is a lightweight copy of the DOM, and manipulation of the VDOM is much faster than it is with the real DOM. After the VDOM is updated, React compares it to a snapshot that was taken from the VDOM before updates were run. After the comparison, React will know which parts have been changed, and only these parts will be updated to the real DOM.

A React component can be defined by using a JavaScript function or the ES6 JavaScript class. We will go more deeply into ES6 in the next section. Here is some simple component source code that renders the Hello World text. This first code block uses the JavaScript function:

```
// Using JavaScript function
function App() {
   return <h1>Hello World</h1>;
}
```

The mandatory return statement in the React function component defines what the component looks like.

The following code uses the ES6 class to create a component:

```
// Using ES6 class
class App extends React.Component {
   render() {
      return <h1>Hello World</h1>;
   }
}
```

The component that was implemented using the class contains the required render() method that shows and updates the rendered output of the component. If you compare the App function and class components, you can see that the render() method is not needed in the function component. Before React version 16.8, you had to use class components to be able to use states. Now, you can use hooks to create states also with function components. We will learn about state and hooks later in this chapter.

In this book, we are creating components using functions. You have to write less code when using function components, but you can still also use class components as well.

> **Important Note**
> The name of the React component should start with a capital letter. It is also recommended to use the *PascalCase* naming convention whereby each word starts with a capital letter.

Let's make changes to our component's `return` statement and add a new `<h2>` element to it, as follows:

```
function App() {
  return (
    <h1>Hello World</h1>
    <h2>This is my first React component</h2>
  );
}
```

When you run the app, you get an `Adjacent JSX elements must be wrapped in an enclosing tag` error, as indicated in the following screenshot:

Figure 7.3 – Adjacent JSX elements error

If your component returns multiple elements, you have to wrap these inside one parent element. To fix this error, we have to wrap the header elements in one element, such as `div`, as illustrated in the following code snippet:

```
// Wrap elements inside the div
function App() {
  return (
    <div>
      <h1>Hello World</h1>
      <h2>This is my first React component</h2>
```

```
    </div>
  );
}
```

Since React version 16.2, we can also use fragments, as shown in the following code snippet:

```
// Using fragments
function App() {
  return (
    <React.Fragment>
      <h1>Hello World</h1>
      <h2>This is my first React component</h2>
    <React.Fragment/>
  );
}
```

There is also shorter syntax for fragments, which look like empty JSX tags. This is shown in the following code snippet:

```
// Using fragments short syntax
function App() {
  return (
    <>
      <h1>Hello World</h1>
      <h2>This is my first React component</h2>
    </>
  );
}
```

Let's look more carefully at the first React app we created in *Chapter 6*, *Setting Up the Environment and Tools – Frontend*, using create-react-app. The source code of the index.js file in the root folder looks like this:

```
import React from 'react';
import ReactDOM from 'react-dom'
import './index.css';
import App from './App';
import reportWebVitals from './reportWebVitals';
```

```
ReactDOM.render(
  <React.StrictMode>
    <App />
  </React.StrictMode>,
  document.getElementById('root')
);
reportWebVitals();
```

At the beginning of the file, there are `import` statements that load components and assets to our file. For example, the second line imports the `react-dom` package from the `node_modules` folder, and the fourth line imports the `App` component (the `App.js` file in the `src` folder). The third line imports the `index.css` style sheet that is in the same folder as the `index.js` file. The `react-dom` package provides DOM-specific methods for us. To render the React component to the DOM, we can use the `render` method from the `react-dom` package. `React.StrictMode` is used to find potential problems in your React app and these are printed in the browser console.

The new **root API** was introduced in React version 18. Here, we first create a root using the `createRoot` method. The root calls the `render` method to render an element to the root. The old root API still works, but you get a warning in the console. In this book, we are using React 18 and the new root API, as indicated in the following code snippet:

```
// New Root API, React 18
import * as ReactDOMClient from 'react-dom/client';
import App from './App';

const container = document.getElementById('root');

// Create a root.
const root = ReactDOMClient.createRoot(container);

// Render an element to the root.
root.render(<App />);
```

The `container` in the root API is `<div id="root"></div>` element, which can be found in the `index.html` file inside the `public` folder. Look at the following `index.html` file:

```html
<!DOCTYPE html>
<html lang="en">
  <head>
    <meta charset="utf-8" />
    <link rel="icon" href="%PUBLIC_URL%/favicon.ico" />
    <meta name="viewport" content="width=device-width,
        initial-scale=1" />
    <meta name="theme-color" content="#000000" />
    <meta
      name="description"
      content="Web site created using create-react-app"
    />
    <link rel="apple-touch-icon" href="%PUBLIC_URL%
        /logo192.png" />
    <link rel="manifest" href="%PUBLIC_URL%/
        manifest.json" />
    <title>React App</title>
  </head>
  <body>
    <noscript>You need to enable JavaScript to run this
        app.</noscript>
    <div id="root"></div>
  </body>
</html>
```

The following source code shows the `App.js` component from our first React app. You can see that import also applies to assets, such as images and style sheets. At the end of the source code, there is an `export` statement that exports the component, and it can be made available to other components by using `import`. There can only be one default `export` statement per file, but there can be multiple named `export` statements:

```js
import logo from './logo.svg';
import './App.css';
```

```
function App() {
  return (
    <div className="App">
      <header className="App-header">
        <img src={logo} className="App-logo" alt="logo" />
        <p>
          Edit <code>src/App.js</code> and save to reload.
        </p>
        <a
          className="App-link"
          href="https://reactjs.org"
          target="_blank"
          rel="noopener noreferrer"
        >
          Learn React
        </a>
      </header>
    </div>
  );
}

export default App;
```

The following example shows how to import default and named exports:

```
import React from 'react' // Import default value
import { name } from … //  Import named value
```

The exports look like this:

```
export default React // Default export
export { name }  //  Named  export
```

Now that we have covered the basics of React components, let's take a look at the basic features of ES6.

Useful ES6 features

ES6 was released in 2015, and it introduced a lot of new features. ECMAScript is a standardized scripting language, and JavaScript is one implementation of it. In this section, we will go through the most important features released in ES6 that we will be using in the following sections.

Constants and variables

Constants, or immutable variables, can be defined by using a `const` keyword, as shown in the following code snippet. When using the `const` keyword, the variable content cannot be reassigned:

```
const PI = 3.14159;
```

Now, you will get an error if you try to reassign the `PI` value, as indicated in the following screenshot:

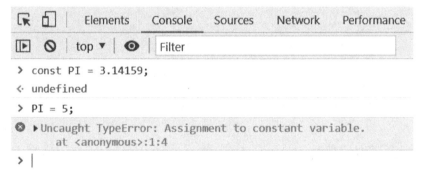

Figure 7.4 – Assignment to constant variable

The scope of `const` is block-scoped. This means that the `const` variable can only be used inside the block in which it is defined. In practice, the block is the area between curly brackets { }. The following sample code shows how the scope works:

```
let count = 10;
if (count > 5) {
  const total = count * 2;
  console.log(total); // Prints 20 to console
}
console.log(total); // Error, outside the scope
```

The second `console.log` statement gives an error because we are trying to use the `total` variable outside the scope.

The following example demonstrates what happens when `const` is an object or array:

```
const myObj = {foo:  3};
myObj.foo = 5; // This is ok
```

When `const` is an object or array, the content can be changed.

The `let` keyword allows you to declare mutable block-scoped variables, therefore the `let` variable can be used inside the block in which they are declared (note that it can also be used inside sub-blocks).

Arrow functions

The traditional way of defining a function in JavaScript is by using a `function` keyword. The following function gets one argument and returns the argument value multiplied by 2:

```
function(x) {
   return x * 2;
}
```

But when we use the ES6 arrow function, the function looks like this:

```
x => x * 2
```

As we can see, by using the arrow function, we have made the declaration of the same function more compact. The function is a so-called anonymous function, and we can't call it. Anonymous functions are often used as an argument for other functions. In JavaScript, functions are *first-class citizens* and you can store functions in variables, as illustrated here:

```
const calc = x => x * 2
```

Now, you can use the variable name to call the function, like this:

```
calc(5); // returns 10
```

When you have more than one argument, you have to wrap the arguments in parentheses and separate the arguments with a comma to use the arrow function effectively. For example, the following function gets two parameters and returns the sum of the parameters:

```
const calcSum = (x, y) => x + y
// function call
calcSum(2, 3); // returns 5
```

If the function body is an expression, then you don't need to use the `return` keyword. The expression is always implicitly returned from the function. When you have multiple lines in the function body, you have to use curly brackets and a `return` statement, as follows:

```
const calcSum = (x, y) => {
   console.log('Calculating sum');
   return x + y;
}
```

If the function doesn't have any arguments, then you should use empty parentheses, like so:

```
const sayHello = () => "Hello"
```

We are going to use lots of arrow functions later in our frontend implementation.

Template literals

Template literals can be used to concatenate strings. The traditional way to concatenate strings is to use the + operator, as follows:

```
let person = {firstName: 'John', lastName: 'Johnson'};
let greeting = "Hello " + ${person.firstName} + " " +
    ${person.lastName};
```

With the template literals, the syntax looks like this. You have to use backticks (` `) instead of single or double quotes:

```
let person = {firstName: 'John', lastName: 'Johnson'};
let greeting = 'Hello ${person.firstName}
    ${person.lastName}';
```

Next, we will learn how to create classes using JavaScript ES6 syntax.

Classes and inheritance

Class definition in ES6 is similar to other **object-oriented** (**OO**) languages, such as Java or C#. The keyword for defining classes is `class`. A class can have fields, constructors, and class methods. The following sample code shows the ES6 class:

```
class Person {
  constructor(firstName, lastName)  {
    this.firstName = firstName;
    this.lastName = lastName;
  }
}
```

Inheritance is performed with an `extends` keyword. The following sample code shows an `Employee` class that inherits a `Person` class. This means that it inherits all fields from the parent class and can have its own fields that are specific to `Employee`. In the constructor, we first call the parent class constructor by using the `super` keyword. That call is required by the rest of the code, and you will get an error if it is missing:

```
class Employee extends Person {
  constructor(firstName, lastName, title, salary)  {
    super(firstName, lastName);
    this.title = title;
    this.salary = salary;
  }
}
```

Although ES6 is already quite old, it is still only partially supported by modern web browsers. **Babel** is a JavaScript compiler that is used to compile ES6 to an older version that is compatible with all browsers. You can test the compiler on the Babel website (`https://babeljs.io`). The following screenshot shows the arrow function compiling back to the older JavaScript syntax:

Figure 7.5 – Babel

Now that we have learned about the basics of ES6, let's take a look at what JSX and styling are all about.

JSX and styling

JSX is the syntax extension for JavaScript. It is not mandatory to use JSX with React, but there are some benefits that make development easier. JSX, for example, prevents injection attacks because all values are escaped in the JSX before they are rendered. The most useful feature is that you can embed JavaScript expressions in the JSX by wrapping it with curly brackets; this technique will be used a lot in the following chapters.

In the following example, we can access the component props when using JSX. Component props are covered in the next section:

```
function App() {
  return <h1>Hello World {props.user}</h1>;
}
```

You can also pass a JavaScript expression as props, as shown in the following code snippet:

```
<Hello count={2+2} />
```

JSX is compiled into regular JavaScript by Babel.

You can use both internal and external styling with React JSX elements. Here are two examples of inline styling. This first one defines the style inside the `div` element:

```
<div style={{ height: 20, width: 200 }}>
  Hello
</div>
```

This second example creates a style object first, which is then used in the `div` element, The object name should use the *camelCase* naming convention:

```
const divStyle = { color: 'red', height: 30 };

const MyComponent = () => (
  <div style={divStyle}>Hello</div>
);
```

As shown in the previous section, you can import a style sheet to a React component. To reference classes from an external **Cascading Style Sheets** (**CSS**) file, you should use a `className` attribute, as shown in the following code snippet:

```
import './App.js';
...
<div className="App-header"> This is my app</div>
```

In the next section, we will learn about React props and state.

Props and state

Props and **state** are the input data for rendering the component. The component is re-rendered when the props or the state change.

Props

Props are inputs to components, and they are a mechanism to pass data from the parent component to its child component. Props are JavaScript objects, therefore they can contain multiple key-value pairs.

Props are immutable, so a component cannot change its props. Props are received from the parent component. A component can access props through the `props` object that is passed to the function component as a parameter. For example, let's take a look at the following component:

```
function Hello() {
   return <h1>Hello John</h1>;
}
```

The component is just rendering a static message, and it is not reusable. Instead of using a hardcoded name, we can pass a name to the `Hello` component by using props, like this:

```
function Hello(props) {
   return <h1>Hello {props.user}</h1>;
}
```

The parent component can send props to the `Hello` component in the following way:

```
<Hello user="John" />
```

Now, when the `Hello` component is rendered, it shows the `Hello John` text.

You can also pass multiple props to a component, as shown here:

```
<Hello firstName="John" lastName="Johnson" />
```

Now, you can access both props in the component using the `props` object, as follows:

```
function Hello(props) {
    return <h1>Hello {props.firstName} {props.lastName}</h1>;
}
```

Now, the component output is `Hello John Johnson`.

State

The state value can be updated inside a component. The state is created using the `useState` hook function. It takes one argument, which is the initial value of the state, and returns an array of two elements. The first element is the name of a state, and the second element is a function that is used to update the state value. The syntax of the `useState` function is shown in the following code snippet:

```
const [state, setState] = React.useState(intialValue);
```

The next code example creates a state variable called `name`, and the initial value is `Jim`:

```
const [name, setName] = React.useState('Jim');
```

You can also import the `useState` function from React, like so:

```
import React, { useState } from 'react';
```

Then, you don't need to type the `React` keyword, as indicated here:

```
const [name, setName] = useState('Jim');
```

The value of the state can now be updated by using the `setName` function, as illustrated in the following code snippet. That is the only way to modify the state value:

```
// Update name state value
setName('John');
```

You should never update the state value directly using the = operator. If you update state directly, React won't re-render the UI and you will also get an error because you cannot re-assign the const variable, as indicated here:

```
// Don't do this, UI won't re-render
name = 'John';
```

If you have multiple states, you can call the useState function multiple times, as shown in the following code snippet:

```
// Create two states: firstName and lastName
const [firstName, setFirstName] = useState('John');
const [lastName, setLastName] = useState('Johnson');
```

Now, you can update states using the setFirstName and setLastName functions, as shown in the following code snippet:

```
// Update state values
setFirstName('Jim');
setLastName('Palmer');
```

You can also define state using an object, as follows:

```
const [name, setName] = useState({
  firstName: 'John',
  lastName: 'Johnson'
});
```

Now, you can update both the firstName and lastName state object parameters using the setName function, as follows:

```
setName({ firstName: 'Jim', lastName: 'Palmer' })
```

If you want to do a partial update of the object, you can use the spread operator. In the following example, we use the object spread syntax (. . .) that was introduced in ES2018. It clones the name state object and updates the firstName value to be Jim:

```
setName({ ...name, firstName: 'Jim' })
```

A state can be accessed by using the state name, as shown in the next example. The scope of the state is the component, so it cannot be used outside the component in which it is defined:

```
// Renders Hello John
import React, { useState } from 'react';


function MyComponent() {
  const [firstName, setFirstName] = useState('John');


  return <div>Hello {firstName}</div>;
}
```

We have now learned the basics of state and props but will learn more about states later in this chapter.

Stateless components

The React **stateless component** is just a pure JavaScript function that takes props as an argument and returns a React element. Here's an example of a stateless component:

```
function HeaderText(props) {
  return (
    <h1>
      {props.text}
    </h1>
  )
}


export default HeaderText;
```

Our `HeaderText` example component is also called a **pure component**. A component is said to be pure if its return value is consistently the same given the same input values. React provides `React.memo()`, which optimizes the performance of pure functional components. In the following code snippet, we wrap our component using `memo()`:

```
import React, { memo } from 'react';


function HeaderText(props) {
```

```
  return (
    <h1>
      {props.text}
    </h1>
  )
}

export default memo(HeaderText);
```

Now, the component is rendered and memoized. In the next render, React renders a memoized result if the props are not changed. The React.memo() phrase also has a second argument, arePropsEqual(), which you can use to customize rendering conditions, but we will not cover that here. The one benefit of the functional components is unit testing, which is straightforward because its return value is always the same for the same input values.

Conditional rendering

You can use a conditional statement to render different UIs if a condition is true or false. This feature can be used, for example, to show or hide some elements, handle authentication, and so on.

In the following example, we will check if props.isLoggedin is true. If so, we will render the <Logout /> component; otherwise, we render the <Login /> component. This is now implemented using two separate return statements:

```
function MyComponent(props) {
  const isLoggedin = props.isLoggedin;

  if (isLoggedin) {
    return (
      <Logout />
    )
  }

  return (
    <Login />
  )
}
```

You can also implement this by using `condition ? true : false` logical operators, and then you need only one `return` statement, as illustrated here:

```
function MyComponent (props) {
  const isLoggedin = props.isLoggedin;

    return (
      <div>
        { isLoggedin ? <Logout /> : <Login /> }
      </div>
    );
}
```

React hooks

There are certain important rules for using hooks in React. You should always call hooks at the top level in your React function component. You shouldn't call hooks inside loops, conditional statements, or nested functions.

useState

We are already familiar with the `useState` hooks function that was used to declare states. Let's create one more example of using the `useState` hook. We will create a counter example that contains a button, and when it is pressed, the counter is increased by 1, as illustrated in the following screenshot:

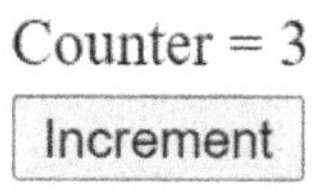

Counter = 3

| Increment |

Figure 7.6 – Counter component

First, we create a `Counter` component and declare a state called `count` with the initial value 0. The value of the counter state can be updated using the `setCount` function. The code is illustrated in the following snippet:

```
import React, { useState } from 'react';

function Counter() {
  // count state with initial value 0
  const [count, setCount] = useState(0);
```

```
    return <div></div>;
};

export default Counter;
```

Next, we render a button element that increments the state by 1. We use the `onClick` event attribute to call the `setCount` function, and the new value is the current value plus 1. We will also render the counter state value. The code is illustrated in the following snippet:

```
import React, { useState } from 'react';

function Counter() {
  const [count, setCount] = useState(0);

  return (
    <div>
      <p>Counter = {count}</p>
      <button onClick={() => setCount(count + 1) }>
        Increment
      </button>
    </div>
  );
};

export default Counter;
```

Now, our `Counter` component is ready, and the counter is incremented by 1 each time the button is pressed. When the state is updated, React re-renders the component, and we can see the new `count` value.

> **Important Note**
> In React, events are named using camelCase—for example, `onClick`.

State updates are asynchronous therefore you have to be careful when a new state value depends on the current state value. To be sure that the latest value is used, you can pass a function to the update function. You can see an example of this here:

```
setCount(prevCount => prevCount + 1)
```

Now, the previous value is passed to the function, and the updated value is returned and saved to the `count` state. There is also a hook function called `useReducer` that is recommended to use when you have a complex state, but we won't cover that in this book.

React also uses batching in state updates to reduce re-renders. Before React version 18, batching only worked in states updated during browser events—for example, a button click. The following example demonstrates the idea of batch updates:

```
import React, { useState } from 'react';

function App() {
  const [count, setCount] = useState(0);
  const [count2, setCount2] = useState(0);

  const increment = () => {
    setCount(count + 1); // No re-rendering yet
    setCount2(count2 + 1);
    // Component re-renders after all state updates
  }

  return (
    <div>
      <p>Counters: {count} {count2}</p>
      <button onClick={increment}>Increment</button>
    </div>
  );
};

export default App;
```

From React version 18 onward, all state updates will be batched. If you don't want to use batch updates in some cases, you can use the `react-dom` library `flushSync` API to avoid batching. For example, you might have a case where you want to update some state before updating the next one. Here's the code you'll need to do this:

```
import { flushSync } from "react-dom";
...
const increment = () => {
  flushSync( () => {
```

```
    setCount(count + 1); // No batch update
  }
}
```

Note—this must be checked when React 18 is released.

useEffect

The `useEffect` hook function can be used to perform side-effects in the React function component. The side-effect can be, for example, a `fetch` request. The `useEffect` hook takes two arguments, as shown here:

```
useEffect(callback, [dependencies])
```

The `callback` function contains side-effect logic, and `dependencies` is an optional array of dependencies.

The following code snippet shows the previous counter example, but we have added the `useEffect` hook. Now, when the button is pressed, the `count` state value increases, and the component is re-rendered. After each render, the `useEffect` callback function is invoked and we can see `Hello from useEffect` in the console, as illustrated in the following code snippet:

```
import React, { useState, useEffect } from 'react';

function Counter() {
  const [count, setCount] = useState(0);

  // Called after every render
  useEffect(() => {
    console.log('Hello from useEffect')
  });

  return (
    <div>
      <p>{count}</p>
      <button onClick={() => setCount(count + 1)}>Increment
      </button>
    </div>
  );
```

```
};
```

```
export default Counter;
```

In the following screenshot, we can see what the console now looks like, and we can see that the useEffect callback is invoked after each render. The first log row is printed after the initial render, and the rest are printed after the button is pressed two times and the component is re-rendered due to state updates:

Figure 7.7 – useEffect

The useEffect hook has a second optional argument that you can use to prevent it from running in every render. In the following code snippet, we define that if the count state value is changed (meaning that the previous and current values differ), the useEffect callback function will be invoked. We can also define multiple states in the second argument. If any of these state values are changed, the useEffect hook will be invoked:

```
// Runs when count value is changed and component is
   re-rendered
useEffect(() => {
  console.log('Counter value is now ' + count);
}, [count]);
```

If you pass an empty array as second argument, the `useEffect` callback function runs only after the first render, as shown in the following code snippet:

```
// Runs only after the first render
useEffect(() => {
   console.log('Hello from useEffect')
}, []);
```

Now, you can see that `Hello from useEffect` is printed only once after the initial render and if you press the button, the text is not printed:

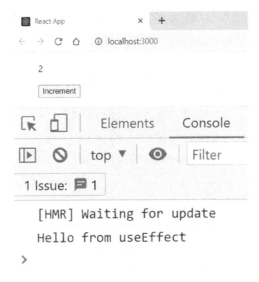

Figure 7.8 – useEffect with an empty array

The `useEffect` function can also return a function that will run before every effect, as shown in the following code snippet. With this mechanism, you can clean up each effect from the previous render before running the effect next time:

```
useEffect(() => {
   console.log('Hello from useEffect');

   return () => {
     console.log('Clean up function');
   }
}, [count]);
```

Now, if you run a counter app with these changes, you can see what happens in the console, as shown in the following screenshot:

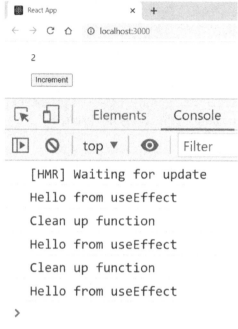

Figure 7.9 – Cleanup function

useRef

The useRef hook returns a mutable ref object and it can be used, for example, to access DOM nodes. You can see it in action here:

```
const ref = useRef(initialValue)
```

The returned ref object has a current property that is initialized with the passed argument (initialValue). In the next example, we create a ref object called inputRef and initialize it to null. Then, we use the JSX element's ref property and pass our ref object to it. Now, it contains our input element, and we can use the current property to execute the input element's focus function:

```
import React, { useRef } from 'react';
import './App.css';

function App() {
  const inputRef = useRef(null);
```

```
  return (
    <div>
      <input ref={inputRef} />
      <button onClick={() => inputRef.current.focus()}>
        Focus input
      </button>
    </div>
  );
}

export default App;
```

There are other useful hook functions, and we will cover some of these later in this book. In this section, we have learned the basics about React hooks, and we will use them in practice when we start to implement our frontend.

Custom hooks

You can also build your own hooks in React. Hooks' names should start with the use-word, and they are JavaScript functions. Custom hooks can also call other hooks. With custom hooks, you can reduce your component code complexity.

Let's go through a simple example of creating a custom hook. We will create a useTitle hook that can be used to update a document title. We will define it in its own file called useTitle.js. First, we define a function, and it gets one argument named title. The code is illustrated in the following snippet:

```
// useTitle.js
function useTitle(title) {
}
```

Next, we will use a useEffect hook to update the document title each time the title argument is changed, as follows:

```
import { useEffect } from 'react';

function useTitle(title) {
  useEffect(() => {
    document.title = title;
```

```
    }, [title]);
}
```

```
export default useTitle;
```

Now, we can start to use our custom hook. Let's use it in our counter example and print the current counter value into the document title. First, we have to import the useTitle hook into our Counter component, like this:

```
import useTitle from './useTitle';
```

```
function Counter() {
  return (
    <div>
    </div>
  );
};
```

```
export default Counter;
```

Then, we will use the useTitle hook to print the count state value into the document title. We can call our hook function in the top level of the Counter component function, and every time the component is rendered, the useTitle hook function is called and we can see the current count value in the document title. The code is illustrated in the following snippet:

```
import React, { useState } from 'react';
import useTitle from './useTitle';

function App() {
  const [count, setCount] = useState(0);

  useTitle('You clicked ${count} times');

  return (
    <div>
      <p>Counter = {count}</p>
      <button onClick={ () => setCount(count + 1) }>
        Increment
```

```
      </button>
    </div>
  );
};

export default App;
```

Now, if you click the button, the count state value is shown also in the document title using our custom hook, as illustrated in the following screenshot:

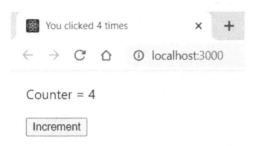

Figure 7.10 – Custom hook

You now have basic knowledge of React hooks and how you can create your own custom hooks.

The Context API

Passing data using props can be cumbersome if your component tree is deep and complex. You have to pass data through all components down the component tree. The Context API solves this problem, and it is recommended to use for *global* data that you might need in multiple components through your component tree—for example, a theme or authenticated user.

Context is created using the createContext method and it takes an argument that defines the default value. You can create your own file for the context, and the code looks like this:

```
import React from 'react';

const AuthContext = React.createContext('');

export default AuthContext;
```

Next, we will use a context provider component that makes our context available for other components. The context provider component has a `value` prop that will be passed to consuming components. In the following example, we have wrapped <MyComponent /> using the context provider component, therefore the `userName` value is available in our component tree under <MyComponent />:

```
import React from 'react';
import AuthContext from './AuthContext';
import MyComponent from './MyComponent';

function App() {
  // User is authenticated and we get the username
  const userName = 'john';

  return (
    <AuthContext.Provider value={userName}>
      <MyComponent />
    </AuthContext.Provider>
  );

};
export default App;
```

Now, we can access the provided value in any component in the component tree by using the `useContext()` hook, as follows:

```
import React from 'react';
import AuthContext from './AuthContext';

function MyComponent() {
  const authContext = React.useContext(AuthContext);

  return(
    <div>
      Welcome {authContext}
    </div>
  );
}
```

```
export default MyComponent;
```

The component now renders `Welcome john` text.

Handling lists with React

For list handling, we will learn about a new JavaScript `map()` method, which is useful when you have to manipulate a list. The `map()` method creates a new array containing the results of calling a function to each element in the original array. In the following example, each array element is multiplied by 2:

```
const arr = [1, 2, 3, 4];
const resArr = arr.map(x => x * 2); // resArr = [2, 4, 6, 8]
```

The `map()` method also has `index` as a second argument, which is useful when handling lists in React. List items in React need a unique key that is used to detect rows that have been updated, added, or deleted.

The following example code demonstrates a component that transforms an array of integers to an array of list items and renders these inside the `ul` element:

```
import React from 'react';

function MyList() {
  const data = [1, 2, 3, 4, 5];

  return (
    <div>
      <ul>
        {
        data.map((number, index) =>
          <li key={index}>Listitem {number}</li>)
        }
      </ul>
    </div>
  );
};

export default MyList;
```

The following screenshot shows what the component looks like when it is rendered:

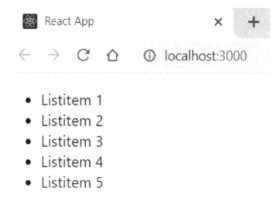

Figure 7.11 – React list component

If the data is an array of objects, it would be nicer to present it in table format. We do this in roughly the same way as we did with the list, but now we just map the array to table rows (`tr` elements) and render these inside the `table` element, as shown in the following component code:

```
import React from 'react';

function MyTable() {
  const data = [
    {brand: 'Ford', model: 'Mustang'},
    {brand: 'VW', model: 'Beetle'},
    {brand: 'Tesla', model: 'Model S'}];

  return (
  <div>
    <table>
      <tbody>
      {
      data.map((item, index) =>
        <tr key={index}>
          <td>{item.brand}</td><td>{item.model}</td>
        </tr>)
      }
      </tbody>
```

```
      </table>
    </div>
  );
};

export default MyTable;
```

The following screenshot shows what the component looks like when it is rendered. Now, you should see the data in the **HyperText Markup Language** (**HTML**) table:

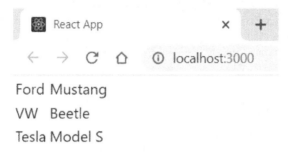

Figure 7.12 – React table

Now, we have learned how to handle list data using the `map()` method and how to render it using, for example, an HTML `table` element.

Handling events with React

Event handling in React is similar to handling DOM element events. The difference compared to HTML event handling is that event naming uses camelCase in React. The following sample component code adds an event listener to a button and shows an alert message when the button is pressed:

```
import React from 'react';

function MyComponent() {
  // This is called when the button is pressed
  const buttonPressed = () => {
    alert('Button pressed');
  }

  return (
```

```
    <div>
      <button onClick={buttonPressed}>Press Me</button>
    </div>
  );
};

export default MyComponent;
```

In React, you cannot return `false` from the event handler to prevent the default behavior. Instead, you should call the `preventDefault()` method. In the following example, we are using a `form` element, and we want to prevent form submission:

```
import React from 'react';

function MyForm() {
  // This is called when the form is submitted
  const handleSubmit = (event) => {
    event.preventDefault(); // Prevents default behavior
    alert('Form submit');
  }

  return (
    <form onSubmit={handleSubmit}>
      <input type="submit" value="Submit" />
    </form>
  );
};

export default MyForm;
```

Now, when you press the **Submit** button, you can see the alert and the form will not be submitted.

Handling forms with React

Form handling is a little bit different with React. An HTML `form` will navigate to the next page when it is submitted. Oftentimes, we want to invoke a JavaScript function that has access to form data after submission and avoid navigating to the next page. We already covered how to avoid submission in the previous section using `preventDefault()`.

Let's first create a minimalistic form with one input field and a **Submit** button. In order to get the value of the input field, we use the onChange event handler. We use the useState hook to create a state variable called text. When the value of the input field is changed, the new value will be saved to the state. This is also called a **controlled component** because form data is handled by React.

The setText(event.target.value) statement gets the value from the input field and saves it to the state. Finally, we will show the typed value when a user presses the **Submit** button. Here is the source code for our first form:

```
import React, { useState } from 'react';

function MyList() {
  const [text, setText] = useState('');

  // Save input element value to state when it has been
     changed
  const inputChanged = (event) => {
    setText(event.target.value);
  }

  const handleSubmit = (event) => {
    alert('You typed: ${text}');
    event.preventDefault();
  }

  return (
    <form onSubmit={handleSubmit}>
      <input type="text" onChange={inputChanged}
          value={text}/>
      <input type="submit" value="Press me"/>
    </form>
  );
};

export default MyList;
```

Here is a screenshot of our form component after the **Submit** button has been pressed:

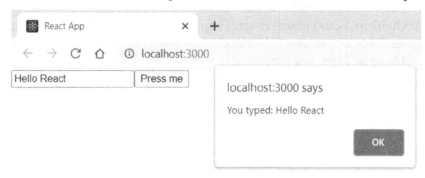

Figure 7.13 – Form component

You can also write an inline onChange handler function using the JSX, as shown in the following example:

```
return (
    <form onSubmit={handleSubmit}>
        <input
            type="text"
            onChange={event => setText(event.target.value)}
            value={text}/>
        <input type="submit" value="Press me"/>
    </form>
);
```

Now is a good time to look at the React developer tools, which are useful for debugging React apps. If we open the React developer tools with our React form app and type something into the input field, we can see how the value of the state changes, and we can inspect the current value of both the props and the state.

The following screenshot shows how the state changes when we type something into the input field:

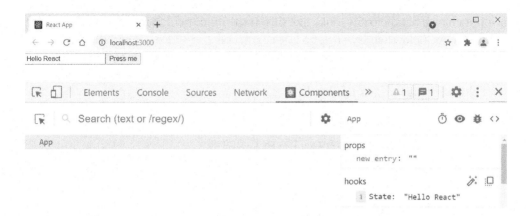

Figure 7.14 – React developer tools

Typically, we have more than one input field in the form. Let's look at how we can handle that using an object state. First, we introduce a state called `user` using the `useState` hook, as shown in the following code snippet. The `user` state is an object with three attributes: `firstName`, `lastName`, and `email`:

```
const [user, setUser] = useState({
  firstName: '',
  lastName: '',
  email: ''
});
```

One way to handle multiple input fields is to add as many change handlers as we have input fields, but this creates a lot of boilerplate code, which we want to avoid. Therefore, we add `name` attributes to our input fields. We can utilize these in the change handler to identify which input field triggers the change handler. The `name` attribute value of the `input` element must be the same as the name of the state object property in which we want to save the value, and the value attribute should be `object.property`—for example, in the first name input element. The code is illustrated here:

```
<input type="text" name="lastName" onChange={inputChanged}
value={user.lastName}/>
```

The input change handler now looks like this. If the input field that triggers the handler is the first name field, then `event.target.name` is `firstName`, and the typed value will be saved to the state object's `firstName` field. Here, we also use the object spread notation that was introduced in the *React hooks* section. In this way, we can handle all input fields with the one change handler:

```
const inputChanged = (event) => {
  setUser({...user, [event.target.name]:
    event.target.value});
}
```

Here is the full source code of the component:

```
import React, { useState } from 'react';

function MyForm() {
  const [user, setUser] = useState({
    firstName: '',
    lastName: '',
    email: ''
  });

  // Save input box value to state when it has been changed
  const inputChanged = (event) => {
    setUser({...user, [event.target.name]:
      event.target.value});
  }

  const handleSubmit = (event) => {
    alert('Hello ${user.firstName} ${user.lastName}');
    event.preventDefault();
  }

  return (
    <form onSubmit={handleSubmit}>
      <label>First name </label>
      <input type="text" name="firstName" onChange=
        {inputChanged}
```

```
            value={user.firstName}/><br/>
        <label>Last name </label>
        <input type="text" name="lastName" onChange=
            {inputChanged}
            value={user.lastName}/><br/>
        <label>Email </label>
        <input type="email" name="email" onChange=
            {inputChanged}
            value={user.email}/><br/>
        <input type="submit" value="Press me"/>
      </form>
  );
};

export default MyForm;
```

Here is a screenshot of our form component after the **Submit** button has been pressed:

Figure 7.15 – React form component

The previous example can be also implemented using separate states instead of one state and object. The following code snippet demonstrates that. Now, we have three states, and in the input element's onChange event handler, we call the correct update function to save values into the states. In this case, we don't need the name input element's name attribute:

```
import React, { useState } from 'react';

function MyForm() {
  const [firstName, setFirstName] = useState('');
  const [lastName, setLastName] = useState('');
```

```
const [email, setEmail] = useState('');

const handleSubmit = (event) => {
  alert('Hello ${firstName} ${lastName}');
  event.preventDefault();
}

return (
  <form onSubmit={handleSubmit}>
    <label>First name </label>
    <input
      onChange={e => setFirstName(e.target.value)}
      value={firstName}/><br/>
    <label>Last name </label>
    <input
      onChange={e => setLastName(e.target.value)}
      value={lastName}/><br/>
    <label>Email </label>
    <input
      onChange={e => setEmail(e.target.value)}
      value={email}/><br/>
    <input type="submit" value="Press me"/>
  </form>
);
};

export default MyForm;
```

We now know how to handle forms with React, and we will use these skills later when we implement our frontend.

Summary

In this chapter, we started to learn about React, which we will be using to build our frontend. Before starting to develop with React, we covered the basics, such as the React component, JSX, props, the state, and hooks. In our frontend development, we used ES6, which makes our code cleaner. We then went through the features we need for further development. We also learned how to handle forms and events with React.

In the next chapter, we will focus on networking with React. We will also be using the GitHub **REpresentational State Transfer** (**REST**) API to learn how to consume a RESTful web service with React.

Questions

1. What is a React component?

2. What are state and props?

3. How does data flow in a React app?

4. What is the difference between stateless and stateful components?

5. What is JSX?

6. What are component life cycle methods?

7. How should we handle events in React?

8. How should we handle forms in React?

Further reading

Packt has the following great resources for learning about React:

*   *React - The Complete Guide*, by *Academind GmbH*: `https://www.packtpub.com/product/react-the-complete-guide-includes-hooks-react-router-and-redux-2021-updated-second-edition-video/9781801812603`

*   *React 17 Design Patterns and Best Practices - Third Edition*, by *Carlos Santana Roldán*: `https://www.packtpub.com/product/react-17-design-patterns-and-best-practices-third-edition/9781800560444`

8
Consuming the REST API with React

This chapter explains networking with React. That is really important skill which we need in most of the React apps. We will learn about promises, which make asynchronous code cleaner and more readable. For networking, we will use the `fetch` and `axios` libraries. As an example, we will use the GitHub REST API to demonstrate how to consume RESTful web services with React.

In this chapter, we will cover the following topics:

- Using promises
- Using the `fetch` API
- Using the `axios` library
- Practical examples
- Handling responses from the REST API

Technical requirements

In this book, we are using the Windows operating system, but all the tools are available for Linux and macOS via Node.js.

The following GitHub link will also be required: `https://github.com/PacktPublishing/Full-Stack-Development-with-Spring-Boot-and-React/tree/main/Chapter08`.

Using promises

The traditional way to handle an asynchronous operation is to use callback functions for the success or failure of the operation. One of these callback functions is called (`success` or `failure`), depending on the result of the call. The following example shows the idea of using a callback function:

```
function doAsyncCall(success,  failure)  {
  // Do some API call
  if (SUCCEED)
    success(resp);
  else
    failure(err);
}

success(response) {
  // Do something with response
}

failure(error) {
  // Handle error
}

doAsyncCall(success, failure);
```

A **promise** is an object that represents the result of an asynchronous operation. The use of promises simplifies the code when you're executing asynchronous calls. Promises are non-blocking.

A promise can be in one of three states:

- **Pending**: Initial state
- **Fulfilled**: Successful operation
- **Rejected**: Failed operation

With promises, we can execute asynchronous calls if the API we are using supports promises. In the following example, the asynchronous call is made and when the response is returned, the callback function inside the `then` method is executed and takes `response` as an argument:

```
doAsyncCall()
.then(response => // Do something with the response)
```

The `then` method returns a promise. You can chain many instances of `then` together, which means that you can run multiple asynchronous operations one after another:

```
doAsyncCall()
.then(response => // Get some data from the response)
.then(data => // Do something with the data
```

You can also add error handling to promises by using `catch()`:

```
doAsyncCall()
.then(response => // Get some data from the response)
.then(data => // Do something with data)
.catch(error => console.error(error))
```

There is a more modern way to handle asynchronous calls that involves `async/await`, which was introduced in ECMAScript 2017. At the time of writing, it is not as widely supported by browsers as promises are. `async/await` is based on promises. To use `async/await`, you must define an `async` function that can contain `await` expressions. The following is an example of an asynchronous call containing `async/await`. As you can see, you can write the code in a similar way to synchronous code:

```
doAsyncCall = async () => {
  const response = await fetch('http://someapi.com');
  const data = await response.json();
  // Do something with the data
}
```

For error handling, you can use `try...catch` with `async/await`, as shown in the following example:

```
doAsyncCall = async () => {
  try {
    const response = await fetch('http://someapi.com');
    const data = await response.json();
    // Do something with the data
  }
  catch(err) {
    console.error(err);
  }
}
```

Now, we can start to learn about the `fetch` API, which we can use to make requests in our React apps.

Using the fetch API

With the `fetch` API, you can make web requests. The idea of the `fetch` API is similar to the traditional `XMLHttpRequest`, but the `fetch` API also supports promises, which makes it more straightforward to use. You don't have to install any libraries if you are using `fetch`.

The `fetch` API provides a `fetch()` method that has one mandatory argument: the path of the resource you are calling. In the case of a web request, it will be the URL of the service. For a simple `GET` method call, which returns a JSON response, the syntax is as follows. The `fetch()` method returns a promise that contains the response. You can use the `json()` method to parse the JSON body from the response:

```
fetch('http://someapi.com')
.then(response => response.json())
.then(data => console.log(data));
.catch(error => console.error(error))
```

To use another HTTP method, such as `POST`, you must define it in the second argument of the `fetch()` method. The second argument is an object where you can define multiple request settings. The following source code makes the request using the `POST` method:

```
fetch('http://someapi.com', {method: 'POST'})
.then(response => response.json())
.then(data => console.log(data))
```

```
.catch(error => console.error(error));
```

You can also add headers inside the second argument. The following `fetch()` call contains the `'Content-Type':'application/json'` header:

```
fetch('http://someapi.com',
  {
    method: 'POST',
    headers: {'Content-Type':'application/json'}
  }
.then(response => response.json())
.then(data => console.log(data))
.catch(error => console.error(error));
```

If you have to send JSON-encoded data inside the request body, the syntax is to do so is as follows:

```
fetch('http://someapi.com',
{
  method: 'POST',
  headers: {'Content-Type':'application/json'},
  body: JSON.stringify(data)
}
.then(response => response.json())
.then(data => console.log(data))
.catch(error => console.error(error));
```

The `fetch` API is not the only way to execute requests in the React app. There are other libraries that you can use as well. In the next section, we will learn how to use one such popular library: `axios`.

Using the axios library

You can also use other libraries for network calls. One very popular library is `axios` (`https://github.com/axios/axios`), which you can install in your React app with npm:

```
npm install axios
```

You must add the following `import` command to your React component before using it:

```
import axios from 'axios';
```

The `axios` library has some benefits, such as automatic transformation for JSON data. The following code shows an example call being made with `axios`:

```
axios.get('http://someapi.com')
.then(response => console.log(response))
.catch(error => console.log(error));
```

The `axios` library has its own call methods for the different HTTP methods. For example, if you want to make a *POST* request and send an object in the body, `axios` provides the `axios.post` method:

```
axios.post('http://someapi.com', { newObject })
.then(response => console.log(response))
.catch(error => console.log(error));
```

Now, we are ready to look at practical examples involving networking with React.

Working on practical examples

In this chapter we will go through two examples of using some open REST APIs in your React app.

OpenWeatherMap API

First, we will make a React app that shows the current weather in London. This weather data will be fetched from **OpenWeatherMap** (https://openweathermap.org/). You need to register with OpenWeatherMap to get an API key. We will use a free account as that is sufficient for our needs. Once you have registered, navigate to your account information to find the **API keys** tab. There, you'll see the API key that you need for your React weather app:

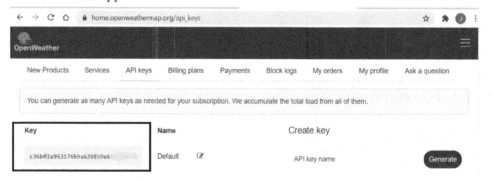

Figure 8.1 – The OpenWeatherMap API key

Let's create a new React app with `create-react-app`:

1. Open a terminal in Windows or Terminal in macOS/Linux, and type the following command:

```
npx create-react-app weatherapp
```

2. Navigate to the `weatherApp` folder:

```
cd weatherapp
```

3. Start your app with the following command:

```
npm start
```

4. Open your project folder with VS Code and open the `App.js` file in the editor view. Remove all the code inside the `<div className="App"></div>` divider. Now, your source code should look as follows:

```
import './App.css';

function App() {
  return (
    <div className="App">
    </div>
  );
}

export default App;
```

5. First, we must add the states that are needed for the response data. We will show the temperature, description, and weather icon in our app. So, we must define three state values. We will also add one Boolean state to indicate the status of fetch loading:

```
import React, { useState } from 'react';
import './App.css';

function App() {
  const [temp, setTemp] = useState('');
  const [desc, setDesc] = useState('');
  const [icon, setIcon] = useState('');
  const [isReady, setReady] = useState(false);
```

```

  return (
    <div className="App">
    </div>
  );
}

export default App;
```

When you are using a REST API, you should inspect the response to be able to get values from the JSON data. In the following example, you can see the address that returns the current weather for London. If you copy the address in a browser, you can view see the JSON response data: `api.openweathermap.org/data/2.5/weather?q=London&units=Metric&APIkey=YOUR_KEY`.

From the response, you can see that `temp` can be accessed using `main.temp`. Then, you can see that `description` and `icon` are inside the weather array, which has only one element, and that we can access it using `weather[0].description` and `weather[0].icon`:

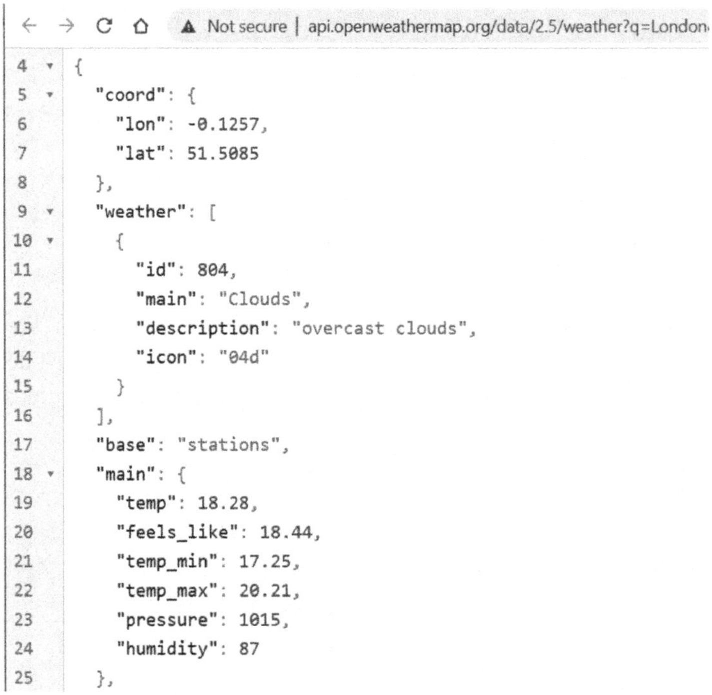


```
{
  "coord": {
    "lon": -0.1257,
    "lat": 51.5085
  },
  "weather": [
    {
      "id": 804,
      "main": "Clouds",
      "description": "overcast clouds",
      "icon": "04d"
    }
  ],
  "base": "stations",
  "main": {
    "temp": 18.28,
    "feels_like": 18.44,
    "temp_min": 17.25,
    "temp_max": 20.21,
    "pressure": 1015,
    "humidity": 87
  },
```

Figure 8.2 – Get weather by city

The REST API call is executed using `fetch` in the `useEffect` hook function, using an empty array as the second argument. Therefore, the fetch is done once, after the first render. After a successful response, we save the weather data to the state and change the `isReady` state to `true`. Once the state values have been changed, the component will be re-rendered. We will implement the `return` statement in the next step.

6. The following is the source code for the `useEffect` hook function, It will execute the fetch function once after the first render::

```
React.useEffect(() => { fetch('http://api.openweathermap.
org/data/2.5/
    weather?q=London&
  APPID=YOUR_KEY&units=metric')
  .then(result => result.json())
  .then(jsonresult => {
    setTemp(jsonresult.main.temp);
    setDesc(jsonresult.weather[0].main);
    setIcon(jsonresult.weather[0].icon);
    setReady(true);
  })
  .catch(err => console.error(err))
}, [])
```

7. Once you have added the `useEffect` function, the request is executed after the first render. We can check that everything has been done correctly using the React developer tool. Open your app in a browser and open your React developer tool's **Component** tab. Now, you can see that the states have been updated with the values from the response:

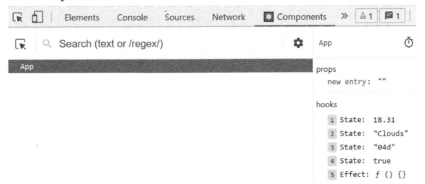

Figure 8.3 – Weather component

You can also check that the request status is 200 OK from the **Network** tab. Finally, we implement the `return` statement to show the weather values. We are using conditional rendering here; otherwise, we will get an error because we don't have image code in the first render call and the image upload won't succeed.

8. To show the weather icon, we must add `http://openweathermap.org/img/wn/` before the icon code, and `@2x.png` after the icon code. Then, we can set the concatenated image URL to the `img` element's `src` attribute. `temperature` and `description` are shown in the paragraph element. The `°C` HTML entity shows the Celsius degree symbol:

```
if (isReady) {
  return (
    <div className="App">
      <p>Temperature: {temp} °C</p>
      <p>Description: {desc}</p>
      <img src={'http://openweathermap.org/img/wn/
          ${icon}@2x.png'}
        alt="Weather icon" />
    </div>
  );
}
else {
  return <div>Loading...</div>
}
```

9. Now, your app should be ready. When you open it in a browser, it should look as follows:

Temperature: 18.38 °C

Description: Clouds

Figure 8.4 – WeatherApp

The source code for the entire `App.js` file is as follows:

```javascript
import React, { useState } from 'react';
import './App.css';


function App() {
  const [temp, setTemp] = useState('');
  const [desc, setDesc] = useState('');
  const [icon, setIcon] = useState('');
  const [isReady, setReady] = useState(false);


  React.useEffect(() => {
      fetch('http://api.openweathermap.org/data
          /2.5/weather?q=London&APPID=c36b03a96
              3176b9a639859e6cf279299&units=metric')
    .then(result => result.json())
    .then(jsonresult => {
      setTemp(jsonresult.main.temp);
      setDesc(jsonresult.weather[0].main);
      setIcon(jsonresult.weather[0].icon);
      setReady(true);
    })
    .catch(err => console.error(err))
  }, [])


  if (isReady) {
    return (
      <div className="App">
        <p>Temperature: {temp} °C</p>
        <p>Description: {desc}</p>
        <img src={'http://openweathermap.
            org/img/wn/${icon}@2x.png'}
          alt="Weather icon" />
      </div>
    );
  }
  else {
```

```
      return <div>Loading...</div>
   }
}
export default App;
```

In this second example, we are going to use the GitHub API to fetch repositories according to a keyword. Following the same steps as in the previous example, create a new React app called `restgithub`:

1. Start the app and open the project folder with VS Code.

2. Remove the extra code inside the `<div className="App"></div>` divider from the `App.js` file. Your `App.js` code should look as follows:

```
import './App.css';

function App() {
  return (
    <div className="App">
    </div>
  );
}
export default App;
```

The URL of the GitHub REST API is as follows:

```
https://api.github.com/search/repositories?q={KEYWORD}.
```

Let's inspect the JSON response by typing the URL into a browser and using the `react` keyword. From the response, we can see that repositories are returned as a JSON array called **items**. From the individual repositories, we will show the `full_name` and `html_url` values. We will present the data in the table and use the `map()` function to transform the values into table rows, as shown in the previous chapter:

```
                api.github.com/search/repositories?q=react
 7   ▾    "items": [
 8   ▾      {
 9          "id": 10270250,
10          "node_id": "MDEwOlJlcG9zaXRvcnkxMDI3MDI1MA==",
11          "name": "react",
12          "full_name": "facebook/react",
13          "private": false,
14   ▾      "owner": {
15            "login": "facebook",
16            "id": 69631,
17            "node_id": "MDEyOk9yZ2FuaXphdGlvbjY5NjMx",
18            "avatar_url": "https://avatars.githubusercontent.com/u/69631?v=4",
19            "gravatar_id": "",
20            "url": "https://api.github.com/users/facebook",
21            "html_url": "https://github.com/facebook",
22            "followers_url": "https://api.github.com/users/facebook/followers",
23            "following_url": "https://api.github.com/users/facebook/following{/other_user}",
24            "gists_url": "https://api.github.com/users/facebook/gists{/gist_id}",
25            "starred_url": "https://api.github.com/users/facebook/starred{/owner}{/repo}",
26            "subscriptions_url": "https://api.github.com/users/facebook/subscriptions",
27            "organizations_url": "https://api.github.com/users/facebook/orgs",
28            "repos_url": "https://api.github.com/users/facebook/repos",
29            "events_url": "https://api.github.com/users/facebook/events{/privacy}",
30            "received_events_url": "https://api.github.com/users/facebook/received_events",
31            "type": "Organization",
32            "site_admin": false
33          },
34          "html_url": "https://github.com/facebook/react",
35          "description": "A declarative, efficient, and flexible JavaScript library for building user interfaces.",
```

Figure 8.5 – GitHub REST API

We are going to make the REST API call with the keyword from the user input. Therefore, we can't make the REST API call in the useEffect() hook function because, in that phase, the user input isn't available. One way to implement this is to create an input field and button.

The user types the keyword into the input field and the REST API call is made when the button is pressed. We need two states – one for the user input and one for the data from the JSON response. The type of the data state is an array because repositories are returned as JSON arrays in the response:

```
import React, { useState } from 'react';
import './App.css';


function App() {
  const [keyword, setKeyword] = useState('');
  const [data, setData] = useState([]);


  return (
```

```
  <div className="App">
  </div>
  );
}
export default App;
```

3. Next, we must implement the input field and the button in the `return` statement. We also have to add a change listener to our input field to be able to save the input value to a state called `keyword`. The button has a click listener that invokes the function that will make the REST API call with the given keyword:

```
const fetchData = () => {
  // REST API call
}

return (
  <div className="App">
    <input
      value={keyword}
      onChange={e => setKeyword(e.target.value)} />
    <button onClick={fetchData}>Fetch</button>
  </div>
);
```

In the `fetchData` function, we concatenate the `url` and `keyword` states by using template literals. Then, we save the `items` array from the response to the `data` state. The following is the source code for the `fetchData` function:

```
const fetchData = () => {
  fetch('https://api.github.com/search/
repositories?q=${keyword}')
    .then(response => response.json())
    .then(data => setData(data))
    .catch(err => console.error(err))
}
```

4. In the `return` statement, we use the `map` function to transform the `data` state into table rows. The `url` property of a repository will be the `href` value of the `<a>` element:

```
return (
  <div className="App">
    <input value={keyword}
      onChange={e => setKeyword(e.target.value)} />
    <button onClick={fetchData}>Fetch</button>
    <table>
      <tbody>
        {
          data.map(repo =>
            <tr>
              <td>{repo.full_name}</td>
              <td>
                <a href={repo.html_url}>
                  {repo.html_url}</a>
              </td>
            </tr>
          )
        }
      </tbody>
    </table>
  </div>
);
```

The following screenshot shows the final app upon using the React keyword in the REST API call:

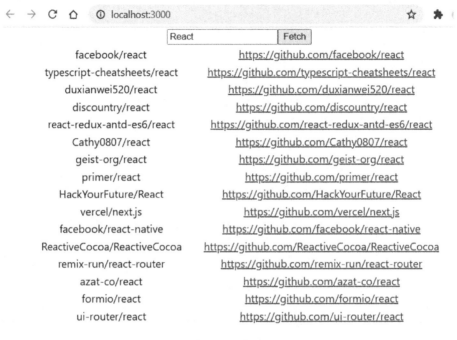

Figure 8.6 – GitHub REST API

The source code for the App.js file looks as follows:

```
import React, { useState } from 'react';
import './App.css';


function App() {
  const [keyword, setKeyword] = useState('');
  const [data, setData] = useState([]);

  const fetchData = () => {
    fetch('https://api.github.com/search/
repositories?q=${
    keyword}')
    .then(response => response.json())
    .then(data => setData(data.items))
    .catch(err => console.error(err))
  }
```

```
    return (
      <div className="App">
        <input value={keyword}
          onChange={e => setKeyword(e.target.value)} />
        <button onClick={fetchData}>Fetch</button>
        <table>
          <tbody>
            {
              data.map(repo =>
                <tr key={repo.id}>
                  <td>{repo.full_name}</td>
                  <td>
                    <a href={repo.html_url}>
                      {repo.html_url}</a>
                  </td>
                </tr>
              )
            }
          </tbody>
        </table>
      </div>
    );
}

export default App;
```

Now that we have learned about networking with React, we can utilize these skills in the frontend implementation.

Summary

In this chapter, we focused on networking with React. We started with promises, which make asynchronous network calls easier to implement. This is a cleaner way to handle calls, and it's much better than using traditional callback functions.

In this book, we are using the **fetch** API for networking. Therefore, we went through the basics of using fetch. We implemented two practical React apps using the fetch API to call REST APIs and we presented the response data in the browser.

In the next chapter, we will look at some useful React components that we are going to use in our frontend.

Questions

Answer the following questions to test your knowledge of this chapter:

1. What is a promise?

2. What is fetch?

3. How should you call the REST API from the React app?

4. How should you handle the response of the REST API call?

Further reading

Packt has other great resources available for learning about React. These are as follows:

*   *React 17 Design Patterns and Best Practices – Third Edition*, by *Carlos Santana Roldán* (https://www.packtpub.com/product/react-17-design-patterns-and-best-practices-third-edition/9781800560444)

*   *Full-Stack React Projects – Second Edition*, by *Shama Hoque* (https://www.packtpub.com/product/full-stack-react-projects-second-edition/9781839215414)

9
Useful Third-Party Components for React

React is component-based, and we can find a lot of useful third-party components that we can use in our apps. In this chapter, we are going to look at several components that we are going to use in our frontend. We will examine how to find suitable components and how you can then use these in your own apps.

In this chapter, we will cover the following topics:

- Using third-party React components
- Working with AG Grid
- Using the **MUI** component library
- Managing routing in React

Technical requirements

In this book, we will be using the Windows operating system, but all the tools are available for Linux and macOS as well.

Node.js also has to be installed, and the following GitHub link will be required: `https://github.com/PacktPublishing/Full-Stack-Development-with-Spring-Boot-and-React/tree/main/Chapter09`.

Using third-party React components

There are lots of nice React components available for different purposes. Our first task is to find a suitable component for your needs. One good site for searching components is `JS.coach` (`https://js.coach/`). You just have to type in a keyword, search, and select **React** from the list of libraries.

In the following screenshot, you can see a search of table components for React:

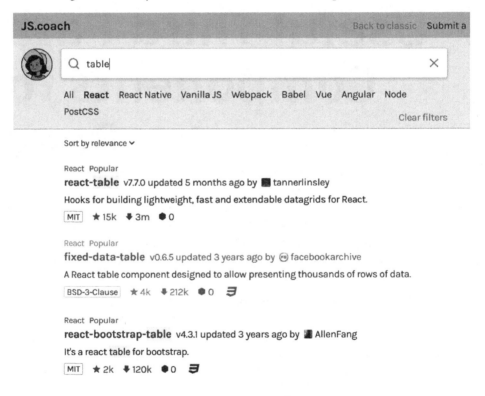

Figure 9.1 – JS.coach

Another good source for React components is `awesome-react-components`
(`https://github.com/brillout/awesome-react-components`).

Components often have good documentation that helps you to utilize them in your own
React app. Let's see how we can install a third-party component to our app and start to use
it, as follows:

1. Navigate to the `JS.coach` site, type `date` in the search input field, and filter by
    React. From the search results, you can find a list component called `react-date-`
    `picker`, as illustrated in the following screenshot:

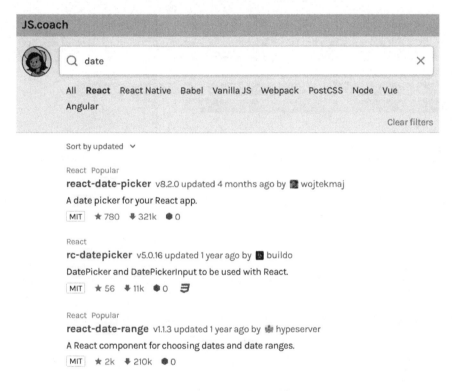

Figure 9.2 – react-date-picker

2.   Click the component link to see more detailed information about the component.

You should find the installation instructions there and some simple examples of how to use the component. You should also check that development of a component is still active. The info page often provides the address of a component's website or GitHub repository, where you can find the full documentation. You can see the info page for react-date-picker in the following screenshot:

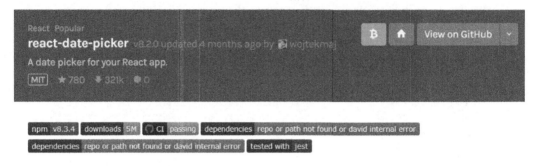

React-Date-Picker

A date picker for your React app.

- Pick days, months, years, or even decades
- Supports virtually any language
- No moment.js needed

Figure 9.3 – react-date-picker

As you can see from the component's info page, components are installed using the npm package. The syntax of the command to install components looks like this:

```
npm install component_name
```

Or, if you are using yarn, it looks like this:

```
yarn add component_name
```

The npm install and yarn add commands save the component's dependency to the package.json file that is in the root folder of your React app.

3. Now, we install the `react-date-picker` component to the `myapp` React app that we created in *Chapter 6, Setting Up the Environment and Tools – Frontend.* You then have to move to your app root folder and type the following command:

```
npm install react-date-picker
```

If you open the `package.json` file from your app root folder, you can see that the component is now added to the `dependencies` section, as illustrated in the following code snippet:

```
{
    "name": "myapp",
    "version": "0.1.0",
    "private": true,
    "dependencies": {
        "@testing-library/jest-dom": "^5.11.4",
        "@testing-library/react": "^11.1.0",
        "@testing-library/user-event": "^12.1.10",
        "react": "^18.0.0",
        "react-dom": "^18.0.0",
        "react-date-picker": "^8.3.4",
        "react-scripts": "4.0.3",
        "web-vitals": "^1.0.1"
    },
```

You can also find the installed version number from the `package.json` file. If you want to install a specific version of a component, you can use the following command:

```
npm install component_name@version
```

And if you want to remove an installed component from your React app, you can use the following command:

```
npm uninstall component_name
```

Installed components are saved to the node_modules folder in your app. If you open that folder, you should find the react-date-picker folder, as illustrated in the following screenshot:

Figure 9.4 – node_modules

4. Now, if you push your React app source code to GitHub, you should not include the node_modules folder because that is too large. create-react-app contains a .gitignore file that excludes the node_modules folder from the repository. The content of the .gitignore file looks like this:

```
# See https://help.github.com/articles/ignoring-files/
for more about ignoring files.

# dependencies
/node_modules
/.pnp
.pnp.js


# testing
/coverage


# production
```

```
/build

# misc
.DS_Store
.env.local
.env.development.local
.env.test.local
.env.production.local

npm-debug.log*
yarn-debug.log*
yarn-error.log*
```

The idea is that when you clone your app from the GitHub repository, you type the `npm install` command, which reads dependencies from the `package.json` file and downloads these to your app.

5. The final step to start using your installed component is to import it into the files where you are using it. The code to achieve this is illustrated in the following snippet:

```
import DatePicker from 'react-date-picker';
```

You have now learned how to install and use React components in your React app.

Working with AG Grid

AG Grid (`https://www.ag-grid.com/`) is a flexible grid component for React apps. It has many useful features, such as filtering, sorting, and pivoting. We will use the community version, which is free to use (**Massachusetts Institute of Technology** (**MIT**) license).

Let's use the GitHub **REST API** app that we created in *Chapter 8, Consuming the REST API with React*. Proceed as follows:

1. To install the `ag-grid` community component, open PowerShell and move to the `restgithub` folder, which is the root folder of the app. Install the component by typing the following command:

```
npm install ag-grid-community ag-grid-react
```

2. Open the `App.js` file with **Visual Studio Code (VS Code)** and remove the `table` element inside the `return` statement. The `App.js` file should now look like this:

```
import React, { useState } from 'react';
import './App.css';

function App() {
  const [keyword, setKeyword] = useState('');
  const [data, setData] = useState([]);

  const fetchData = () => {
fetch('https://api.github.com/search/
    repositories?q=${keyword}')
    .then(response => response.json())
    .then(data => setData(data.items))
    .catch(err => console.error(err))
  }

  return (
    <div className="App">
      <input value={keyword}
      onChange={e => setKeyword(e.target.value)} />
      <button onClick={fetchData}>Fetch</button>
    </div>
  );
}

export default App;
```

3. Import the `ag-grid` component and style sheets by adding the following lines of code at the beginning of the `App.js` file. `ag-grid` provides different predefined styles, and we are using a material design:

```
import { AgGridReact } from 'ag-grid-react';

import 'ag-grid-community/dist/styles/ag-grid.css';
import 'ag-grid-community/dist/styles/
    ag-theme-material.css';
```

4. Next, we add the imported `AgGridReact` component to the `return` statement. To fill the `ag-grid` component with data, you have to pass the `rowData` prop to the component. Data can be an array of objects, and therefore we can use our state, called `data`. The `ag-grid` component should be wrapped inside the `div` element that defines the style. The code is illustrated in the following snippet:

```
return (
    <div className="App">
      <input value={keyword}
        onChange={e => setKeyword(e.target.value)} />
      <button onClick={fetchData}>Fetch</button>
      <div className="ag-theme-material"
        style={{height: 500, width: '90%'}}>
        <AgGridReact
          rowData={data}
          columnDefs={columns}
        />
      </div>
    </div>
  );
```

5. Next, we will define columns for `ag-grid`. We will define a constant called `columns` that is an array of column objects. In a column object, you have to define at least the data accessor by using `field` props. `field` values come from our REST API response data. You can see in the following code snippet that our response data contains an object called `owner`, and we can show these values using the `owner.field_name` syntax:

```
const columns = [
    {field: 'full_name'},
    {field: 'html_url'},
    {field: 'owner.login'}
]
```

6. Finally, we will use `ag-grid` `columnDefs` props to define these columns, as follows:

```
<AgGridReact
  rowData={data}
  columnDefs={columns}
/>
```

7. Run the app and navigate to `http://localhost:3000`. The table looks quite nice by default, as shown in the following screenshot:

Figure 9.5 – ag-grid component

8. Sorting and filtering are disabled by default, but you can enable them using `sortable` and `filter` props in `ag-grid` columns, as follows:

```
const columns = [
  {field: 'full_name', sortable: true, filter:
    true},
  {field: 'html_url', sortable: true, filter: true},
  {field: 'owner.login', sortable: true, filter:
    true}
]
```

9. Now, you can sort and filter any columns in the grid by clicking the column header, as illustrated in the following screenshot:

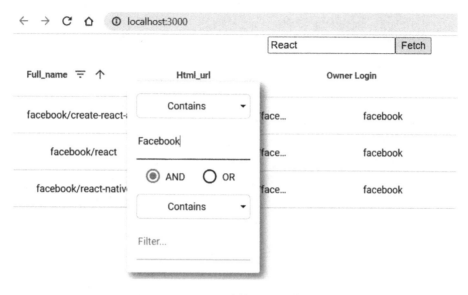

Figure 9.6 – ag-grid filtering and sorting

10. You can also enable paging and set the page size in `ag-grid` by using `pagination` and `paginationPageSize` props, as follows:

```
<AgGridReact
  rowData={data}
  columnDefs={columns}
  pagination={true}
  paginationPageSize={8}
/>
```

11. Now, you should see pagination in your table, as illustrated in the following screenshot:

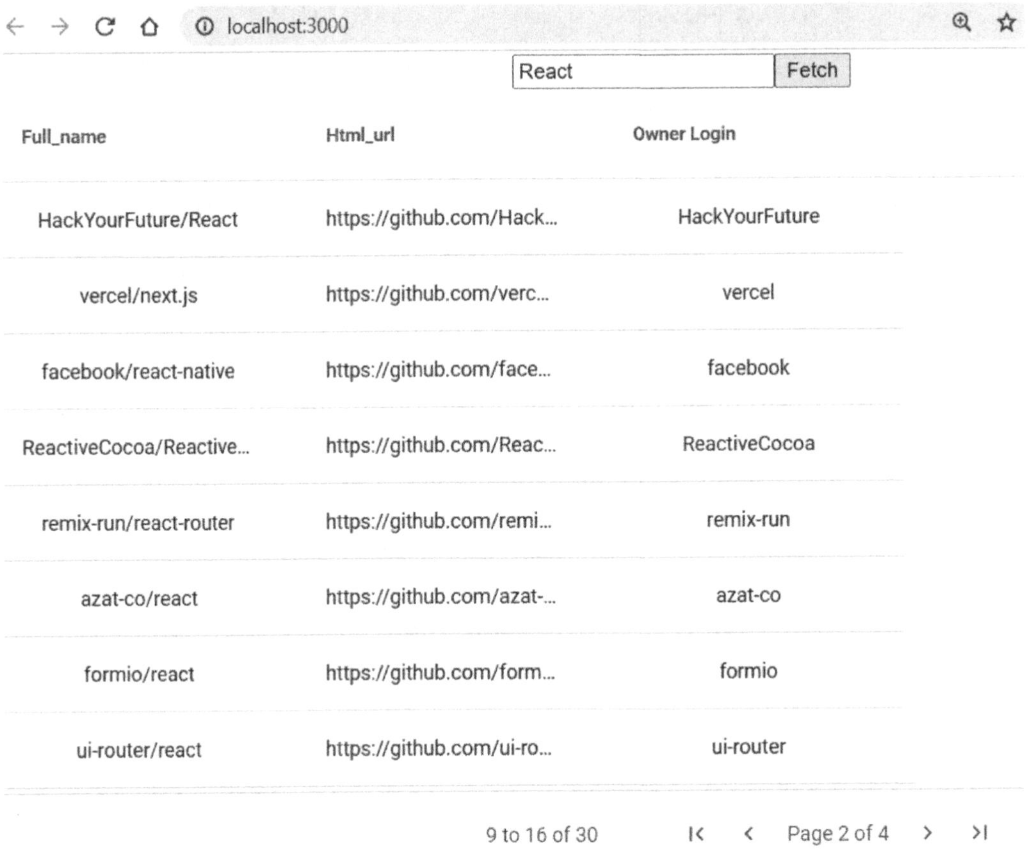

Figure 9.7 – ag-grid pagination

You can find documentation for different grid and column props from the *AG Grid* website.

`cellRendererFramework` props can be used to customize the content of a table cell. The following example shows how you can render a button to a grid cell. The function in the cell renderer passes `params` as an argument. `params.value` will be the value of the `full_name` cell, which is defined in the accessor of the column. You can also use `params.row`, which is the whole row object. When the button is pressed, it will open an alert that shows the value of the `full_name` cell:

```
const columns = [
  {field: 'full_name', sortable: true, filter: true},
```

```
{field: 'html_url', sortable: true, filter: true},
{field: 'owner.login', sortable: true, filter: true},
{
  field: 'full_name',
  cellRenderer: params =>
    <button
      onClick={() => alert(params.value)}>
      Press me
    </button>
}
]
```

Next is a screenshot of the table with buttons. You can try to press any button, and you should see an alert that shows the value of the `full_name` cell:

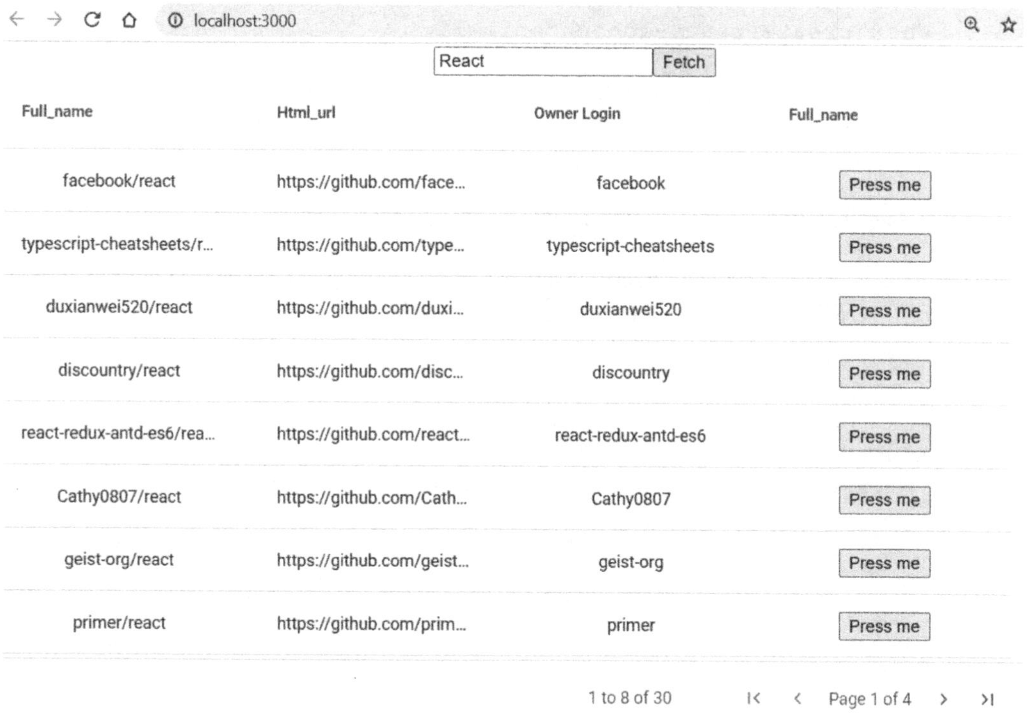

Figure 9.8 – Grid with buttons

Now, the button column has a `Full_name` header because, by default, the field name will be used as the header name. If you want to use something else, you can use the `headerName` prop in the column definition.

Next, we will start to use the MUI component library, which is one of the most popular React component libraries.

Using the MUI component library

MUI (`https://mui.com/`) is the React component library that implements Google's Material Design language. In this book, we are using MUI version 5, and if you are using some other version, you should follow the official documentation. MUI contains a lot of different components—such as buttons, lists, tables, and cards—that you can use to achieve a nice and uniform **user interface** (**UI**).

We will create a small shopping list app and style the UI using MUI components, as follows:

1. Create a new React app called `shoppinglist` by running the following command:

   ```
   npx create-react-app shoppinglist
   ```

2. Open the shopping list app with VS Code. Install MUI by typing the following command in the project root folder to PowerShell or any suitable terminal you are using:

   ```
   npm install @mui/material @emotion/react @emotion/styled
   ```

3. Open the App.js file and remove all the code inside the App div tag. Now, your App.js file should look like this, and you should see an empty page in the browser:

   ```
   import './App.css';

   function App() {
     return (
       <div className="App">
       </div>
     );
   }

   export default App;
   ```

4. MUI provides different layout components, and the basic layout component is
    `Container`. This is used to center your content horizontally, and you can specify
    the maximum width of a container using the `maxWidth` prop; the default value is
    `lg`, which is suitable for us. Let's use the `Container` component in our `App.js`
    file, as follows:

```
import Container from '@mui/material/Container';

function App() {
  return (
    <Container>
    </Container>
  );
}

export default App;
```

5. We will use the MUI `AppBar` component to show the toolbar in our app. Import
    the `AppBar`, `ToolBar`, and `Typography` components into your `App.js` file.
    We also import `React` and `useState`, which we will need later. The code is
    illustrated in the following snippet:

```
import React, { useState } from 'react';
import Container from '@mui/material/Container';
import AppBar from '@mui/material/AppBar';
import Toolbar from '@mui/material/Toolbar';
import Typography from '@mui/material/Typography';
```

6. Add the following code to your `App` component's `return` statement. The
    `Typography` component provides predefined text sizes, and we will use this in our
    toolbar text. `variant` props can be used to define text size:

```
function App() {
  return (
    <Container>
      <AppBar position="static">
        <Toolbar>
          <Typography variant="h6">
            Shopping List
          </Typography>
```

```
        </Toolbar>
      </AppBar>
   </Container>
 );
}
```

Your app should now look like this:

Figure 9.9 – AppBar component

7. In the App component, we only require one state to keep the shopping list items. One shopping list item contains two fields: product and amount. We also need a method to add a new item to the items state. Here is the source code to define the state and a function for adding a new item to the state. In the addItem function, we are using spread notation (. . .), which is used to add a new item at the beginning of an existing array:

```
const [items, setItems] = useState([]);

const addItem = (item) => {
    setItems([item, ...items]);
}
```

8. Add a new component for adding shopping items. Create a new file called AddItem.js in the root folder of the app and add the following code to your AddItem.js file. The AddItem component function also receives props from its parent component. The code is illustrated in the following snippet:

```
import React from 'react';

function AddItem(props) {
  return(
    <div></div>
  );
}

export default AddItem;
```

The AddItem component will use the MUI modal dialog for collecting data. In the form, we will add two input fields (product and amount) and a button that calls the App component's addItem function. To be able to call the addItem function, which is in the App component, we have to pass it in props when rendering the AddItem component. Outside the modal Dialog component, we will add a button that opens the modal form when it is pressed. This button is the only visible element when the component is rendered initially.

The Dialog component has one prop called open, and if the value is true, the dialog is visible. The default value of open props is false, and the dialog is hidden. The button that opens the modal dialog sets the open state value to true, and the dialog opens. We also have to handle the change event of input elements so that we can access values that have been typed. When the button inside the modal form is clicked, the addItem function is called, and the modal form is closed by setting the open state value to false. The function creates an object from the input field values and calls the App component's addItem function, which finally adds a new item to the state array and re-renders the UI.

The following steps describe the implementation of the modal form:

1. We have to import the following MUI components for the modal form: Dialog, DialogActions, DialogContent, and DialogTitle. And as regards the UI of the modal form, we require the following components: Button and TextField. Add the following imports to your AddItem.js file:

    ```
    import Button from '@mui/material/Button';
    import TextField from '@mui/material/TextField';
    import Dialog from '@mui/material/Dialog';
    import DialogActions from '@mui/material/DialogActions';
    import DialogContent from '@mui/material/DialogContent';
    import DialogTitle from '@mui/material/DialogTitle';
    ```

2. Next, we will declare one state called open and two functions for opening and closing the modal dialog. The default value of the open state is false. The handleOpen function sets the open state to true, and the handleClose function sets it to false. The code is illustrated in the following snippet:

    ```
    // AddItem.js
    const [open, setOpen] = React.useState(false);

    const handleOpen = () => {
      setOpen(true);
    }
    ```

```
const handleClose = () => {
  setOpen(false);
}
```

3. We will add `Dialog` and `Button` components inside the `return` statement. We have one button outside the dialog that will be visible when the component is rendered for the first time. When the button is pressed, it calls the `handleOpen` function, which opens the dialog. Inside the dialog, we have two buttons—one for canceling and one for adding a new item. The **Add** button calls the `addItem` function, which we will implement later. The code is illustrated in the following snippet:

```
return(
    <div>
        <Button onClick={handleOpen}>
          Add Item
        </Button>
        <Dialog open={open} onClose={handleClose}>
            <DialogTitle>New Item</DialogTitle>
            <DialogContent>
            </DialogContent>
            <DialogActions>
                <Button onClick={handleClose}>
                  Cancel
                </Button>
                <Button onClick={addItem}>
                  Add
                </Button>
            </DialogActions>
        </Dialog>
    </div>
);
```

4. To collect data from a user, we have to declare one more state. The state is an object with two attributes – `product` and `amount`. Add the following line of code after the line where you declared the `open` state:

```
const [item, setItem] = React.useState({
  product: '',
```

```
    amount: ''
  });
```

5. Inside the `DialogContent` component, we will add two inputs to collect data from a user. There, we use the `TextField` MUI component that we have already imported. The `margin` prop is used to set the vertical spacing of text fields, and the `fullwidth` prop is used to make input take the full width of its container. You can find all props from the *Material Design* documentation. `value` props of text fields must be the same as the state where we want to save the typed value. In the `product` field, it is `item.product`, and in the `amount` field, it is `item.amount`. We will also use `name` props, as we did earlier with forms. The code is illustrated in the following snippet:

```
<DialogContent>
  <TextField value={item.product} margin="dense"
    onChange={handleChange} name="product"
    label="Product" fullWidth />
  <TextField value={item.amount} margin="dense"
    onChange={handleChange} name="amount"
    label="Amount" fullWidth />
</DialogContent>
```

6. Next, we have to implement the `handleChange` function, which is invoked when we type something into the input fields. As we have already learned in *Chapter 7, Getting Started with React,* the following function saves values from the input field to the `item` state:

```
const handleChange = (e) => {
  setItem({...item, [e.target.name]: e.target.value})
}
```

7. Finally, we have to add a function that calls the `addItem` function that we get in the `props` field and pass a new item into that function. The new item is now the `item` state that contains the shopping item that the user typed in. Because we get the `addItem` function from the props, we can call it using the `props` keyword. We will also call the `handleClose` function, which closes the modal dialog. The code is illustrated in the following snippet:

```
// Calls addItem function (in props) and pass item state
// into it
const addItem = () => {
```

```
    props.addItem(item);
    setItem({product: '', amount: ''}); // Clear text
        fields
    handleClose();
}
```

8. Our `AddItem` component is now ready, and we have to import it into our `App.js` file and render it there. Add the following `import` statement to your `App.js` file:

```
import AddItem from './AddItem';
```

9. Add the `AddItem` component to the `return` statement in the `App.js` file. Pass the `addItem` function in a prop to the `AddItem` component, as follows:

```
// App.js
return (
  <Container>
    <AppBar position="static">
      <Toolbar>
        <Typography variant="h6">
          Shopping List
        </Typography>
      </Toolbar>
    </AppBar>
    <AddItem addItem={addItem}/>
  </Container>
);
```

10. If we want to center the **ADD ITEM** button, we can use the MUI `Stack` layout component. It can be used to define the layout of its child components. The default direction is `column`, and you can change that using the `direction` prop. You can use the `alignItems` prop to define horizontal alignment. The code is illustrated in the following snippet:

```
// App.js
// Import Stack component
import Stack from '@mui/material/Stack';


// Render Stack component
```

```
return (
  <Container>
    <AppBar position="static">
      <Toolbar>
        <Typography variant="h6">
          Shopping List
        </Typography>
      </Toolbar>
    </AppBar>
    <Stack alignItems="center">
      <AddItem addItem={addItem} />
    </Stack>
  </Container>
);
```

11. Now, if you open your app in the browser and press the **ADD ITEM** button, you
    will see the modal form opening and you can type a new item, as illustrated in the
    following screenshot. The modal form is closed when you press the **ADD** button:

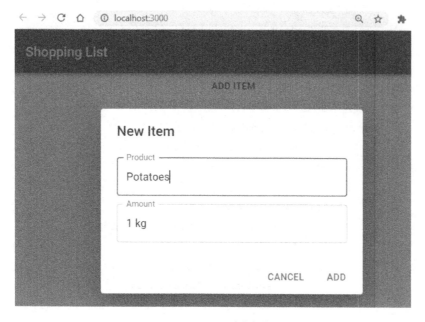

Figure 9.10 – Modal dialog

12. Next, we will add a list to the `App` component that shows our shopping items. For that, we will use the MUI `List`, `ListItem`, and `ListItemText` components. Import the components into the `App.js` file. Here's the code you'll need:

```
// App.js
import List from '@mui/material/List';
import ListItem from '@mui/material/ListItem';
import ListItemText from '@mui/material/ListItemText';
```

13. Then, we will render the `List` component, and inside that, we use the `map` function to generate `ListItem` components. Each `ListItem` component should have a unique `key` prop, and we use a `divider` prop to get a divider at the end of each list item. We will show the product in the primary text and an amount in the secondary text of the `ListItemText` component. The code is illustrated in the following snippet:

```
// App.js
return (
    <Container>
        <AppBar position="static">
            <Toolbar>
                <Typography variant="h6">
                    Shopping List
                </Typography>
            </Toolbar>
        </AppBar>
        <Stack alignItems="center">
            <AddItem addItem={addItem} />
            <List>
            {
                items.map((item, index) =>
                    <ListItem key={index} divider>
                        <ListItemText
                            primary={item.product}
                            secondary={item.amount}/>
                    </ListItem>
                )
            }
            </List>
```

```
        </Stack>
    </Container>
  );
```

Now, the UI looks like this:

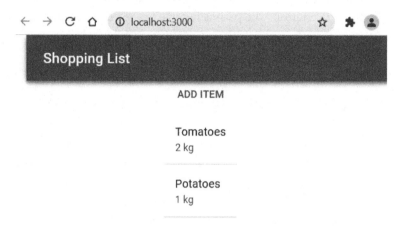

Figure 9.11 – Shopping list

The MUI `Button` component has three variants: `text`, `contained`, and `outlined`. The `text` variant is the default, and you can change it using the `variant` prop. For example, if we want to have an outlined **ADD ITEM** button, change the button's `variant` prop in the `AddItem.js` file, like this:

```
<Button variant="outlined" onClick={handleOpen}>
    Add Item
</Button>
```

Next, we will learn how to use React Router, a popular routing library.

Managing routing in React

There are multiple solutions available for routing in React. The most popular one, which we are using, is **React Router** (`https://github.com/ReactTraining/react-router`). For web applications, React Router provides a package called `react-router-dom`.

To start using React Router, we have to install dependencies using the following command. In this book, we are using version React Router version 6:

```
npm install react-router-dom@6 history@5
```

Four different components in the `react-router-dom` library are required to implement routing. `BrowserRouter` is the router for web-based applications. The `Route` component renders the defined component if the given locations match.

The following code snippet provides an example of the `Route` component. The `element` prop defines a rendered component when the user navigates to the `contact` endpoint that is defined in the `path` prop. The path is relative to the parent route that renders them:

```
<Route path="contact" element={<Contact />} />
```

You can use an `*` wildcard at the end of the `path` prop, like this:

```
<Route path="/contact/*" element={<Contact />} />
```

Now, it will match all endpoints under the contact—for example, `contact/mike`, `contact/john`, and so on.

The `Routes` component wraps multiple `Route` components. The `Link` component provides navigation to your application. The following example shows the `Contact` link and navigates to the `/contact` endpoint when the link is clicked:

```
<Link to="/contact">Contact</Link>
```

The following example shows how to use these components in practice. Let's create a new React app called `routerapp`, using `create-react-app`, as follows:

1. Open the `src` folder with VS Code and open the `App.js` file to editor view. Import components from the `react-router-dom` package and remove extra code from the `return` statement. Following these modifications, your `App.js` source code should look like this:

    ```
    import React from 'react';
    import {BrowserRouter, Routes, Route, Link} from 'react-
    router-dom';
    import './App.css';

    function App() {
      return (
        <div className="App">
        </div>
      );
    }
    ```

```
export default App;
```

2. Let's first create two simple components that we can use in routing. Create two new files, Home.js and Contact.js, in the application src folder. Then, add headers to the return statements to show the name of the component. The code of the components looks like this:

```
// Home.js
function Home() {
    return <h1>Home.js</h1>;
}
export default Home;
```

```
// Contact.js
function Contact() {
    return <h1>Contact.js</h1>;
}

export default Contact;
```

3. Open the App.js file, and then add a router that allows us to navigate between the components, as follows:

```
import React from 'react';
import { BrowserRouter, Routes, Route, Link } from
'react-router-dom';
import Home from './Home';
import Contact from './Contact';
import './App.css';

function App() {
  return (
    <div className="App">
      <BrowserRouter>
        <nav>
          <Link to="/">Home</Link>{' '}
            <Link to="/contact">Contact</Link>{' '}
        </nav>
```

```
        <Routes>
            <Route path="/" element={<Home />} />
            <Route path="contact" element={<Contact />} />
        </Routes>
      </BrowserRouter>
  </div>
  );
}

export default App;
```

4. Now, when you start the app, you will see the links and the Home component, which is shown in the root endpoint (localhost:3000), as defined in the first Route component. You can see a representation of this in the following screenshot:

Home.js

Figure 9.12 – React router

5. When you click the **Contact** link, the Contact component is rendered, as illustrated here:

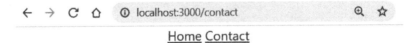

Contact.js

Figure 9.13 – React router (continued)

You can have a PageNotFound route by using an * wildcard at the path prop. In the following example, if any other route doesn't match, the last one is used:

```
<Routes>
  <Route path="/" element={<Home />} />
  <Route path="contact" element={<Contact />} />
```

```
    <Route path="*" element={<PageNotFound />} />
  </Routes>
```

You can also have nested routes such as the ones shown in the next example:

```
<Routes>
  <Route path="contact" element={<Contact />}>
      <Route path="london" element={<ContactLondon />} />
      <Route path="paris" element={<ContactParis />} />
  </Route>
</Routes>
```

You can also use a `useRoutes()` hook to declare routes using JavaScript objects instead of React elements, but we are not covering that in this book.

At this point, you have learned how to install and use third-party components with React. These skills will be required in the following chapters when we start to build our frontend.

Summary

In this chapter, we learned how to use third-party React components. We familiarized ourselves with several components that we are going to use in our frontend. `ag-grid` is the table component with built-in features, such as sorting, paging, and filtering.

MUI is the component library that provides multiple UI components that implement Google's Material Design language. We also learned how to use React Router for routing in React applications.

In the next chapter, we will build an environment for frontend development.

Questions

1. How can you find components for React?
2. How should you install components?
3. How can you use the `ag-grid` component?
4. How can you use the MUI component library?
5. How can you implement routing in a React application?

Further reading

Packt Publishing has other great resources available for learning about React. Some of these are listed here:

- *React – The Complete Guide*, by *Academind GmbH*: `https://www.packtpub.com/product/react-the-complete-guide-includes-hooks-react-router-and-redux-2021-updated-second-edition-video/9781801812603`

- *React 17 Design Patterns and Best Practices – Third Edition*, by *Carlos Santana Roldán*: `https://www.packtpub.com/product/react-17-design-patterns-and-best-practices-third-edition/9781800560444`

Part 3: Full Stack Development

In this part, we will combine the Spring Boot backend and the React frontend. We will use the Spring Boot backend that we created in *Part 1, Backend Programming with Spring Boot*, to create a frontend with React. The frontend provides all the CRUD operations for us.

We will cover the following chapters in this section:

10

Setting up the Frontend for Our Spring Boot RESTful Web Service

This chapter explains the steps that are required to start the development of the frontend part. We will first define the functionalities that we are developing. Then, we will do a mock-up of the UI. As a backend, we will use our Spring Boot application from *Chapter 5, Securing and Testing Your Backend*. We will begin development using the unsecured version of the backend. Finally, we will create the React app that we will use in our frontend development.

In this chapter, we will cover the following topics:

- Why a mock-up is necessary and how to go about it
- Preparing our Spring Boot backend for frontend development
- Creating the React app for the frontend

Technical requirements

The Spring Boot application that we created in *Chapter 5, Securing and Testing Your Backend*, is required.

Node.js also has to be installed, and the code samples available at the following GitHub link will be required to follow along with the examples in this chapter: `https://github.com/PacktPublishing/Full-Stack-Development-with-Spring-Boot-and-React/tree/main/Chapter10`.

Check out the following video to see the Code in Action: `https://bit.ly/3NzdSxs`

Mocking up the UI

In the first few chapters of this book, we created a car database backend that provides the RESTful API. Now, it is time to start building the frontend for our application. We will create a frontend that lists cars from the database and provides paging, sorting, and filtering. There is a button that opens the modal form to add new cars to the database. In each row of the car table, there is a button to delete or edit the car from the database. The frontend contains a link or button to export data from the table to a CSV file.

Let's create a mock-up from our UI. There are lots of different applications for creating mock-ups, or you can even use a pencil and paper. You can also create interactive mock- ups to demonstrate a number of functionalities. If you have done a mock-up, it is much easier to discuss requirements with the client before you start to write any actual code. With the mock-up, it is also easier for the client to understand the idea of the frontend and suggest corrections for it. Changes to the mock-up are really easy and fast to implement, compared to modifications involving actual frontend source code.

The following screenshot shows the mock-up of our car list frontend:

Brand	Model	Color	Year	Price		
Tesla	Model X	White	2022	87900	✏	🗑
Toyota	Prius	Black	2019	29000	✏	🗑
Ford	Mustang	Black	2021	65000	✏	🗑

Figure 10.1 – The frontend mock-up

The modal form that is opened when the user presses the **New Car** button looks like the following:

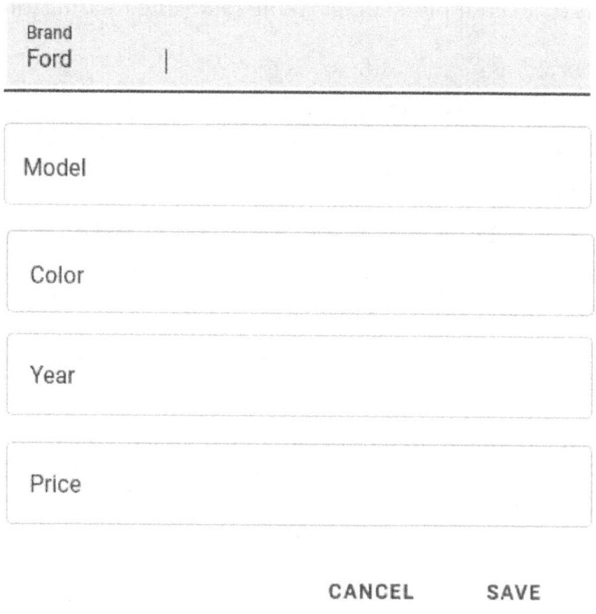

Figure 10.2 – The frontend mock-up

Now that we have our mock-up from our UI ready, let's look at how we can prepare our Spring Boot backend.

Preparing the Spring Boot backend

We are beginning frontend development with the unsecured version of our backend. In the first phase, we will implement all CRUD functionalities and test that these are working correctly. In the second phase, we will enable security in our backend, make the modifications that are required, and finally, implement authentication.

Open the Spring Boot application with Eclipse, which we created in *Chapter 5, Securing and Testing Your Backend*. Open the `SecurityConfig.java` file that defines the Spring Security configuration. Temporarily comment out the current configuration and give everyone access to all endpoints. Refer to the following modifications:

```java
@Override
protected void configure(HttpSecurity http) throws Exception {
    // Add this row
    http.csrf().disable().cors().and()
      .authorizeRequests().anyRequest().permitAll();

    /* Comment this out
    http.csrf().disable().cors().and()
    .sessionManagement()
    .sessionCreationPolicy
        (SessionCreationPolicy.STATELESS).and()
    .authorizeRequests()
    .antMatchers(HttpMethod.POST, "/login").permitAll()
    .anyRequest().authenticated().and().exceptionHandling()
    .authenticationEntryPoint(exceptionHandler).and()
    .addFilterBefore(authenticationFilter,
    UsernamePasswordAuthenticationFilter.class);
    */
}
```

Now, if you start the MariaDB database, run the backend, and send the GET request to the `http:/localhost:8080/api/cars` endpoint with Postman, you should get all cars in the response, as shown in the following screenshot:

Figure 10.3 – The GET request

Now, we are ready to create our React project for the frontend.

Creating the React project for the frontend

Before we start coding the frontend, we have to create a new React app:

1. Open PowerShell, or any other suitable terminal. Create a new React app by typing the following command:

    ```
    npx create-react-app carfront
    ```

2. Move to the `project` folder and install the Material-UI component library by typing the following commands:

    ```
    cd carfront
    npm install @mui/material @emotion/react @emotion/styled
    ```

3. Run the app by typing the following command in the project's `root` folder:

```
npm start
```

Alternatively, if you are using `yarn`, type in the following:

```
yarn start
```

4. Open the `src` folder with Visual Studio Code, remove any superfluous code, and use the MUI `AppBar` component in the `App.js` file to get the toolbar for your app. Following the modifications, your `App.js` file source code should appear as follows:

```
import './App.css';
import AppBar from '@mui/material/AppBar';
import Toolbar from '@mui/material/Toolbar';
import Typography from '@mui/material/Typography';


function App() {
  return (
    <div className="App">
      <AppBar position="static">
        <Toolbar>
          <Typography variant="h6">
            Carshop
          </Typography>
        </Toolbar>
      </AppBar>
    </div>
  );
}


export default App;
```

Your frontend starting point will look like the following:

Figure 10.4 – Carshop

We have now created the React project for our frontend and can continue with further development.

Summary

In this chapter, we started the development of our frontend using the backend that we created in *Chapter 5, Securing and Testing Your Backend*. We defined the functionalities of the frontend and created a mock-up of the UI. We started frontend development with an unsecured version of the backend and, therefore, made some modifications to our Spring Security configuration class. We also created the React app that we are going to use during development.

In the next chapter, we will start to add CRUD functionalities to our frontend.

Questions

1. Why should you do a mock-up of the UI?
2. How do you disable Spring Security from the backend?

Further reading

Packt has other great resources available for learning about React. These are as follows:

- *React – The Complete Guide* by *Academind GmbH*: `https://www.packtpub.com/product/react-the-complete-guide-includes-hooks-react-router-and-redux-2021-updated-second-edition-video/9781801812603`

- *React 17 Design Patterns and Best Practices – Third Edition* by *Carlos Santana Roldán*: `https://www.packtpub.com/product/react-17-design-patterns-and-best-practices-third-edition/9781800560444`

11
Adding CRUD Functionalities

This chapter describes how we can implement CRUD functionalities in our frontend. We are going to use the components that we learned about in *Chapter 9, Useful Third-Party Components for React*. We will fetch data from our backend and present the data in a table. Then, we will implement the delete, edit, and add functionalities. In the final part of this chapter, we will add features so that we can export data to a CSV file.

In this chapter, we will cover the following topics:

- Creating the list page
- Deleting, adding, and updating data using the REST API
- How to show toast messages to the user
- Exporting data to the CSV file from the React app

Technical requirements

The Spring Boot application that we created in *Chapter 10, Setting Up the Frontend for Our Spring Boot RESTful Web Service* (**the unsecured backend**), is required, as is the React app that we created in the same chapter (**carfront**).

The following GitHub link will also be required: `https://github.com/PacktPublishing/Full-Stack-Development-with-Spring-Boot-and-React/tree/main/Chapter11`.

Check out the following video to see the Code in Action: `https://bit.ly/3z78Fcj`

Creating the list page

In the first phase, we will create the list page to show cars with paging, filtering, and sorting features. Run your unsecured Spring Boot backend. The cars can be fetched by sending the `GET` request to the `http://localhost:8080/api/cars` URL, as shown in *Chapter 4*, *Creating a RESTful Web Service with Spring Boot*.

Figure 11.1 – Fetching cars

Now, let's inspect the JSON data from the response. The array of cars can be found in the `_embedded.cars` node of the JSON response data.

Once we know how to fetch cars from the backend, we are ready to implement the list page to show the cars. The following steps describe this in practice:

1. Open the `carfront` React app with VS Code (the React app we created in the previous chapter).

2. When the app has multiple components, it is recommended that you create a folder for them. Create a new folder called `components` in the `src` folder. With VS Code, you can create a folder by right-clicking the folder in the sidebar file explorer and selecting **New Folder** from the menu:

Figure 11.2 – New folder

3. Create a new file called `Carlist.js` in the `components` folder. Your project structure should look like the following:

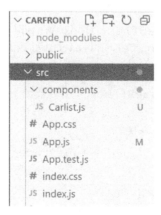

Figure 11.3 – Project structure

4. Open the `Carlist.js` file in the editor view and write the base code of the component, as follows:

```
import React from 'react';

function Carlist() {
  return(
    <div></div>
  );
}

export default Carlist;
```

5. We need a state for the fetched cars from the REST API. Therefore, we have to declare a state called `cars` and the initial value is an empty array:

```
import React, { useState } from 'react';

function Carlist() {
  const [cars, setCars] = useState([]);

  return(
    <div></div>
  );
}

export default Carlist;
```

6. Execute `fetch` in the `useEffect` Hook. We will pass an empty array as the second argument; therefore, `fetch` is executed only once after the first render. The cars from the JSON response data will be saved to the state, called `cars`:

```
import React, { useEffect, useState } from 'react';

function Carlist() {
  const [cars, setCars] = useState([]);

  useEffect(() => {
```

```
      fetch('http://localhost:8080/api/cars')
      .then(response => response.json())
      .then(data => setCars(data._embedded.cars))
      .catch(err => console.error(err));
    }, []);

    return (
      <div></div>
    );
  }

  export default Carlist;
```

7. Use the map function to transform car objects into table rows in the return statement and add the table element:

```
return (
  <div>
    <table>
      <tbody>
        {
          cars.map((car, index) =>
            <tr key={index}>
              <td>{car.brand}</td>
              <td>{car.model}</td>
              <td>{car.color}</td>
              <td>{car.year}</td>
              <td>{car.price}</td>
            </tr>)
        }
      </tbody>
    </table>
  </div>
);
```

8. Finally, we have to import and render the `Carlist` component in our `App.js` file. In the `App.js` file, add the `import` statement, and then add the `Carlist` component to the `return` statement:

```
import './App.css';
import AppBar from '@mui/material/AppBar';
import Toolbar from '@mui/material/Toolbar';
import Typography from '@mui/material/Typography';
import Carlist from './components/Carlist';

function App() {
  return (
    <div className="App">
      <AppBar position="static">
        <Toolbar>
          <Typography variant="h6">
            Carshop
          </Typography>
        </Toolbar>
      </AppBar>
      <Carlist />
    </div>
  );
}

export default App;
```

9. Now, if you start the React app with the `npm start` command, you should see the following list page. Note, your backend should be also running:

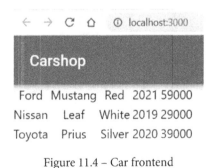

Figure 11.4 – Car frontend

The server URL address can repeat multiple times when we create more CRUD functionalities, and it will change when the backend is deployed to a server other than the local host; therefore, it is better to define it as a constant. Then, when the URL value changes, we have to modify it in one place. With `create-react-app`, you can also create a `.env` file in the root of your project and define environment variables there, but that is not covered here.

Let's create a new file, `constants.js`, to the `src` folder of our app:

1. Open the file in the editor and add the following line to the file:

    ```
    export const SERVER_URL='http://localhost:8080/';
    ```

2. Then, we will import `SERVER_URL` to our `Carlist.js` file and use it in the `fetch` method:

    ```
    //Carlist.js
    // Import server url (named import)
    import { SERVER_URL } from '../constants.js'


    // Use imported constant in the fetch method
    fetch(SERVER_URL + 'api/cars')
    ```

3. Finally, your `Carlist.js` file source code should appear as follows:

    ```
    import React, { useEffect, useState } from 'react';
    import { SERVER_URL } from  '../constants.js';

    function Carlist() {
      const [cars, setCars] = useState([])

      useEffect(() => {
        fetch(SERVER_URL + 'api/cars')
        .then(response => response.json())
        .then(data => setCars(data._embedded.cars))
        .catch(err => console.error(err));
      }, []);

      return(
        <div>
    ```

```
      <table>
        <tbody>
          {
            cars.map((car, index) =>
            <tr key={index}>
              <td>{car.brand}</td>
              <td>{car.model}</td>
              <td>{car.color}</td>
              <td>{car.year}</td>
              <td>{car.price}</td>
            </tr>)
          }
        </tbody>,
      </table>
    </div>
  );
}

export default Carlist;
```

We have already used the `ag-grid` component to implement data grid and that can be used here as well. But, we will use the new MUI data grid component to get the paging, filtering, and sorting features out of the box:

1. Stop the development server by pressing *Ctrl* + *C* in the terminal and installing the MUI data grid community version. The following is the current installation command but you should check the latest installation command and usage from MUI documentation. Post-installation, restart the app:

```
npm install @mui/x-data-grid
```

2. Then, import the `DataGrid` component to your `Carlist.js` file:

```
import { DataGrid } from '@mui/x-data-grid';
```

3. We also have to define the columns of the data grid, where `field` is the property of the car object. The `headerName` prop can be used to set the title of the columns. We also set the width of the columns:

```
const columns = [
  {field: 'brand', headerName: 'Brand', width: 200},
  {field: 'model', headerName: 'Model', width: 200},
  {field: 'color', headerName: 'Color', width: 200},
  {field: 'year', headerName: 'Year', width: 150},
  {field: 'price', headerName: 'Price', width: 150},
];
```

4. Then, remove `table` and all its child elements from the component's `return` statement and add the `DataGrid` component. The data source of the data grid is the `cars` state, which contains fetched cars, and that is defined using the `rows` prop. The data grid component requires all rows to have a unique ID property that is defined using the `getRowId` prop. We can use our `link` field of the car object because that contains the unique car ID (`_links.self.href`). We also have to define the width and height of the grid in the `div` element. Refer to the source code of the following `return` statement:

```
return (
  <div style={{ height: 500, width: '100%' }}>
    <DataGrid
      rows={cars}
      columns={columns}
      getRowId={row => row._links.self.href}/>
  </div>
);
```

5.   With the MUI data grid component, we acquired all the necessary features (such as sorting, filtering, and paging) for our table with a small amount of coding. Now, the list page looks like the following:

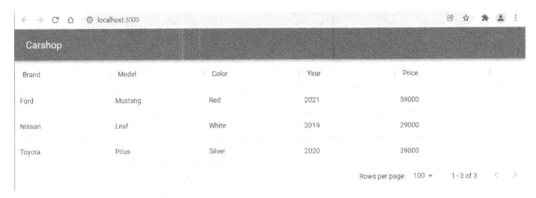

Figure 11.5 – Car frontend

Data grid columns can be filtered using the column menu and clicking the **Filter** menu item. You can also set the visibility of the columns from the column menu:

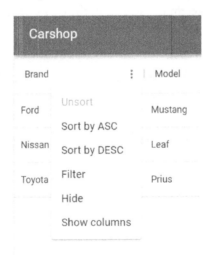

Figure 11.6 – Column menu

Next, we will implement the `delete` functionality.

The delete functionality

Items can be deleted from the database by sending the DELETE method request to the `http://localhost:8080/api/cars/{carId}` endpoint. If we look at the JSON response data, we can see that each car contains a link to itself and it can be accessed from the `_links.self.href` node, as shown in the following screenshot. We already used the `link` field to set a unique ID for every row in the grid. That row ID can be used in deletion, as we can see later:

Figure 11.7 – Car link

The following steps demonstrate how to implement the `delete` functionality:

1. Here, we will create a button for each row in the table. The field of the button will be `_links.self.href`, which is a link to a car. If you need more complex cell content, you can use a `renderCell` prop that you can use to define how a cell content is rendered.

    Let's add a new column to the table using `renderCell` to render the `button` element. The `row` argument that is passed to the function is a row object that contains all values from a row. In our case, it contains a link to a car in each row, and that is needed in deletion. The link is in the row's `id` property, and we will pass this value to a `delete` function. Refer to the following source code. We don't want to enable sorting and filtering for the `button` column, therefore, the `filterable` and `sortable` props are set to `false`. The button invokes the `onDelClick` function when pressed and passes a link (`row.id`) to the function as an argument:

    ```
    const columns = [
      {field: 'brand', headerName: 'Brand', width: 200},
      {field: 'model', headerName: 'Model', width: 200},
      {field: 'color', headerName: 'Color', width: 200},
      {field: 'year', headerName: 'Year', width: 150},
      {field: 'price', headerName: 'Price', width: 150},
      {
        field: '_links.self.href',
        headerName: '',
        sortable: false,
        filterable: false,
        renderCell: row =>
          <button
            onClick={() => onDelClick(row.id)}>Delete
          </button>
      }
    ];
    ```

2. Next, we implement the onDelClick function. But first, let's take the fetch method out of the useEffect Hook. This is necessary because we also want to call fetch after the car has been deleted in order to show an updated list of cars to the user. Create a new function called fetchCars, and copy the code from the useEffect Hook into a new function. Then, call the fetchCars function from the useEffect Hook to fetch cars:

```
useEffect(() => {
  fetchCars();
}, []);

const fetchCars = () => {
  fetch(SERVER_URL + 'api/cars')
  .then(response => response.json())
  .then(data => setCars(data._embedded.cars))
  .catch(err => console.error(err));
}
```

3. Implement the onDelClick function. We send the DELETE request to a car link, and when the DELETE request succeeds, we refresh the list page by calling the fetchCars function:

```
const onDelClick = (url) => {
  fetch(url, {method: 'DELETE'})
  .then(response => fetchCars())
  .catch(err => console.error(err))
}
```

When you start your app, the frontend should look like the following screenshot. The car disappears from the list when the **Delete** button is pressed. Note that after deletions, you can restart the backend to reset the database:

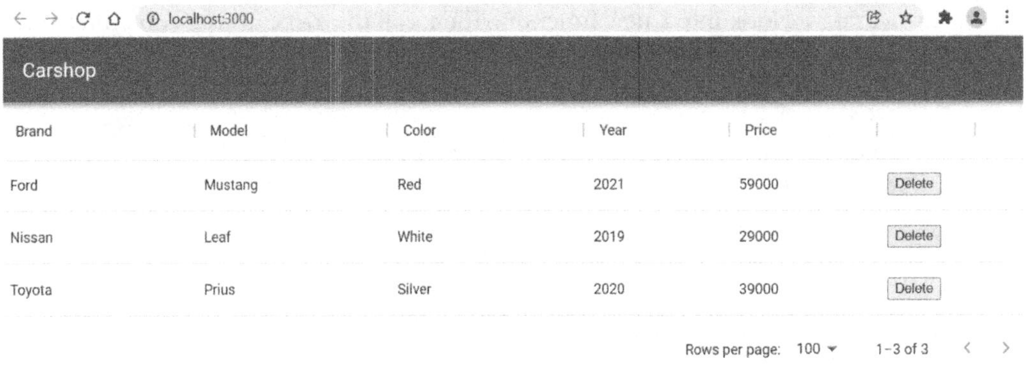

Brand	Model	Color	Year	Price		
Ford	Mustang	Red	2021	59000	Delete	
Nissan	Leaf	White	2019	29000	Delete	
Toyota	Prius	Silver	2020	39000	Delete	

Rows per page: 100 ▼   1–3 of 3   <   >

Figure 11.8 – Car frontend

You can also see that when you click any row in the grid, the row is selected. You can disable that by setting the `disableSelectionOnClick` prop in the grid to `true`:

```
<DataGrid
  rows={cars}
  columns={columns}
  disableSelectionOnClick={true}
  getRowId={row => row._links.self.href} />
```

It would be nice to show the user some feedback in the case of successful deletion, or if there are any errors.

4. Let's implement a toast message to show the status of the deletion. For that, we are going to use the MUI `Snackbar` component. We have to import the `Snackbar` component by adding the following `import` statement to your `Carlist.js` file:

```
import Snackbar from '@mui/material/Snackbar';
```

The `Snackbar` component open prop value is a Boolean, and if it is `true`, the component is shown. Let's declare one state called `open` to handle the visibility of our `Snackbar` component. The initial value is `false` because the message is shown only after the deletion:

```
//Carlist.js
const [open, setOpen] = useState(false);
```

5. Next, we add the `Snackbar` component in the `return` statement after the MUI data grid component. The `autoHideDuration` prop defines the time in milliseconds when the `onClose` function is called automatically, and the message disappears. The `message` prop defines the message to display:

```
<Snackbar
    open={open}
    autoHideDuration={2000}
    onClose={() => setOpen(false)}
    message="Car deleted"
/>
```

6. Finally, we set the `open` state to `true` after the deletion and toast message opens:

```
const onDelClick = (url) => {
  fetch(url, {method: 'DELETE'})
  .then(response => {
    fetchCars();
    setOpen(true);
  })
  .catch(err => console.error(err))
}
```

Now, you will see the toast message when the car is deleted, as shown in the following screenshot:

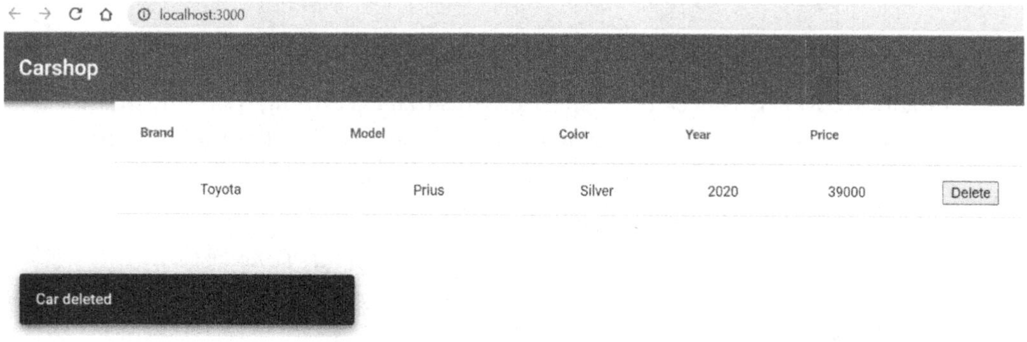

Figure 11.9 – Toast message

7.   To avoid the accidental deletion of the car, it would be nice to have a confirmation dialog after the **Delete** button has been pressed. We will implement this using the window object's `confirm` method. Add `confirm` to the `onDelClick` method:

```
const onDelClick = (url) => {
  if (window.confirm("Are you sure to delete?")) {
    fetch(url, {method: 'DELETE'})
    .then(response => {
      fetchCars()
      setOpen(true);
    })
    .catch(err => console.error(err))
  }
}
```

If you press the **Delete** button now, the confirmation dialog will be opened and the car will only be deleted if you press the **OK** button:

Figure 11.10 – Confirm dialog

Finally, we will also check the response status that everything went fine in the deletion. As we have already learned, the `response` object has the `ok` property, which we can use to check that the response was successful:

```
const onDelClick = (url) => {
  if (window.confirm("Are you sure to delete?")) {
    fetch(url, {method: 'DELETE'})
    .then(response => {
      if (response.ok) {
        fetchCars();
        setOpen(true);
```

```
        }
        else {
          alert('Something went wrsong!');
        }
      })
      .catch(err => console.error(err))
   }
}
```

Next, we will begin the implementation of the functionality to add a new car.

The add functionality

The next step is to create an add functionality for the frontend. We will implement this using the MUI modal dialog. We already went through the utilization of the MUI modal form in *Chapter 9, Useful Third-Party Components for React*. We will add the **New Car** button to the user interface, which opens the modal form when it is pressed. The modal form contains all the fields that are required to add a new car, as well as the button for saving and canceling.

We have already installed the MUI component library to our frontend app in *Chapter 10, Setting Up the Frontend for Our Spring Boot RESTful Web Service*.

The following steps show you how to create the add functionality using the modal dialog component:

1. Create a new file called AddCar.js in the components folder and write some function component base code to the file, as shown here. Add the imports for the MUI Dialog component:

```
import React from 'react';
import Dialog from '@mui/material/Dialog';
import DialogActions from '@mui/material/DialogActions';
import DialogContent from '@mui/material/DialogContent';
import DialogTitle from '@mui/material/DialogTitle';

function AddCar(props) {
  return(
    <div></div>
  );
```

```
}

export default AddCar;
```

2. Declare a state that contains all car fields using the useState Hook. For the dialog, we also need a Boolean state to define the visibility of the dialog form:

```
import React, { useState } from 'react';
import Dialog from '@mui/material/Dialog';
import DialogActions from '@mui/material/DialogActions';
import DialogContent from '@mui/material/DialogContent';
import DialogTitle from '@mui/material/DialogTitle';

function AddCar(props) {
  const [open, setOpen] = useState(false);
  const [car, setCar] = useState({
    brand: '',
    model: '',
    color: '',
    year: '',
    fuel: '',
    price: ''
  });

  return(
    <div></div>
  );
}

export default AddCar;
```

3. Next, we add two functions to close and open the dialog form. The handleClose and handleOpen functions set the value of the open state, which affects the visibility of the modal form:

```
// AddCar.js
// Open the modal form
const handleClickOpen = () => {
```

```
    setOpen(true);
  };
```

```
  // Close the modal form
  const handleClose = () => {
    setOpen(false);
  };
```

4. Add a `Dialog` component inside the `AddCar` component's `return` statement. The form contains the MUI `Dialog` component with buttons and the input fields that are required to collect the car data. The button that opens the modal window, which will be shown on the car list page, must be outside of the `Dialog` component. All input fields should have the `name` attribute with a value that is the same as the name of the state the value will be saved to. Input fields also have the `onChange` prop, which saves the value to `state` by invoking the `handleChange` function:

```
// AddCar.js
const handleChange = (event) => {
  setCar({...car, [event.target.name]:
    event.target.value});
}

return (
  <div>
    <button onClick={handleClickOpen}>New Car</button>
    <Dialog open={open} onClose={handleClose}>
      <DialogTitle>New car</DialogTitle>
      <DialogContent>
        <input placeholder="Brand" name="brand"
          value={car.brand} onChange={handleChange}
          /><br/>
        <input placeholder="Model" name="model"
          value={car.model} onChange={handleChange}
          /><br/>
        <input placeholder="Color" name="color"
          value={car.color} onChange={handleChange}/>
          <br/>
```

```
        <input placeholder="Year" name="year"
            value={car.year} onChange={handleChange}/>
            <br/>
        <input placeholder="Price" name="price"
            value={car.price} onChange={handleChange}/>
            <br/>
      </DialogContent>
      <DialogActions>
        <button onClick={handleClose}>Cancel</button>
        <button onClick={handleClose}>Save</button>
      </DialogActions>
    </Dialog>
  </div>
);
```

5. Implement the addCar function to the Carlist.js file, which will send the
   POST request to the backend api/cars endpoint. The request will include the new
   car object inside the body and the 'Content-Type':'application/json'
   header. The header is required because the car object is converted into a JSON
   string using the JSON.stringify() method:

```
// Carlist.js

// Add a new car
const addCar = (car) => {
  fetch(SERVER_URL + 'api/cars',
  {
    method: 'POST',
    headers: { 'Content-Type':'application/json' },
    body: JSON.stringify(car)
  })
  .then(response => {
    if (response.ok) {
      fetchCars();
    }
    else {
      alert('Something went wrong!');
```

```
        }
    })
    .catch(err => console.error(err))
}
```

6. Import the `AddCar` component into the `Carlist.js` file:

```
import AddCar from './AddCar.js';
```

7. Add the `AddCar` component to the `Carlist.js` file's `return` statement and
pass the `addCar` function as props to the `AddCar` component. This allows us to
call this function from the `AddCar` component. Now, the `return` statement of the
`CarList.js` file should appear as follows:

```
// Carlist.js
return(
  <React.Fragment>
    <AddCar addCar={addCar} />
    <div style={{ height: 500, width: '100%' }}>
      <DataGrid
        rows={cars}
        columns={columns}
        disableSelectionOnClick={true}
        getRowId={row => row._links.self.href}
      />
      <Snackbar
        open={open}
        autoHideDuration={2000}
        onClose={() => setOpen(false)}
        message="Car deleted"
      />
    </div>
  </React.Fragment>
);
```

8. If you start the `carshop` app, it should now look like the following, and if you press the **New Car** button, it should open the modal form:

Figure 11.11 – Carshop

9. Create a function called `handleSave` in the `AddCar.js` file. The `handleSave` function calls the `addCar` function, which can be accessed using `props`, and pass the `car` state object to it. Finally, the modal form is closed and the car list is updated:

```
// AddCar.js

// Save car and close modal form
const handleSave = () => {
  props.addCar(car);
  handleClose();
}
```

10. Finally, you have to change the `AddCar` component's `onClick` save button to call the `handleSave` function:

```
// AddCar.js

<DialogActions>
  <button onClick={handleClose}>Cancel</button>
  <button onClick={handleSave}>Save</button>
</DialogActions>
```

11. Now, you can open the modal form by pressing the **New Car** button. Then, you can fill the form with data and press the **Save** button. At this point, the form doesn't have a nice appearance, but we are going to style it in the next chapter:

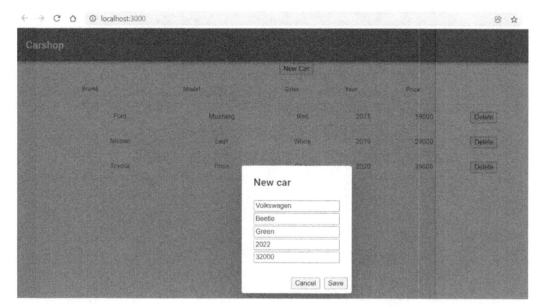

Figure 11.12 – Add new car

After saving, the list page is refreshed, and the new car can be seen in the list:

Figure 11.13 – Carshop

Next, we will begin to implement the edit functionality in relation to our frontend.

The edit functionality

We will implement the edit functionality by adding the **Edit** button to each table row. When the row **Edit** button is pressed, it opens the modal form, where the user can edit the existing car and finally save the changes:

1. First, we will create a skeleton of the EditCar component, which will be the form for editing an existing car. Create a new file called EditCar.js in the components folder. The EditCar component code is similar to the AddCar component, but for now, in the handleSave function, we should call the update function that we will implement later:

```javascript
import React, { useState } from 'react';
import Dialog from '@mui/material/Dialog';
import DialogActions from '@mui/material/DialogActions';
import DialogContent from '@mui/material/DialogContent';
import DialogTitle from '@mui/material/DialogTitle';

function EditCar(props) {
  const [open, setOpen] = useState(false);
  const [car, setCar] = useState({
    brand: '', model: '', color: '',
    year: '', fuel:'', price:   ''
  });

  // Open the modal form
  const handleClickOpen = () => {
    setOpen(true);
  };

  // Close the modal form
  const handleClose = () => {
    setOpen(false);
  };

  const handleChange = (event) => {
    setCar({...car,
      [event.target.name]: event.target.value});
```

```
    }

    // Update car and close modal form
    const handleSave = () => {
    }

    return(
      <div></div>
    );
}

export default EditCar;
```

2. Then, we render the edit dialog form in the `return` statement:

```
// EditCar.js
return(
  <div>
    <button onClick={handleClickOpen}>Edit</button>
    <Dialog open={open} onClose={handleClose}>
      <DialogTitle>Edit car</DialogTitle>
      <DialogContent>
        <input placeholder="Brand" name="brand"
          value={car.brand}onChange={handleChange}
            /><br/>
        <input placeholder="Model" name="model"
          value={car.model}onChange={handleChange}
            /><br/>
        <input placeholder="Color" name="color"
          value={car.color}onChange={handleChange}
            /><br/>
        <input placeholder="Year" name="year"
          value={car.year}
onChange={handleChange}/><br/>
        <input placeholder="Price" name="price"
          value={car.price}onChange={handleChange}
            /><br/>
```

```
        </DialogContent>
        <DialogActions>
          <button onClick={handleClose}> Cancel
          </button>
          <button onClick={handleSave}>Save</button>
        </DialogActions>
      </Dialog>
    </div>
  );
```

3. To update the car data, we have to send the PUT request to the http://
   localhost:8080/api/cars/[carid] URL. The link will be the same as it is
   for the delete functionality. The request contains the updated car object inside the
   body, and the 'Content-Type': 'application/json' header that we had in
   the add functionality. Create a new function called updateCar in the Carlist.
   js file. The source code of the function is shown in the following code snippet.

   The function gets two arguments—the updated car object and the request URL.
   Following a successful update, we will fetch the cars and the list is updated:

```js
// Carlist.js
// Update car
const updateCar = (car, link) => {
  fetch(link,
    {
      method: 'PUT',
      headers: { 'Content-Type':  'application/json' },
      body: JSON.stringify(car)
    })
    .then(response => {
      if (response.ok) {
        fetchCars();
      }
      else {
        alert('Something went wrong!');
      }
    })
    .catch(err => console.error(err))
}
```

4. Next, we will import the `EditCar` component into the `Carlist` component so
    that we are able to show it in the car list. Add the following `import` statement to
    the `Carlist.js` file:

    ```
    import EditCar from './EditCar.js';
    ```

5. Now, add the `EditCar` component to the table columns in the same way that
    we did with the `delete` functionality. The `EditCar` component is rendered to
    table cells, and it only shows the **Edit** button. This is because the modal form is
    not visible before the button is pressed. When the user presses the **Edit** button, it
    updates the `open` state value to `true` in the `EditCar` component, and the modal
    form is shown. We pass two props to the `EditCar` component. The first prop is
    `row`, which will be the row object that contains the link and car data that we need in
    the update. The second one is the `updateCar` function, which we have to call from
    the `EditCar` component in order to be able to save changes:

    ```
    // Carlist.js
    const columns = [
      {field: 'brand', headerName: 'Brand', width: 200},
      {field: 'model', headerName: 'Model', width: 200},
      {field: 'color', headerName: 'Color', width: 200},
      {field: 'year', headerName: 'Year', width: 150},
      {field: 'price', headerName: 'Price', width: 150},
      {
        field: '_links.car.href',
        headerName: '',
        sortable: false,
        filterable: false,
        renderCell: row =>
          <EditCar
            data={row}
            updateCar={updateCar} />
      },
      {
        field: '_links.self.href',
        headerName: '',
        sortable: false,
        filterable: false,
    ```

```
renderCell: row =>
    <button
        onClick={() =>
        onDelClick(row.id)}>Delete
    </button>
    }
];
```

6. We have now added the **Edit car** button to the data grid, and we are able to open the edit form. Our goal is to populate edit form fields using the data from a row where the **Edit** button is pressed. We passed one prop called `data` to the `EditCar` component and let's now find out what the value of this prop is. Open the app in the browser and open the React developer tools **Components** tab.

7. Click the **Edit** button and open the edit form in any of the rows, and find `EditCar` from the developer tools component tree. You should now see the value of passed `props` in the developer tools. We will find out that we can get car data from `data.row` and the link to a car from `data.id`, and we will use these values in the next step:

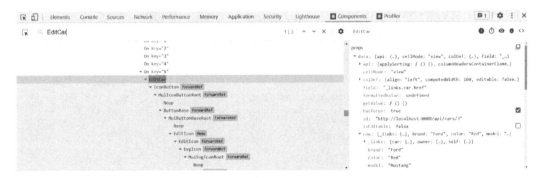

Figure 11.14 – React developer tools

8. Next, we will perform the final modifications to the EditCar.js file. We get the car to be edited from the data prop, which we use to populate the form with the existing car values. Change the handleClickOpen function in the EditCar.js file. Now, when the form is opened, the car state is updated with the values from the data prop. The data prop has a row property that contains the car object:

```
// EditCar.js
// Open the modal form and update the car state
const handleClickOpen = () => {
  setCar({
    brand: props.data.row.brand,
    model: props.data.row.model,
    color: props.data.row.color,
    year: props.data.row.year,
    fuel: props.data.row.fuel,
    price: props.data.row.price
  })
  setOpen(true);
}
```

9. Finally, we will change the handleSave function in the EditCar.js file and call the updateCar function using props. The first argument is the car state that contains the updated car object. The second argument is the id property of the data props, and that is the link to a car:

```
// EditCar.js
// Update car and close modal form
const handleSave = () => {
  props.updateCar(car, props.data.id);
  handleClose();
}
```

10. If you press the **Edit** button in the table, it opens the modal edit form and shows the car from that row. The updated values are saved to the database when you press the **Save** button:

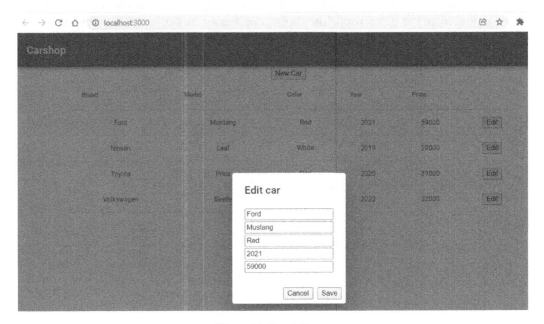

Figure 11.15 – Edit car

Now, we have implemented all CRUD functionalities in relation to our frontend.

Other functionalities

One feature that we will also implement is a **comma-separated values (CSV)** export of the data. We don't need any extra library for the export because the MUI data grid provides this feature:

1. First, we will import the following components to the `Carlist.js` file:

```
import { DataGrid, GridToolbarContainer, GridToolbarExport,
  gridClasses } from '@mui/x-data-grid';
```

2. Next, we will create the `toolbar` component that renders the **Export** button using the MUI `GridToolbarContainer` and `GridToolbarExport` components:

```
// Carlist.js
function CustomToolbar() {
  return (
    <GridToolbarContainer
      className={gridClasses.toolbarContainer}>
      <GridToolbarExport />
    </GridToolbarContainer>
  );
}
```

3. Finally, we have to enable our toolbar that contains the **Export** button. To enable the toolbar in the MUI data grid, you have to use the `components` prop and set the value to `Toolbar: CustomToolbar`:

```
return(
    <React.Fragment>
      <AddCar addCar={addCar} />
      <div style={{ height: 500, width: '100%' }}>
        <DataGrid
          rows={cars}
          columns={columns}
          disableSelectionOnClick={true}
          getRowId={row => row._links.self.href}
          components={{ Toolbar: CustomToolbar }}
        />
        <Snackbar
          open={open}
          autoHideDuration={2000}
          onClose={() => setOpen(false)}
          message="Car deleted"
        />
      </div>
    </React.Fragment>
  );
```

Now, you will see the **Export** button in the grid. If you press the button and select **Download as CSV**, the grid data is exported to a CSV file. You can also print your grid using the **Export** button:

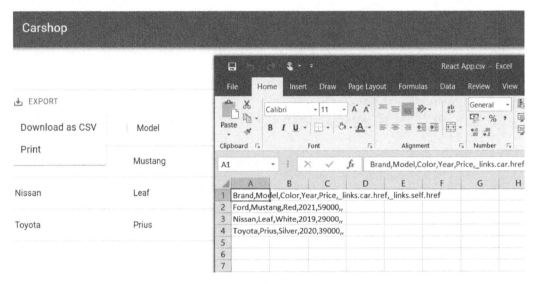

Figure 11.16 – Export CSV

Now, all the functionalities have been implemented. In *Chapter 12*, *Styling the Frontend with React MUI*, we will focus on styling the frontend.

Summary

In this chapter, we implemented all the functionalities for our app. We started with fetching the cars from the backend and showing these in the MUI data grid, which provides paging, sorting, and filtering features. Then, we implemented the `delete` functionality and used the `toast` component to give feedback to the user.

The `add` and `edit` functionalities were implemented using the MUI modal `dialog` component. Finally, we implemented the ability to export data to a CSV file.

In the next chapter, we are going to style the rest of our frontend using the React MUI component library.

Questions

1. How do you fetch and present data using the REST API with React?

2. How do you delete data using the REST API with React?

3. How do you add data using the REST API with React?

4. How do you update data using the REST API with React?

5. How do you show toast messages with React?

6. How do you export data to a CSV file with React?

Further reading

Packt has other great resources available for learning about React. These are as follows:

- *React - The Complete Guide*, by *Academind GmbH*: `https://www.packtpub.com/product/react-the-complete-guide-includes-hooks-react-router-and-redux-2021-updated-second-edition-video/9781801812603`

- *React 17 Design Patterns and Best Practices – Third Edition*, by *Carlos Santana Roldán*: `https://www.packtpub.com/product/react-17-design-patterns-and-best-practices-third-edition/978800560444`

12
Styling the Frontend with React MUI

This chapter explains how to use MUI components in our frontend. We will use the `Button` component to show the styled buttons. We will also use MUI icons and the `IconButton` component. The modal form input fields are replaced by `TextField` components.

In this chapter, we will cover the following topics:

- Using the MUI `Button` component in our frontend
- Using the MUI `Icon` and `IconButton` components in our frontend
- Using the MUI `TextField` component in our frontend

Technical requirements

The Spring Boot application that we created in *Chapter 5, Securing and Testing Your Backend*, is required, together with the modification from *Chapter 10, Setting Up the Frontend for Our Spring Boot RESTful Web Service* (the unsecured backend).

We also need the React app that we used in *Chapter 11, Adding CRUD Functionalities*.

The following code samples available at the GitHub link will also be required: https://github.com/PacktPublishing/Full-Stack-Development-with-Spring-Boot-and-React/tree/main/Chapter12.

Check out the following video to see the Code in Action: https://bit.ly/3x04wnw

Using the Button component

Execute the following steps to implement the Button component:

1. Let's first change all the buttons to use the MUI Button component. Import Button to the AddCar.js file:

```
// AddCar.js
import Button from '@mui/material/Button';
```

2. Change the buttons to use the Button component. In the list page, we are using the **contained** button (variant="contained") and in the modal form, we use the text buttons (default).

The following code shows the AddCar component's return statement with the changes:

```
// AddCar.js
return(
    <div>
        <Button variant="contained"
onClick={handleClickOpen}>
            New Car
        </Button>
        <Dialog open={open} onClose={handleClose}>
            <DialogTitle>New car</DialogTitle>
            <DialogContent>
                <input placeholder="Brand" name="brand"
                    value={car.brand}
                        onChange={handleChange}/><br/>
                <input placeholder="Model" name="model"
                    value={car.model}
```

```
                    onChange={handleChange}/><br/>
          <input placeholder="Color" name="color"
            value={car.color}
                    onChange={handleChange}/><br/>
          <input placeholder="Year" name="year"
            value={car.year} onChange={handleChange}
               /><br/>
          <input placeholder="Price" name="price"
            value={car.price} onChange=
               {handleChange}/><br/>
        </DialogContent>
        <DialogActions>
          <Button onClick={handleClose}>Cancel
          </Button>
          <Button onClick={handleSave}>Save</Button>
        </DialogActions>
       </Dialog>
     </div>
  );
```

Now, the **NEW CAR** button is also rendered using the MUI `Button` component, but the layout is not looking good because the button is touching the toolbar.

3. We will add some margins to the button by using the MUI `Stack` layout component. Import the MUI `Stack` component to the `Carlist.js` file:

```
import Stack from '@mui/material/Stack';
```

4. Then, wrap the `AddCar` component inside the `Stack` component and add top and bottom margins using the `mt` and `mb` props:

```
// Carlist.js
<Stack mt={2} mb={2}>
    <AddCar addCar={addCar} />
</Stack>
```

Now, the **NEW CAR** button should look as shown in the following screenshot:

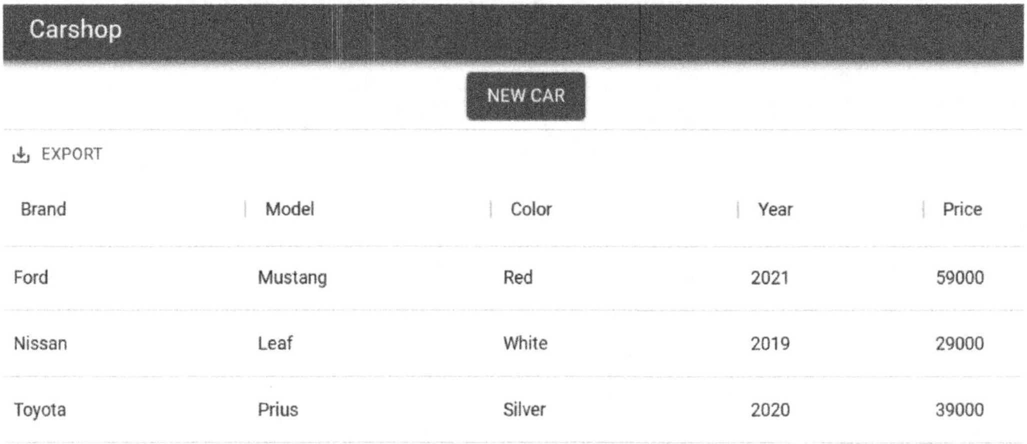
Carshop
NEW CAR
EXPORT
Brand
Model
Color
Year
Price
Ford
Mustang
Red
2021
59000
Nissan
Leaf
White
2019
29000
Toyota
Prius
Silver
2020
39000

Figure 12.1 – The Carlist buttons

The modal form buttons should look like the following:

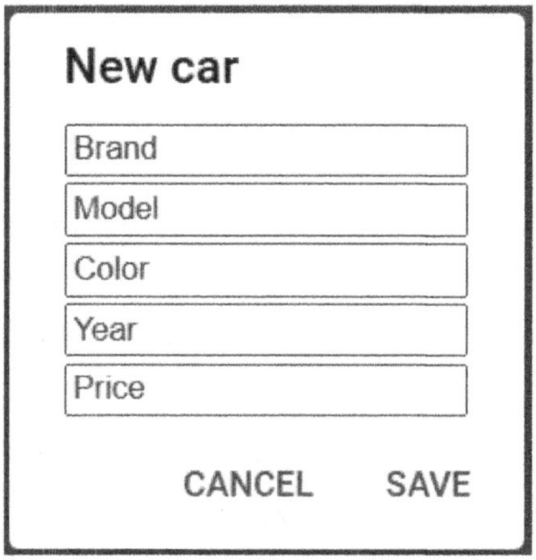
New car
Brand
Model
Color
Year
Price
CANCEL
SAVE

Figure 12.2 – The AddCar buttons

We also need to change the buttons in the `EditCar` component. The button that opens the modal form is the **Edit** button, which is shown in the table, and that will be changed later using icons.

Let's change **CANCEL** and **SAVE** buttons as we did with the new car form:

1. Import the `Button` component to the `EditCar.js` file:

```
// EditCar.js
import Button from '@mui/material/Button';
```

2. Then, change the **SAVE** and **CANCEL** buttons to use the MUI `Button` component:

```
return (
    <div>
        <button onClick={handleClickOpen}>Edit</button>
        <Dialog open={open} onClose={handleClose}>
            <DialogTitle>Edit car</DialogTitle>
            <DialogContent>
                <input placeholder="Brand" name="brand"
                    value={car.brand}
                        onChange={handleChange}/><br/>
                <input placeholder="Model" name="model"
                    value={car.model} onChange=
                        {handleChange}/><br/>
                <input placeholder="Color" name="color"
                    value={car.color} onChange=
                        {handleChange}/><br/>
                <input placeholder="Year" name="year"
                    value={car.year} onChange=
                        {handleChange}/><br/>
                <input placeholder="Price" name="price"
                    value={car.price} onChange=
                        {handleChange}/><br/>
            </DialogContent>
            <DialogActions>
                <Button onClick={handleClose}>Cancel
                </Button>
                <Button onClick={handleSave}>Save</Button>
            </DialogActions>
        </Dialog>
    </div>
);
```

Now, the buttons in the edit form are also implemented using the MUI `Button` component. Next, we will use the `IconButton` component for the **Edit** and **DELETE** buttons in the grid.

Using icon components

MUI provides prebuilt SVG icons that we have to install by using the following command in the terminal:

```
npm install @mui/icons-material
```

Let's first implement the **DELETE** button in the grid. The MUI `IconButton` component can be used to render icon buttons. The `@mui/icons-material` package that we just installed contains lots of icons that can be used with MUI.

You can find the list of icons available from the MUI documentation. We need an icon for our **DELETE** button; therefore, we will use an icon called `DeleteIcon`:

1. Open the `Carlist.js` file and add the following imports:

    ```
    // Carlist.js
    import IconButton from '@mui/material/IconButton';
    import DeleteIcon from '@mui/icons-material/Delete';
    ```

2. Next, we will render the `IconButton` component in our grid. We will modify the **DELETE** button in the code where we define the grid columns. We change the `button` element to the `IconButton` component and render `DeleteIcon` inside the `IconButton` component. To get the red delete icon, we can use the `color` prop of `DeleteIcon`:

    ```
    // Carlist.js
    const columns = [
      {field: 'brand', headerName: 'Brand', width: 200},
      {field: 'model', headerName: 'Model', width: 200},
      {field: 'color', headerName: 'Color', width: 200},
      {field: 'year', headerName: 'Year', width: 150},
      {field: 'price', headerName: 'Price', width: 150},
      {
        field: '_links.car.href',
        headerName: '',
        sortable: false,
        filterable: false,
        renderCell: row =>
          <EditCar
            data={row}
    ```

```
            updateCar={updateCar} />
  },
  {
    field: '_links.self.href',
    headerName: '',
    sortable: false,
    filterable: false,
    renderCell: row =>
        <IconButton onClick={() => onDelClick
            (row.id)}>
          <DeleteIcon color="error" />
        </IconButton>
  }
];
```

Now, the **DELETE** button in the grid should look like the following screenshot:

Figure 12.3 – The Delete icon button

Next, we will implement the **Edit** button using the IconButton component.

3. Open the EditCar.js file and import the IconButton component and the EditIcon icon:

```
// EditCar.js
import IconButton from '@mui/material/IconButton';
import EditIcon from '@mui/icons-material/Edit';
```

4. Then, render `IconButton` in the `return` statement. The icon color is the MUI primary color, which is blue:

```
// EditCar.js return
<IconButton onClick={handleClickOpen}>
    <EditIcon color="primary" />
</IconButton>
```

Finally, both buttons are rendered as icons, as shown in the following screenshot:

Figure 12.4 – Icon buttons

Next, we will implement text fields using the MUI `TextField` component.

Using the TextField components

In this section, we'll change the text inputs in the modal forms using the MUI `TextField` and `Stack` components:

1. Add the following import statement to the `AddCar.js` and `EditCar.js` files:

```
import TextField from '@mui/material/TextField';
import Stack from '@mui/material/Stack';
```

2. Then, change the input elements to the `TextField` components in the add and edit forms. We are using the `label` prop to set the labels of the `TextField` components. The first `TextField` component contains the `autoFocus` prop, and the input will be focused on this field. There are three different variants available, and we are using the `standard` one.

The text fields are wrapped inside the `Stack` component to get spacing between the components and to set the top margin:

```
// AddCar.js, do the same modifications to the EditCar.js
file
return(
    <div>
      <Button variant="contained"
  onClick={handleClickOpen}>New Car</Button>
      <Dialog open={open} onClose={handleClose}>
          <DialogTitle>New car</DialogTitle>
          <DialogContent>
            <Stack spacing={2} mt={1}>
              <TextField label="Brand" name="brand"
                 autoFocus
                 variant="standard" value={car.brand}
                 onChange={handleChange}/>
              <TextField label="Model" name="model"
                 variant="standard" value={car.model}
                 onChange={handleChange}/>
              <TextField label="Color" name="color"
                 variant="standard" value={car.color}
                 onChange={handleChange}/>
              <TextField label="Year" name="year"
                 variant="standard" value={car.year}
                 onChange={handleChange}/>
              <TextField label="Price" name="price"
                 variant="standard" value={car.price}
                 onChange={handleChange}/>
            </Stack>
          </DialogContent>
        <DialogActions>
          <Button onClick={handleClose}>Cancel
          </Button>
          <Button onClick={handleSave}>Save</Button>
```

```
            </DialogActions>
        </Dialog>
    </div>
);
```

After the modifications, the modal form should look like the following:

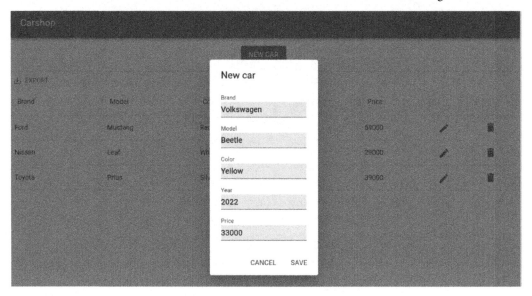

Figure 12.5 – Text fields

Now, we have completed the styling of our frontend using MUI components.

Summary

In this chapter, we finalized our frontend using MUI, which is the React component library that implements Google's Material Design. We replaced the buttons with the MUI Button and IconButton components. Our modal form got a new look by using the MUI TextField component. After these modifications, our frontend looks more professional and uniform.

In the next chapter, we will focus on frontend testing.

Questions

1. What is MUI?

2. How should you use different Material-UI components?

3. How do you use MUI icons?

Further reading

Packt has other great resources available for learning about React. These are as follows:

- *React – The Complete Guide* by *Academind GmbH*: https://www.packtpub.com/product/react-the-complete-guide-includes-hooks-react-router-and-redux-2021-updated-second-edition-video/9781801812603

- *React 17 Design Patterns and Best Practices – Third Edition* by *Carlos Santana Roldán*: https://www.packtpub.com/product/react-17-design-patterns-and-best-practices-third-edition/978800560444

13
Testing Your Frontend

This chapter explains the basics of testing React apps. It will give us an overview of using Jest, which is a JavaScript testing framework developed by Facebook. We will look at how you can create new test suites and tests, and also how to run a test and work with the results. Unit tests make it easier to refactor and maintain code. Unit tests are also easy to automate, which allows us to run tests frequently.

In this chapter, we will cover the following topics:

- Using Jest
- Firing events in tests
- Understanding snapshot testing

Technical requirements

The Spring Boot application that we created in *Chapter 5, Securing and Testing Your Backend*, is required, as is the React app that we used in *Chapter 12, Styling the Frontend with React MUI*.

The code samples available at the following GitHub link will also be required to follow along with this chapter: `https://github.com/PacktPublishing/Full-Stack-Development-with-Spring-Boot-and-React/tree/main/Chapter13`.

Check out the following video to see the Code in Action: `https://bit.ly/3NLSHIK`

Using Jest

Jest is a testing framework for JavaScript developed by Facebook (`https://jestjs.io/`). Jest is widely used with React and provides lots of useful features for testing. You can create a snapshot test, whereby you can take snapshots from React trees and investigate how states are changing. Jest also has mock functionalities that you can use to test, for example, your asynchronous REST API calls. Jest also provides functions that are required for assertions in your test cases.

We will first see how you can create a simple test case for a basic JavaScript function that performs some simple calculations. The following function takes two numbers as arguments and returns the product of the numbers:

```
// multi.js
export const calcMulti = (x, y) => {
  x * y;
}
```

The following code snippet shows a Jest test for the preceding function. The test case starts with a `test` method that runs the test case. The `test` method has an alias, called `it`, that can be used as well. The `test` method gets the two required arguments—the test name and the function that contains the test. `expect` is used when you want to test values, and it gives you access to multiple matchers.

The `toBe` function shown in the following code snippet is one matcher that checks whether the result from the function equals the value in the matcher. There are many different matchers available in Jest and you can find these from the Jest documentation:

```
// multi.test.js
import { calcMulti } from './multi';

test('2 * 3 equals 6', () => {
  expect(calcMulti(2, 3)).toBe(6);
});
```

Jest comes with `create-react-app`, so we don't have to do any installations or configurations to start testing. It is recommended to create a folder called __test__ for your test files. The test files should have the `.test.js` extension. If you look at your React frontend in the **Visual Studio Code (VS Code)** file explorer, you can see that in the `src` folder, there is already one test file automatically created, and it is called `App.test.js`. You can see a representation of this in the following screenshot:

Figure 13.1 – Test file

The source code of the test file looks like this:

```
import { render, screen } from '@testing-library/react';
import App from './App';


test('renders learn react link', () => {
  render(<App />);
  const linkElement = screen.getByText(/learn react/i);
  expect(linkElement).toBeInTheDocument();
});
```

The following test file renders the App component and tests whether the component renders a link element with `'learn react'` text. This test case also uses **React Testing Library** (https://testing-library.com/), which comes with `create-react-app`. The `screen` object that we have imported from React Testing Library has different queries that are bound to `document.body`. For example, `getByText` is used to find `'learn react'` substring text, and `'i'` ignores case.

> **Important Note**
>
> React 18 requires React Testing Library version 13 or later. You can check the installed version from the `package.json` file.

You can run your tests by typing the following command into your terminal:

```
npm test
```

Or, if you are using `yarn`, type the following command:

```
yarn test
```

If the `App.js` file is modified and there is no link element, the test will fail. You will also see a reason for failure in the terminal, as illustrated in the following screenshot:

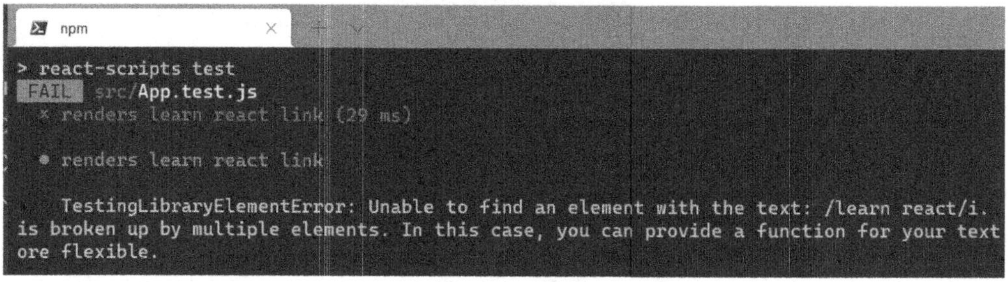

Figure 13.2 – Failed test run

If you create a React app using `create-react-app` and run the test without removing the link, the test will pass, as illustrated here:

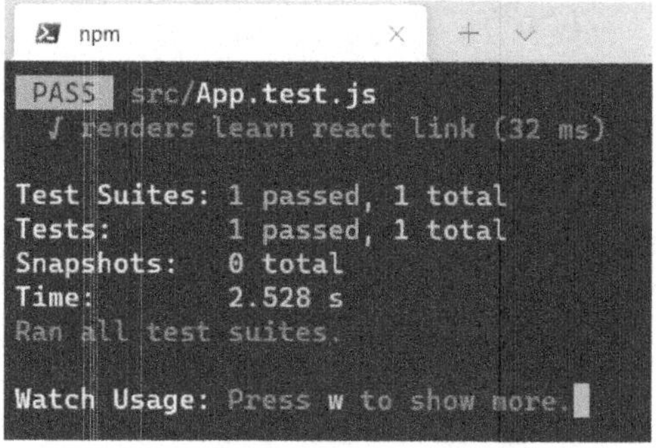

Figure 13.3 – Passed test run

Tests are run in watch mode, and every time your JavaScript files are modified and saved, it will rerun your tests automatically. You can stop the watch mode by pressing *Q* in the terminal.

We have now learned the basics of Jest and how to run tests in a React app.

Firing events in tests

React Testing Library provides a `fireEvent` method that can be used to fire **Document Object Model** (**DOM**) events in your test cases. In the following example, we will create a test case that opens our car addition modal form.

First, add the following imports to the `App.test.js` file:

```
import { render, screen, fireEvent } from '@testing-library/
react';
import App from './App';
```

Next, we will create a new test case in the `App.test.js` file, as follows:

```
test('open add car modal form', () => {
});
```

Then, we use `fireEvent.click`, which creates a click event to a given DOM element. In our case, the DOM element is the button to open the modal form, and we can find it by using a `getByText` query, like this:

```
test('open add car modal form', async () => {
    render(<App />);
    fireEvent.click(screen.getByText('New Car'));
});
```

Finally, we verify that the modal dialog form is opened and there is `'New Car'` text rendered (our modal form header text). We use the `getByRole` query to find our modal dialog. It can be used to query elements with a given role, and to check whether our **MUI** dialog component that we use in our modal form has a `dialog` role, as illustrated in the following code snippet:

```
test('open add car modal form', async () => {
  render(<App />);
  fireEvent.click(screen.getByText('New Car'));
  expect(screen.getByRole('dialog')).toHaveTextContent
      ('New car');
});
```

Now, if you run the tests, you should see that two test cases are passed, as illustrated in the following screenshot:

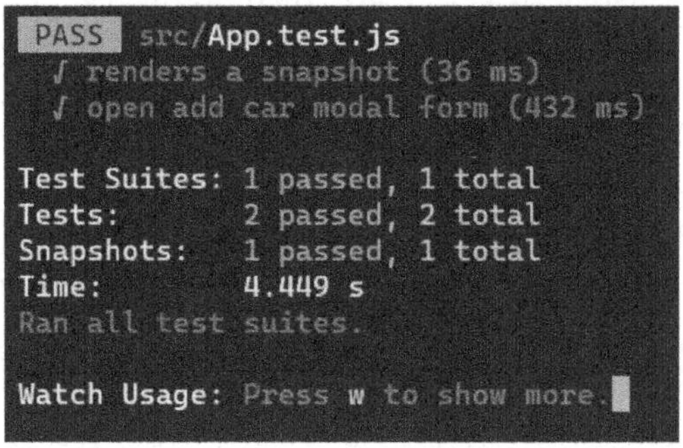

Figure 13.4 – Test run

There is also a `user-event` library available that contains more tools to simulate browser interactions than `fireEvent`.

Understanding snapshot testing

Snapshot testing is a useful way to test that there are no unwanted changes in your **user interface** (**UI**). Jest generates snapshot files when snapshot tests are executed. The next time tests are executed, the new snapshot is compared to the previous one. If there are changes between the content of the files, the test case fails, and an error message is shown in the terminal.

To start snapshot testing, perform the following steps:

1. Install the `react-test-renderer` package. The `--save-dev` parameter means that this dependency is saved to the `package.json` file's `devDependencies` part, and it is only used for development purposes. If you type the `npm install --production` command in the installation phase, dependencies in the `devDependencies` part are not installed. So, all dependencies that are only required in the development phase should be installed using the `--save-dev` parameter, like this:

```
npm install react-test-renderer --save-dev
```

2. After the installation, your `package.json` file contains the new `devDependencies` part, as illustrated in the following code snippet:

```
"devDependencies": {
    "react-test-renderer": "^17.0.2"
}
```

3. Let's now add a new snapshot test case to our `App.test.js` file. Remove the default test case from the file. The test case will create a snapshot test of our `AddCar` component. First, we add the following imports:

```
import TestRenderer from 'react-test-renderer';
import AddCar from './components/AddCar';
```

4. Add the following test case to the `App.test.js` file. The test case takes a snapshot from our `AddCar` component and then compares whether the snapshot differs from the previous snapshot:

```
test('renders a snapshot', () => {
  const tree = TestRenderer.create
    (<AddCar/>).toJSON();
  expect(tree).toMatchSnapshot();
});
```

5. Run the test cases again by typing the following command in your terminal:

```
npm test
```

6. Now, you can see the following message in the terminal. The test suite tells us the number of test files, and the tests tell us the number of test cases. We can also see that one snapshot file was written:

```
PASS  src/App.test.js
  √ renders a snapshot (38 ms)

  › 1 snapshot written.
Snapshot Summary
  › 1 snapshot written from 1 test suite.

Test Suites: 1 passed, 1 total
Tests:       1 passed, 1 total
Snapshots:   1 written, 1 total
Time:        3.024 s
Ran all test suites related to changed files.
```

Figure 13.5 – Snapshot test

When a test is executed for the first time, a _snapshots_ folder is created. This folder contains all snapshot files that are generated from test cases. Now, you can see that there is one snapshot file generated, as shown in the following screenshot:

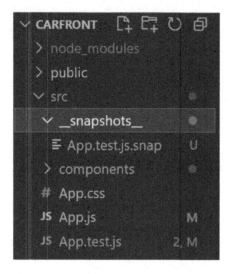

Figure 13.6 – Snapshots folder

The snapshot file now contains the React tree of our AddCar component. You can see part of the snapshot file in the following code block:

```
// Jest Snapshot v1, https://goo.gl/fbAQLP
exports['renders  a  snapshot 1'] = '
<div>
  <button
    className="MuiButton-root MuiButton-contained MuiButton
        -containedPrimary MuiButton-sizeMedium MuiButton
        -containedSizeMedium MuiButtonBase-root
        css-sghohy-MuiButtonBase-root-MuiButton-root"
    disabled={false}
    onBlur={[Function]}
    onClick={[Function]}
    onContextMenu={[Function]}
    onDragLeave={[Function]}
  … continues
```

Now, we are ready with the basics of React testing.

Summary

In this chapter, we provided a basic overview of how to test React apps. Jest is a testing framework developed by Facebook, and it is already available in our frontend because we created our app with `create-react-app`.

We created a couple of tests with Jest and ran those tests to see how you can check the results of tests. We also learned the principles of snapshot testing.

In the next chapter, we will secure our application and add the login functionality to the frontend.

Questions

1. What is Jest?
2. How should you create test cases using Jest?
3. How can you fire events in test cases?
4. How should you create a snapshot test using Jest?

Further reading

Packt Publishing has other great resources available for learning about React and testing. A couple of them are listed here:

- *Simplify Testing with React Testing Library*, by *Scottie Crump* (`https://www.packtpub.com/product/simplify-testing-with-react-testing-library/9781800564459`)

- *Mastering React Test-Driven Development*, by *Daniel Irvine* (`https://www.packtpub.com/product/mastering-react-test-driven-development/9781789133417`)

14
Securing Your Application

This chapter will explain how to implement authentication to our frontend when we are using **JSON Web Token (JWT)** authentication in the backend. In the beginning, we will switch on security in our backend to enable JWT authentication. Then, we will create a component for the login functionality. Finally, we will modify our CRUD functionalities to send the token in the request's authorization header to the backend. We will learn how to secure our application in this chapter.

In this chapter, we will cover the following topics:

- Securing the backend
- Securing the frontend

Technical requirements

The Spring Boot application that we created in *Chapter 5, Securing and Testing Your Backend*, is required (located on GitHub at `https://github.com/ PacktPublishing/Full-Stack-Development-with-Spring-Boot-2-and- React/tree/main/Chapter05`), as is the React app that we used in *Chapter 12, Styling the Frontend with React MUI* (located on GitHub at `https://github.com/ PacktPublishing/Full-Stack-Development-with-Spring-Boot-2-and- React/tree/main/Chapter12`).

The following GitHub link will also be required: `https://github.com/PacktPublishing/Full-Stack-Development-with-Spring-Boot-and-React/tree/main/Chapter14`.

Check out the following video to see the Code in Action: `https://bit.ly/38RFOOX`

Securing the backend

We have implemented CRUD functionalities in our frontend using an unsecured backend. Now, it is time to switch on security for our backend and go back to the version that we created in *Chapter 5, Securing and Testing Your Backend*:

1. Open your backend project with the Eclipse IDE and open the `SecurityConfig.java` file in the editor view. We have commented the security out and have allowed everyone access to all endpoints. Now, we can remove that line and also remove the comments from the original version. Now, the `configure` method of your `SecurityConfig.java` file should look like the following:

    ```
    @Override
    protected void configure(HttpSecurity http) throws
    Exception {
       http.csrf().disable().cors().and()
        .sessionManagement()
      .sessionCreationPolicy(SessionCreationPolicy.
         STATELESS).and()
        .authorizeRequests()
        .antMatchers(HttpMethod.POST, "/login").permitAll()
        .anyRequest().authenticated().and()
        .exceptionHandling()
        .authenticationEntryPoint(exceptionHandler).and()
        .addFilterBefore(authenticationFilter,
        UsernamePasswordAuthenticationFilter.class);
    }
    ```

    Let's test what happens when the backend is secured again.

2. Run the backend by pressing the **Run** button in Eclipse, and check from the Console view that the application started correctly. Run the frontend by typing the `npm start` command into your terminal, and the browser should be opened to the address `localhost:3000`.

3. You should now see that the list page and the car list are empty. If you open the developer tools and the **Network** tab, you will notice that the response status is `401 Unauthorized`. This is actually what we wanted because we haven't yet executed authentication in relation to our frontend:

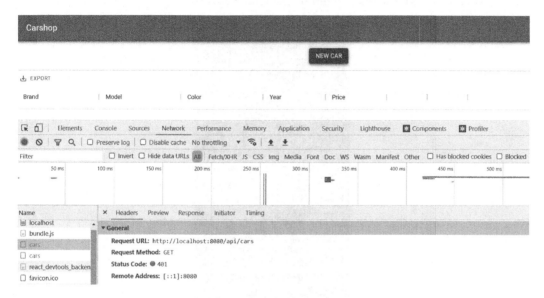

Figure 14.1 – 401 Unauthorized

Now, we are ready to work with the frontend.

Securing the frontend

The authentication was implemented in the backend using JWT. In *Chapter 5*, *Securing and Testing Your Backend*, we created JWT authentication, and everyone is allowed access to the /login endpoint without authentication. On the frontend's login page, we have to first call the /login endpoint using the user credentials to get the token. After that, the token will be included in all requests that we send to the backend, as demonstrated in *Chapter 5*, *Securing and Testing Your Backend*.

Let's first create a login component that asks for credentials from the user to get a token from the backend:

1. Create a new file, called Login.js, in the components folder. Now, the file structure of the frontend should be the following:

Figure 14.2 – Project structure

2. Open the file in the VS Code editor view and add the following base code to the Login component. We are also importing SERVER_URL, because it is required in a login request:

```
import React, { useState } from 'react';
import { SERVER_URL } from '../constants.js';

function Login() {
  return (
    <div></div>
  );
}

export default Login;
```

3. We need three state values for the authentication: two for the credentials (username and password), and one Boolean value to indicate the status of the authentication. The initial value of the authentication status state is `false`:

```
const [user, setUser] = useState({
  username: '',
  password: ''
});
const [isAuthenticated, setAuth] = useState(false);
```

4. In the user interface, we are going to use the **Material UI (MUI)** component library, as we did with the rest of the user interface. We need some `TextField` components for the credentials, the `Button` component to call a login function, and the `Stack` component for layout. Add imports for the components to the `login.js` file:

```
import Button from '@mui/material/Button';
import TextField from '@mui/material/TextField';
import Stack from '@mui/material/Stack';
```

5. Add imported components to a user interface by adding these to the `return` statement. We need two `TextField` components: one for the username and one for the password. One `Button` component is needed to call the login function that we are going to implement later in this section:

```
return(
    <div>
        <Stack spacing={2} alignItems='center' mt={2}>
            <TextField
                name="username"
                label="Username"
                onChange={handleChange} />
            <TextField
                type="password"
                name="password"
                label="Password"
                onChange={handleChange}/>
            <Button
                variant="outlined"
                color="primary"
```

```
            onClick={login}>
                Login
        </Button>
    </Stack>
    </div>
 );
```

6. Implement the change handler function for the TextField components, in order to save typed values to the states:

```
const handleChange = (event) => {
  setUser({...user,
     [event.target.name] : event.target.value});
}
```

7. As shown in *Chapter 5*, *Securing and Testing Your Backend*, the login is done by calling the /login endpoint using the POST method and sending the user object inside the body. If authentication succeeds, we get a token in a response Authorization header. We will then save the token to session storage and set the isAuthenticated state value to true. The session storage is similar to local storage, but it is cleared when a page session ends. When the isAuthenticated state value is changed, the user interface is re-rendered:

```
const login = () => {
    fetch(SERVER_URL + 'login', {
      method: 'POST',
      headers: { 'Content-Type':'application/json' },
      body: JSON.stringify(user)
    })
    .then(res => {
      const jwtToken = res.headers.get
          ('Authorization');
      if (jwtToken !== null) {
        sessionStorage.setItem("jwt", jwtToken);
        setAuth(true);
      }
    })
    .catch(err => console.error(err))
}
```

8. We can implement conditional rendering that renders the `Login` component
    if the `isAuthenticated` state is `false`, or the `Carlist` component if
    the `isAuthenticated` state is `true`. We first have to import the `Carlist`
    component to the `Login.js` file:

```
import Carlist from './Carlist';
```

9. Then, we have to implement the following changes to the `return` statement:

```
if (isAuthenticated) {
  return <Carlist />;
}
else {
  return (
    <div>
      <Stack spacing={2} alignItems='center' mt={2} >
        <TextField
          name="username"
          label="Username"
          onChange={handleChange} />
        <TextField
          type="password"
          name="password"
          label="Password"
          onChange={handleChange}/>
        <Button
          variant="outlined"
          color="primary"
          onClick={login}>
            Login
        </Button>
      </Stack>
    </div>
  );
}
```

10. To show the login form, we have to render the Login component instead of the Carlist component in the App.js file:

```
import './App.css';
import AppBar from '@mui/material/AppBar';
import Toolbar from '@mui/material/Toolbar';
import Typography from '@mui/material/Typography';
import Login from './components/Login';

function App() {
  return (
    <div className="App">
      <AppBar position="static">
        <Toolbar>
          <Typography variant="h6">
            Carshop
          </Typography>
        </Toolbar>
      </AppBar>
      <Login />
    </div>
  );
}

export default App;
```

Now, when your frontend and backend are running, your frontend should look like the following screenshot:

Figure 14.3 – Login page

If you log in using the *user/user* or *admin/admin* credentials, you should see the car list page. If you open the developer tools' **Application** tab, you can see that the token is now saved to the session storage:

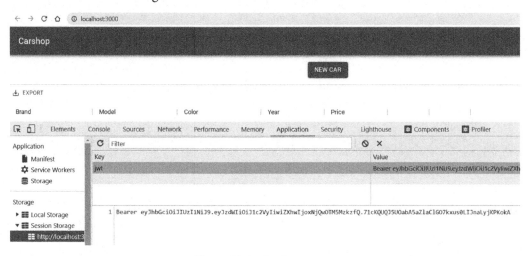

Figure 14.4 – Session storage

The car list is still empty, but that is correct because we haven't included the token in the GET request yet. That is required for the JWT authentication, which we will implement in the next phase:

1. Open the `Carlist.js` file in the VS Code editor view. To fetch the cars, we first have to read the token from the session storage and then add the `Authorization` header with the token value to the GET request. You can see the source code of the `fetchCars` function here:

```js
const fetchCars = () => {
    // Read the token from the session storage
    // and include it to Authorization header
    const token = sessionStorage.getItem("jwt");

    fetch(SERVER_URL + 'api/cars', {
        headers: { 'Authorization' : token }
    })
    .then(response => response.json())
    .then(data => setCars(data._embedded.cars))
    .catch(err => console.error(err));
}
```

2. If you log in to your frontend, you should see the car list populated with cars from the database:

Carshop							

NEW CAR

⬇ EXPORT

Brand	Model	Color	Year	Price			
Ford	Mustang	Red	2021	59000		✏	🗑
Nissan	Leaf	White	2019	29000		✏	🗑
Toyota	Prius	Silver	2020	39000		✏	🗑

Figure 14.5 – Car list

3. Check the request content from the developer tools; you can see that it contains the `Authorization` header with the token value:

Figure 14.6 – Request headers

All other CRUD functionalities require the same modification to work correctly. The source code of the onDelClick function appears as follows, after the modifications:

```
// Carlist.js
const onDelClick = (url) => {
    if (window.confirm("Are you sure to delete?")) {
        const token = sessionStorage.getItem("jwt");

        fetch(url, {
            method: 'DELETE',
            headers: { 'Authorization' : token }
        })
        .then(response => {
            if (response.ok) {
                fetchCars();
                setOpen(true);
            }
            else {
                alert('Something went wrong!');
            }
        })
        .catch(err => console.error(err))
    }
}
```

The source code of the addCar function appears as follows, after the modifications:

```
// Carlist.js
// Add a new car
```

```
const addCar = (car) => {
    const token = sessionStorage.getItem("jwt");

    fetch(SERVER_URL + 'api/cars',
      {
        method: 'POST',
        headers: {
          'Content-Type':'application/json',
          'Authorization' : token
        },
        body: JSON.stringify(car)
    })
    .then(response => {
      if (response.ok) {
        fetchCars()
      }
      else {
        alert('Something went wrong!');
      }
    })
    .catch(err => console.error(err))
}
```

Finally, the source code of the updateCar function looks like this:

```
// Carlist.js
// Update car
const updateCar = (car, link) => {
    const token = sessionStorage.getItem("jwt");

    fetch(link,
      {
        method: 'PUT',
        headers: {
          'Content-Type':'application/json',
          'Authorization' : token
        },
```

```
    body: JSON.stringify(car)
  })
  .then(response => {
    if (response.ok) {
      fetchCars();
    }
    else {
      alert('Something went wrong!');
    }
  })
  .catch(err => console.error(err))
}
```

Now, all the CRUD functionalities will be working after you have logged in to the application.

In the final phase, we are going to implement an error message that is shown to a user if authentication fails. We are using the Snackbar MUI component to show the message:

1. Add the following import to the Login.js file:

```
import Snackbar from '@mui/material/Snackbar';
```

2. Add a new state called open to control the Snackbar visibility:

```
const [open, setOpen] = useState(false);
```

3. Add the Snackbar component to the return statement:

```
<Snackbar
  open={open}
  autoHideDuration={3000}
  onClose={() => setOpen(false)}
  message="Login failed: Check your username and
     password"
/>
```

4. Open the `Snackbar` component if authentication fails, by setting the `open` state value to `true`:

```
const login = () => {
    fetch(SERVER_URL + 'login', {
      method: 'POST',
      headers: { 'Content-Type':'application/json' },
      body: JSON.stringify(user)
    })
    .then(res => {
      const jwtToken = res.headers.get('Authorization');
      if (jwtToken !== null) {
        sessionStorage.setItem("jwt", jwtToken);
        setAuth(true);
      }
      else {
        setOpen(true);
      }
    })
    .catch(err => console.error(err))
}
```

If you now log in with the wrong credentials, you will see the following message:

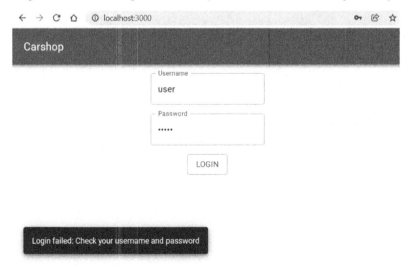

Figure 14.7 – Login failed

The logout functionality is much more straightforward to implement. You basically just have to remove the token from the session storage and change the `isAuthenticated` state value to `false`, as shown in the following source code:

```
const logout = () => {
    sessionStorage.removeItem("jwt");
    setAuth(false);
}
```

Now, we are ready with our car application.

Summary

In this chapter, we learned how to implement a login functionality for our frontend when we are using JWT authentication. Following successful authentication, we used session storage to save the token that we received from the backend. The token was then used in all requests that we sent to the backend; therefore, we had to modify our CRUD functionalities to work with authentication properly.

In the next chapter, we will deploy our application to Heroku, as we demonstrate how to create Docker containers.

Questions

1. How should you create a login form?
2. How should you log in to the backend using JWT?
3. How should you store tokens in session storage?
4. How should you send a token to the backend in CRUD functions?

Further reading

Packt has other great resources available for learning about React. These are as follows:

*   *React - The Complete Guide*, by *Academind GmbH*: `https://www.packtpub.com/product/react-the-complete-guide-includes-hooks-react-router-and-redux-2021-updated-second-edition-video/9781801812603`

*   *React 17 Design Patterns and Best Practices - Third Edition*, by *Carlos Santana Roldán*: `https://www.packtpub.com/product/react-17-design-patterns-and-best-practices-third-edition/978800560444`

15
Deploying Your Application

This chapter will explain how to deploy your backend and frontend to a server. Successful deployment is a key part of the software development process, and it is important to learn how a modern deployment process works. There are a variety of cloud servers or **PaaS** (short for **Platform-as-a-Service**) providers available, such as **Amazon Web Services (AWS)**, DigitalOcean, and Microsoft Azure. In this book, we are using Heroku and AWS, which support multiple programming languages that are used in web development. We will also show you how to use Docker containers in deployment.

In this chapter, we will cover the following topics:

- Deploying the backend
- Deploying the frontend
- Using Docker containers

Technical requirements

The Spring Boot application that we created in *Chapter 5, Securing and Testing Your Backend* is required (it is available on GitHub at `https://github.com/PacktPublishing/Full-Stack-Development-with-Spring-Boot-and-React/tree/main/Chapter05`), as is the React app that we used in *Chapter 13, Testing Your Frontend* (it is available on GitHub at `https://github.com/PacktPublishing/Full-Stack-Development-with-Spring-Boot-and-React/tree/main/Chapter13`).

Docker installation is necessary, and the following GitHub link will also be required: `https://github.com/PacktPublishing/Full-Stack-Development-with-Spring-Boot-and-React/tree/main/Chapter15`.

Deploying the backend

If you are going to use your own server, the easiest way to deploy the Spring Boot application is to use an executable **Java ARchive (JAR)** file. If you use Maven, an executable JAR file can be created using the Spring Boot Maven plugin and adding the following lines of code to your `pom.xml` file:

```
<plugin>
    <groupId>org.springframework.boot</groupId>
    <artifactId>spring-boot-maven-plugin</artifactId>
    <configuration>
        <executable>true</executable>
    </configuration>
</plugin>
```

Next, we have to build our project using the `mvn clean install` command. You can run a custom maven command in the Eclipse **integrated development environment (IDE)** by right-clicking **Project** in the project explorer, selecting **Run as | Maven Build…**, and typing `clean install` in the **Goals** field. That command creates a JAR file in the `target` folder, as illustrated in the following screenshot:

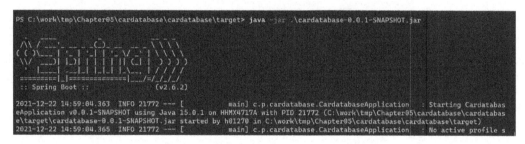

Name	Date modified	Type	Size
classes	22.12.2021 14:54	File folder	
generated-sources	22.12.2021 14:54	File folder	
generated-test-sources	22.12.2021 14:54	File folder	
maven-archiver	22.12.2021 14:54	File folder	
maven-status	22.12.2021 14:54	File folder	
surefire-reports	22.12.2021 14:54	File folder	
test-classes	22.12.2021 14:54	File folder	
cardatabase-0.0.1-SNAPSHOT.jar	22.12.2021 14:54	Executable Jar File	40 052 KB
cardatabase-0.0.1-SNAPSHOT.jar.original	22.12.2021 14:54	ORIGINAL File	20 KB

Figure 15.1 – Executable JAR file

In this case, you don't have to install a separate application server, because it is embedded in your JAR file. Then, you just have to run the JAR file using the `java -jar your_appfile.jar` Java command, as illustrated in the following screenshot:

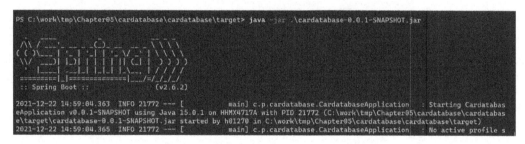

Figure 15.2 – Running the executable JAR files

Nowadays, cloud servers are the principal means of providing your application to end users. Next, we are going to deploy our backend to the **Heroku** cloud server (`https://www.heroku.com/`). Heroku offers a free account that you can use to deploy your own applications. With the free account, your applications go to sleep after 30 minutes of inactivity, and it takes a little bit more time to restart the application. However, the free account is sufficient for testing and hobby purposes.

For deployment, you can use Heroku's web-based **user interface (UI)**. The following steps will take you through the deployment process:

1. After you have created an account with Heroku, log in to the Heroku website. Navigate to the dashboard, which shows a list of your applications. There is a **New** button that opens a menu. Select the **Create new app** option from the menu, as illustrated in the following screenshot:

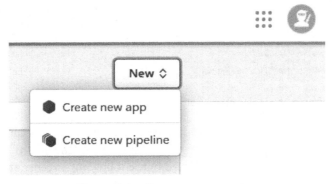

Figure 15.3 – Create new app option

2. Name your app, select a region, and press the **Create app** button, as illustrated in the following screenshot:

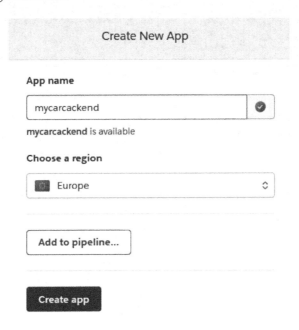

Figure 15.4 – Create app button

3. Select a deployment method. There are several options; in the following example, we are using the **GitHub** option. In this method, you first have to push your application to GitHub, and then link your GitHub repository to Heroku:

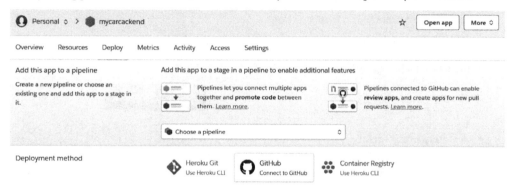

Figure 15.5 – Deployment method

4. Search for a repository you want to deploy to, as illustrated in the following screenshot, and then press the appropriate connect button. In our case, we're using the **Connect to GitHub** option:

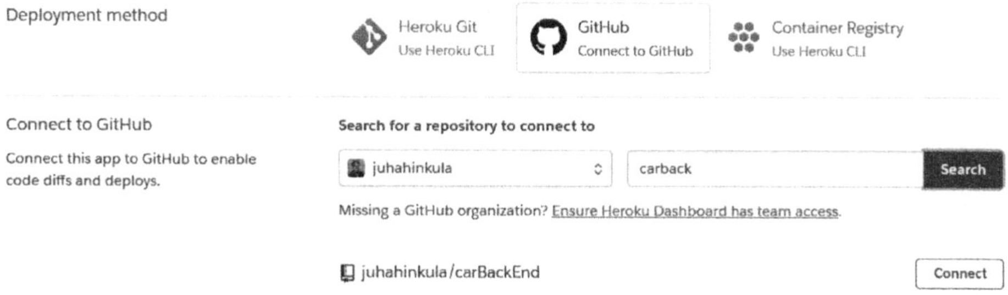

Figure 15.6 – Connect to GitHub option

5. Choose between an automatic and manual deployment. The automatic option deploys your app automatically when you push a new version to the connected GitHub repository. You also have to select a branch you want to deploy. We will use the manual option, which deploys the app when you press the **Deploy Branch** button. The options are illustrated in the following screenshot:

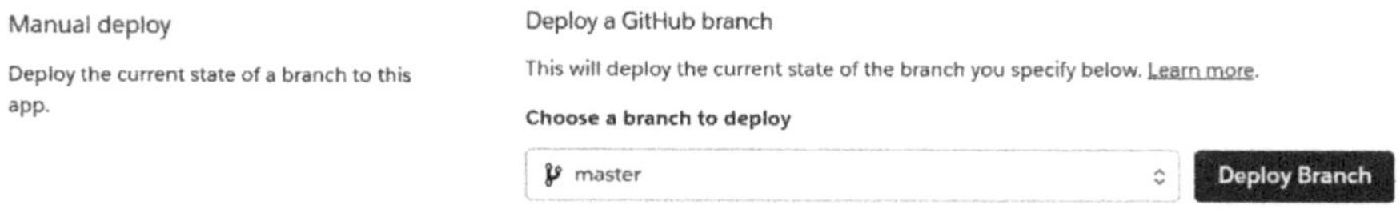

Figure 15.7 – Manual deployment

6.   Deployment starts, and you can see a build log. You should see a message that says **Your app was successfully deployed.**, as illustrated in the following screenshot:

Deploy a GitHub branch

This will deploy the current state of the branch you specify below. Learn more.

Choose a branch to deploy

⌥ master	⌄	Deploy Branch

Receive code from GitHub	⊘
Build **master** `6bcad422`	⊘
Release phase	⊘
Deploy to Heroku	✓

Your app was successfully deployed.

[📤 View]

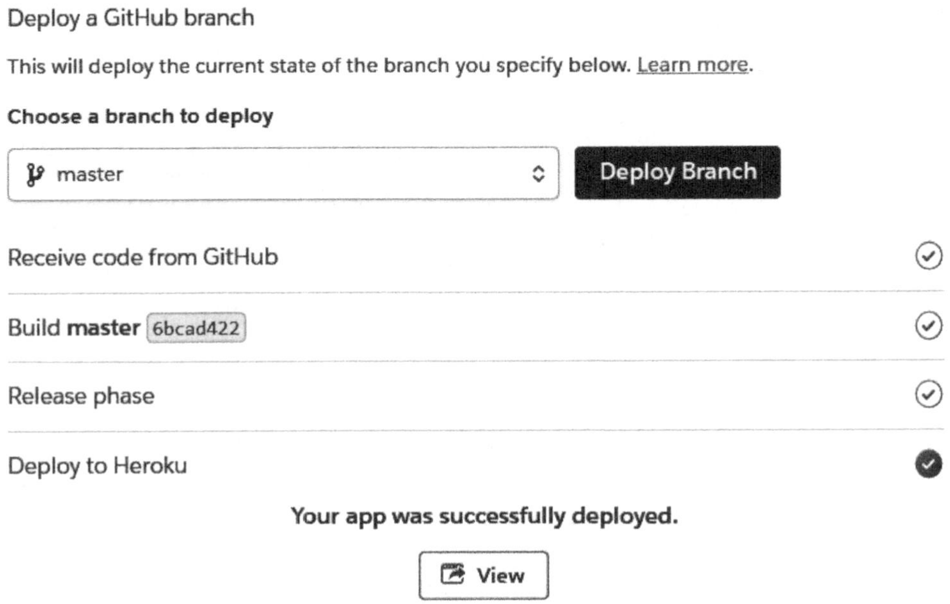

Figure 15.8 – Successful deployment

Now, your application is deployed to the Heroku cloud server. If you are using the **H2** in-memory database, this will be enough, and your application should work. We are using MariaDB; therefore, we have to install the database.

In Heroku, we can use **JawsDB**, which is available in Heroku as an add-on. JawsDB is a **Database as a Service (DBaaS)** provider that offers the MariaDB database, which can be used in Heroku. The following steps describe how to start using the database:

1.   Open a **Resources** tab in your Heroku app page and type jawsdb into the **Add-ons** search field, as illustrated in the following screenshot:

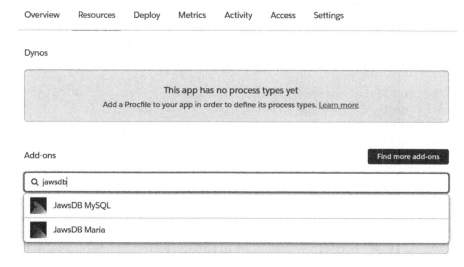

Figure 15.9 – JawsDB

2. Select **JawsDB Maria** from the drop-down list. Select a free plan and press the **Submit Order Form** button. Note that this step requires you to fill in the billing information in Heroku. After JawsDB is connected to your Heroku app, you can see the connection information of your database, as illustrated in the following screenshot:

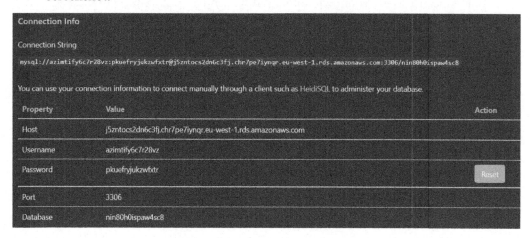

Figure 15.10 – Connection Info page

3. Change the database connection definition in the `application.properties` file to the values from the JawsDB **Connection Info** page. In the following example, we use a plain password, but it is recommended that you encrypt a password using—for example—the **Java Simplified Encryption (JASYPT)** library:

```
spring.datasource.url=jdbc:mariadb://j5zntocs2dnc3fj.
chr7pe6iynr.eu-west-1.rds.amazonaws.com:3306/
nik920iia4sc7
```
```
spring.datasource.username=arimtyfj6cag78vz
```
```
spring.datasource.password=zkjeftjukktfxtor
```
```
spring.datasource.driver-class-name=org.mariadb.jdbc.
Driver
```

4. With the free account, we can have a maximum of 10 concurrent connections to our database; therefore, we also have to add the following line of code to the `application.properties` file:

```
spring.datasource.max-active=10
```

5. Push your changes to GitHub and deploy your app in Heroku. Now, your application is ready, and you can test that with Postman. The **Uniform Resource Locator (URL)** of the app is `https://mycarbackend.herokuapp.com/`, but you can also use your own domain. If we send a `POST` request to the `/login` endpoint with the credentials, we can get a token in the response header. So, everything seems to work properly, as we can see here:

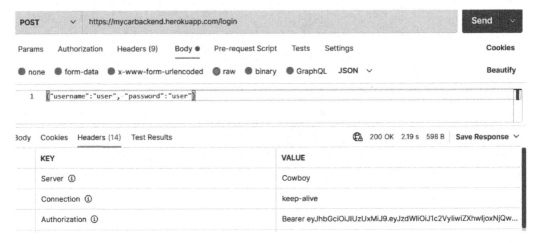

Figure 15.11 – Postman request

We can also connect to the JawsDB database using HeidiSQL.

We can watch application logs by selecting the **View logs** from the Heroku **More** menu, as illustrated in the following screenshot:

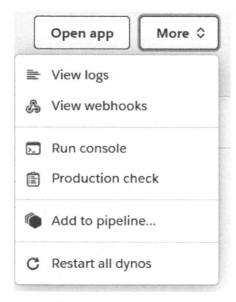

Figure 15.12 – More menu

The application log view looks like this:

```
Application Logs                                                                                                         ALL PROCESSES ◇

2021-12-23T10:54:49.769451+00:00 app[web.1]: Hibernate: update hibernate_sequence set next_val= ? where next_val=?
2021-12-23T10:54:49.773781+00:00 app[web.1]: Hibernate: insert into car (brand, color, model, owner, price, register_number, year, id) values (?, ?, ?, ?, ?, ?, ?, ?)
2021-12-23T10:54:49.781354+00:00 app[web.1]: Hibernate: insert into user (password, role, username) values (?, ?, ?)
2021-12-23T10:54:49.789597+00:00 app[web.1]: Hibernate: insert into user (password, role, username) values (?, ?, ?)
2021-12-23T10:56:07.300042+00:00 app[web.1]: 2021-12-23 10:56:07.299  INFO 4 --- [io-37459-exec-3] o.a.c.c.C.[Tomcat].[localhost].[/]       : Initializing Spring
FrameworkServlet 'dispatcherServlet'
2021-12-23T10:56:07.300162+00:00 app[web.1]: 2021-12-23 10:56:07.300  INFO 4 --- [io-37459-exec-3] o.s.web.servlet.DispatcherServlet        : FrameworkServlet
'dispatcherServlet': initialization started
2021-12-23T10:56:07.319174+00:00 app[web.1]: 2021-12-23 10:56:07.318  INFO 4 --- [io-37459-exec-3] o.s.web.servlet.DispatcherServlet        : FrameworkServlet
'dispatcherServlet': initialization completed in 18 ms
2021-12-23T10:56:08.614814+00:00 app[web.1]: 2021-12-23 10:56:08.614  INFO 4 --- [io-37459-exec-3] o.h.h.i.QueryTranslatorFactoryInitiator  : HHH000397: Using
ASTQueryTranslatorFactory
```

Figure 15.13 – Log view

Now, we are ready to deploy our frontend.

Deploying the frontend

You can deploy your frontend to Heroku as well, but we will now use **AWS Amplify** for the deployment.

First, we have to change our REST API URL. Open your frontend project with **Visual Studio Code** (**VS Code**) and open the `constants.js` file in the editor. Change the `SERVER_URL` constant to match your backend's URL, as follows, and save the changes:

```
export const SERVER_URL = 'https://carbackend.herokuapp.com/';
```

Then, push your code to GitHub and follow the next steps:

1. Log in to the Amplify console (`https://console.aws.amazon.com/amplify/home`).

2. Press the **Get started** button under **Amplify Hosting**, as illustrated in the following screenshot:

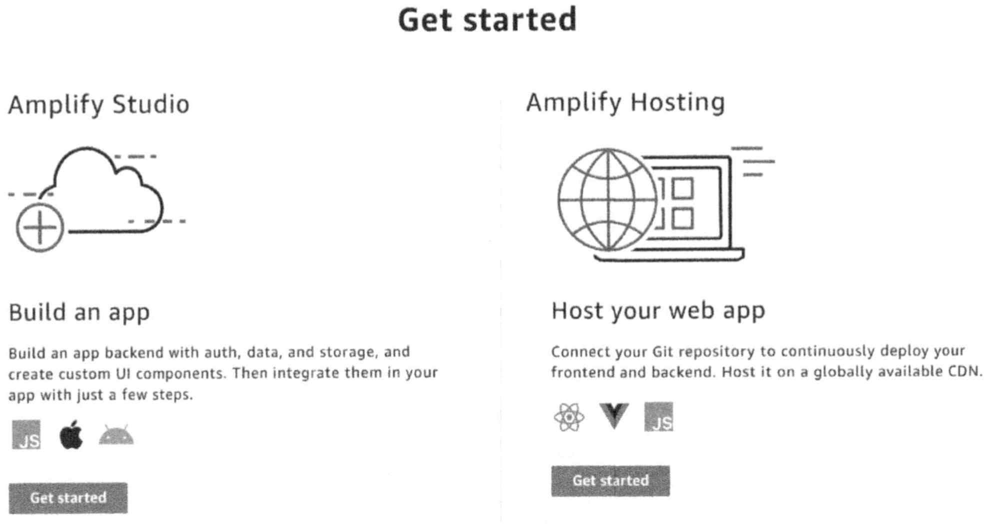

Figure 15.14 – Amplify Hosting

3. Select **GitHub** and press the **Continue** button, as illustrated in the following screenshot. First, you have to link your GitHub account to Amplify:

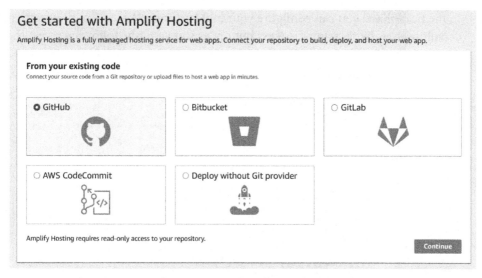

Figure 15.15 – GitHub repository

4. Next, select the repository and branch where your frontend exists and press the **Next** button, as illustrated in the following screenshot:

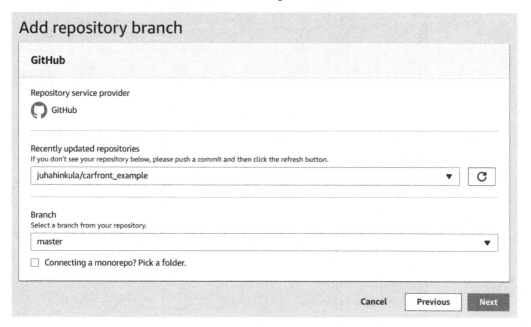

Figure 15.16 – Selecting a repository

5. In the next phase, you can configure your build settings. We can continue with the default settings by pressing the **Next** button, as shown in the following screenshot:

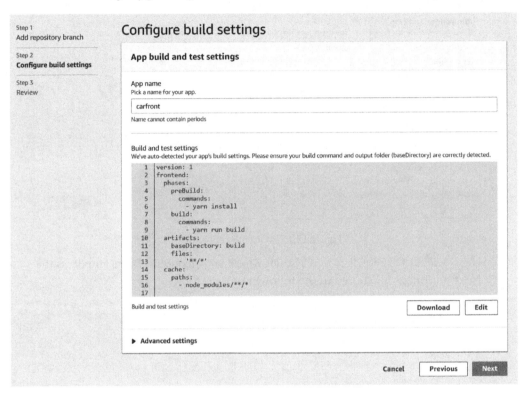

Figure 15.17 – Build settings

6. Then, you can review your settings and start deployment by pressing the **Save and deploy** button, as shown in the following screenshot:

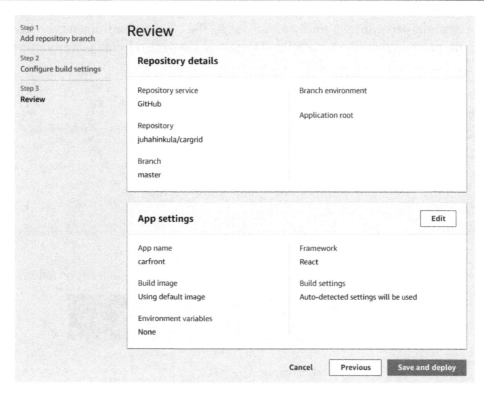

Figure 15.18 – Review settings

7. Now, the deployment starts, and you can see a progress graph on this page, as illustrated in the following screenshot:

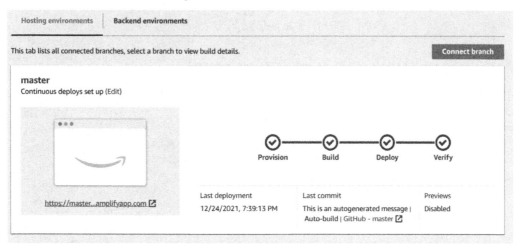

Figure 15.19 – Deployment

After the deployment is finished, you can get the URL of your frontend app from the previous screen or by selecting **Domain management** from the **App settings** menu, as illustrated in the following screenshot:

Figure 15.20 – Domain management

If you navigate to your frontend URL, you should see the login form, as follows:

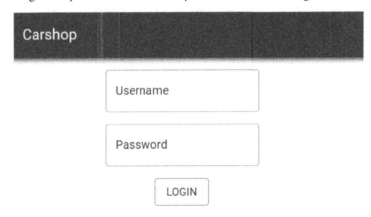

Figure 15.21 – Login screen

We have now deployed our frontend and we can continue with containers.

Using Docker containers

Docker is a container platform that makes software development, deployment, and shipping easier. Containers are lightweight and executable software packages that include everything that is needed to run software. In this section, we are creating a container from our Spring Boot backend, as follows:

1. Install Docker on your workstation. You can find the installation packages at `https://www.docker.com/get-docker`. There are installation packages for multiple platforms, and if you have a Windows operating system, you can go through the installation wizard using the default settings. After the installation, you can check the current version by typing the following command in the terminal:

```
heroku --version
```

2. First, we have to create an executable JAR file from our Spring Boot application, just as we did at the beginning of this chapter. Right-click your project in the project explorer and select **Run as | Maven build...** from the menu. Select your project in the **Base directory** field, using the **Workspace...** button. Type `clean install` into the **Goals** field and press the **Run** button. The process is illustrated in the following screenshot:

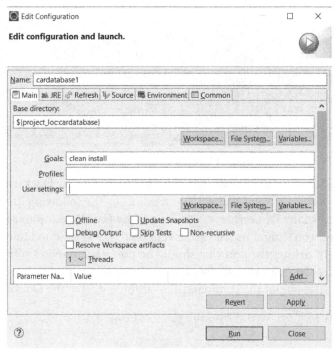

Figure 15.22 – Edit configuration and launch

3. Once the build is finished, you can find the executable JAR file from the /target folder, as follows:

classes	22.12.2021 15:06	File folder	
generated-sources	22.12.2021 14:54	File folder	
generated-test-sources	22.12.2021 14:54	File folder	
maven-archiver	22.12.2021 14:54	File folder	
maven-status	22.12.2021 14:54	File folder	
surefire-reports	22.12.2021 14:54	File folder	
test-classes	22.12.2021 14:54	File folder	
cardatabase-0.0.1-SNAPSHOT.jar	22.12.2021 14:54	Executable Jar File	40 052 KB

Figure 15.23 – Executable JAR file

4. You can test that the build has executed correctly by running the JAR file with the following command:

```
java -jar .\cardatabase-0.0.1-SNAPSHOT.jar
```

5. You'll see the application's starting messages, and finally, your application will be running, as illustrated in the following screenshot:

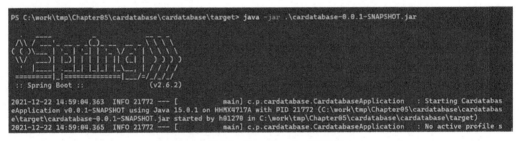

Figure 15.24 – Running the JAR file

6. Containers are defined by using **Dockerfiles**. Create a new Dockerfile in the root folder of your project and name it Dockerfile. The following lines of code show the contents of the Dockerfile. FROM defines the **Java Development Kit (JDK)** version, and you should use the same version that you used to build your JAR file. EXPOSE defines the port that should be published outside of the container. COPY copies the JAR file to the container's filesystem and renames it app.jar. ENTRYPOINT defines the command-line arguments that the Docker container runs:

```
FROM adoptopenjdk/openjdk11:latest

VOLUME /tmp

EXPOSE 8080
```

```
ARG JAR FILE
COPY target/cardatabase-0.0.1-SNAPSHOT.jar app.jar
ENTRYPOINT ["java","-jar","/app.jar"]
```

7. Create a container with the following command. With the -t argument, we can give a friendly name to our container:

```
docker build -t carbackend .
```

At the end of the build, you should see a Building FINISHED message, as illustrated in the following screenshot:

Figure 15.25 – Docker build

8. Check the list of containers using the docker image ls command, as follows:

Figure 15.26 – Docker images

9. Run the container with the following command:

```
docker run -p 4000:8080 carbackend
```

The Spring Boot application starts, but it ends with an error because we are trying to access the localhost database. The localhost now points to the container itself, and there is no MariaDB database installed.

10. We will create our own container for MariaDB. You can pull the latest MariaDB database from Docker Hub using the following command:

```
docker pull mariadb:latest
```

After the `pull` command has finished, you can check that a new `mariadb` container exists by typing the `docker image ls` command again, as follows:

```
PS C:\work\tmp\Chapter05\cardatabase\cardatabase> docker image ls
REPOSITORY      TAG       IMAGE ID        CREATED         SIZE
carbackend      latest    5e0f78efc3d2    18 minutes ago  146MB
mariadb         latest    e2278f24ac88    6 weeks ago     410MB
PS C:\work\tmp\Chapter05\cardatabase\cardatabase>
```

Figure 15.27 – Docker images

11. Next, we run the `mariadb` container. The following command sets the root user password and creates a new database, called `cardb`, that we need for our Spring Boot application:

```
docker run –name cardb -e MYSQL_ROOT_PASSWORD=your_pwd -e
MYSQL_DATABASE=cardb mariadb
```

12. Now, we have to change the data source URL of our Spring Boot application. Open the `application.properties` file of your application and change the `spring.datasource.url` value to the following:

```
spring.datasource.url=jdbc:mariadb://mariadb:3306/cardb
```

After the changes, you have to recreate the JAR file and Spring Boot container, as we did previously. Before you can recreate the container, you have to delete the old one first by using the following command:

```
docker image rm carbackend --force
```

13. After you have created a new `carbackend` container, we can run our Spring Boot container and link the MariaDB container to it using the following command. This command defines that our Spring Boot container can access the MariaDB container using the `mariadb` name:

```
docker run -p 8080:8080 --name carapp --link
cardb:mariadb -d carbackend
```

14. Now, when our application and database are running, we can access the Spring Boot application logs using the following command:

```
docker logs carapp
```

15. And we can see here that our application is up and running:

```
Hibernate: select nextval(hibernate_sequence)
Hibernate: select nextval(hibernate_sequence)
Hibernate: insert into owner (firstname, lastname, ownerid) values (?, ?, ?)
Hibernate: insert into owner (firstname, lastname, ownerid) values (?, ?, ?)
Hibernate: select nextval(hibernate_sequence)
Hibernate: select nextval(hibernate_sequence)
Hibernate: select nextval(hibernate_sequence)
Hibernate: insert into car (brand, color, model, owner, price, register_number, year, id) values (?, ?, ?, ?, ?, ?, ?, ?
)
Hibernate: insert into car (brand, color, model, owner, price, register_number, year, id) values (?, ?, ?, ?, ?, ?, ?, ?
)
Hibernate: insert into car (brand, color, model, owner, price, register_number, year, id) values (?, ?, ?, ?, ?, ?, ?, ?
)
Hibernate: select car0_.id as id1_0_, car0_.brand as brand2_0_, car0_.color as color3_0_, car0_.model as model4_0_, car0
_.owner as owner8_0_, car0_.price as price5_0_, car0_.register_number as register6_0_, car0_.year as year7_0_ from car c
ar0_
2021-12-25 18:15:27.794  INFO 1 --- [           main] c.p.cardatabase.CardatabaseApplication   : Ford Mustang
2021-12-25 18:15:27.795  INFO 1 --- [           main] c.p.cardatabase.CardatabaseApplication   : Nissan Leaf
2021-12-25 18:15:27.795  INFO 1 --- [           main] c.p.cardatabase.CardatabaseApplication   : Toyota Prius
Hibernate: insert into user (password, role, username) values (?, ?, ?)
Hibernate: insert into user (password, role, username) values (?, ?, ?)
```

Figure 15.28 – Application log

We can see that our application has started successfully, and the demonstration data has been inserted into the database that exists in the MariaDB container.

Summary

In this chapter, you learned how to deploy the Spring Boot application. We went through the different deployment options for the Spring Boot application and deployed the application to Heroku. Next, we deployed our React frontend using AWS Amplify. Finally, we used Docker to create containers from our Spring Boot application and the MariaDB database.

In the next chapter, we will cover some more technologies and best practices that you should explore.

Questions

1. How should you create a Spring Boot executable JAR file?

2. How should you deploy a Spring Boot application to Heroku?

3. How should you deploy a React app using AWS Amplify?

4. What is Docker?

5. How should you create a Spring Boot application container?

6. How should you create a MariaDB container?

Further reading

Packt Publishing has other great resources available for learning about React, Spring Boot, and Docker. A couple of them are listed here:

- *Mastering Docker*, by *Russ McKendrick* (`https://subscription.packtpub.com/book/cloud_and_networking/9781839216572/1`)

- *Docker for Developers*, by *Russ McKendrick* and *Scott Gallagher* (`https://subscription.packtpub.com/book/cloud_and_networking/9781789536058/1`)

16
Best Practices

This chapter will go through some points that you should know if you want to become a full stack developer, or if you want to progress further in your software development career. We will also go over some best practices that are worth keeping in mind when you're working in the field of software development.

In this chapter, we will answer the following questions:

- What kind of technologies should you know?
- Which best practices are important to you?

What to learn next

To become a full stack developer, you have to be able to work with both the backend and the frontend. That sounds like quite a challenging task, but if you focus on the right things and don't try to master everything, it is possible. Nowadays, the technology stack available is huge, and you might often wonder what you should learn next. There are multiple factors that can give you a few hints about where to go next. One way to find out is to browse job opportunities and see which technologies companies are looking for.

There are multiple approaches, and no single right path, when it comes to setting out on learning new technology. Studying a course in web programming is a really popular starting point, and it gives you the basic knowledge to start the learning process. The process is never-ending because technologies are developing and changing all the time.

An understanding of the following technologies is necessary if you want to become a full stack developer. This is not a complete list, but it is a good starting point.

HTML

HTML is the most fundamental thing that you should learn in web development. You don't have to master all the details of HTML, but you should have a good basic knowledge of it. HTML5 introduced a lot of new features that are also worth learning.

CSS

CSS is also a very basic thing to learn. One good aspect is the fact that there are lots of good tutorials available for both HTML and CSS. It is worthwhile learning about the use of some CSS libraries, such as Bootstrap, which is widely used. CSS preprocessors, such as SASS and Less, are also worth learning.

HTTP

The **HTTP** protocol is key to developing web applications and RESTful web services. You have to understand the basics of HTTP and know its limitations. You should also know what kinds of methods exist and how to use these with different programming languages.

JavaScript

JavaScript is definitely a programming language that you should master. Without JavaScript skills, it is really hard to work with modern frontend development. ES6 is also good to learn because it makes JavaScript coding cleaner and more efficient.

A backend programming language

It's hard to survive without knowing a few programming languages. If JavaScript is used for frontend development, it can also be used in the backend with Node.js. That is the benefit of Node.js; you can use one programming language in both the frontend and the backend. Other popular languages for backend development are Java, C#, Python, and PHP. All these languages also have good backend frameworks you can use.

Some frontend libraries and frameworks

In this book, we used React.js in the frontend, which is currently a popular option, but there are many other options that are also good, such as Angular and Vue.js.

Databases

You should also know how to use databases with your backend programming language. The database can be either a SQL or a NoSQL database, and it is good to know both options. You should also know how performance can be optimized with the database you are using and the queries you are executing.

Version control

Version control is something that you can't live without. Nowadays, Git is a really popular version control system, and it's really important to know how to use it. It is also worthwhile getting familiar with repository management services, such as GitHub and GitLab.

Useful tools

There are also many different tools that can help to make your development process more efficient. Here, we are just mentioning a number of tools that might be useful for you. Gulp.js is an open source JavaScript toolkit to automate your tasks in the development process. Grunt is similar to the JavaScript task runner, which you can use to automate your process. webpack is a JavaScript module bundler that creates static assets from your dependencies. `create-react-app`, which we used in the previous chapters, actually uses webpack under the hood.

Security

You have to know the basics of web security and how to handle these issues in web development. A good way to start learning is to read the *OWASP Top 10* project (`https://owasp.org/www-project-top-ten/`). Then, you have to learn how to handle these issues with the frameworks you are using.

Best practices

Software development always involves teamwork, and therefore, it is really important that everyone in a team uses common best practices. Here, we will go through some basic things that you have to take into account. This is not the whole list, but we will try to concentrate on some basic things that you should know.

Coding conventions

Coding conventions are guidelines that describe how the code should be written in a specific programming language. It makes the code more readable and easier to maintain. Naming conventions define how variables, methods, and more should be named. Naming is really important because it helps developers understand the purpose of a certain unit in a program.

The layout convention defines how the structure of the source code should look – for example, indenting and the use of spaces. The commenting convention defines how the source code should be commented on. Quite often, it is good to use some standardized ways of commenting, such as Javadoc with Java.

Most software development environments and editors offer tools that help you with code conventions. You can also use code formatters, such as Prettier for JavaScript.

Choosing the proper tools

You should always choose the proper tools that best fit your software development process. This makes your process more efficient and also helps you in the development life cycle. There are many tools to automate tasks in the development process, and it is a good way of avoiding mistakes that occur in repetitive tasks. Of course, the tools you use will depend on the process and the technologies you're using.

Choosing the proper technologies

When starting to develop an application, one of the first things to decide is which technologies (programming language, frameworks, databases, and so on) you should use. Quite often, it feels safe to select technologies that you have always used, but that's not always the optimal choice. The application itself normally imposes a number of limitations in relation to the technologies that you can use.

For example, if you have to create a mobile application, there are several technologies that you can use; but if you have to develop a similar application that you have made many times, it might be wiser to use technologies that you are already very familiar with.

Minimizing the amount of coding

A common good practice is to minimize the amount of coding. This is really sensible because it makes code maintenance and testing much easier. DRY (short for **Don't Repeat Yourself**) is a common principle in software development. The basic idea of DRY is to reduce the amount of code by avoiding repetition in it.

It is always a good practice to split your source code into smaller components because smaller units are always easier to manage. Of course, the optimal structure depends on the programming language you are using. One good statement is also **Keep it Simple, Stupid (KISS)**, which should guide you in the right direction.

Summary

In this book, we covered the technologies that you should be familiar with if you want to become a full stack developer. We started to develop our backend using the Spring Boot framework. We also learned to create the REST API and how to secure your backend. Next, we started to learn the basics of the React frontend library. Then, we developed a frontend to our existing backend using React. We also learned the basics of unit testing and how to deploy your frontend and backend.

Questions

1. Why are coding conventions important?
2. Why should you try to avoid excessive coding?
3. Why are naming conventions important?

Further reading

Packt has other great resources available for learning about full stack development. These are as follows:

- *The Complete JavaScript Developer: A Primer to Full Stack JS [Video]*, by *Full Stack Training Limited* (`https://www.packtpub.com/product/the-complete-javascript-developer-a-primer-to-full-stack-js-video/9781789346022`)

- *Full Stack Development with JHipster*, by *Deepu K Sasidharan* and *Sendil Kumar N* (`https://www.packtpub.com/application-development/full-stack-development-jhipster`)

- *Fundamentals of Continuous Delivery Pipeline [Video]*, by *Rafał Leszko* (`https://www.packtpub.com/networking-and-servers/fundamentals-continuous-delivery-pipeline-video`)

Assessments

Chapter 1

1. **Spring Boot** is a Java-based web application framework that is based on Spring. With Spring Boot, you can develop standalone web applications with embedded application servers.

2. **Eclipse** is an open source **integrated development environment** (**IDE**), and it is mostly used for Java programming, but it supports multiple other programming languages as well.

3. **Maven** is an open source software project-management tool. Maven can manage builds, documentation, testing, and more in the software development project.

4. The easiest way to start a new Spring Boot project is to create it with the Spring Initializr web page. This creates a skeleton for your project with the modules that you need.

5. If you are using the Eclipse IDE, you just activate your main class and press the **Run** button. You can also use the Maven `mvn spring-boot:run` command to run an application.

6. The Spring Boot starter package provides logging features for you. You can define the level of logging in the `application.properties` settings file.

7. The error and log messages can be seen in the Eclipse IDE console after you run the application.

Chapter 2

1. **Depenency Injection** (**DI**) is software development technology that helps the interaction between the classes, but at the same time keeps the classes independent.

2. The easiest way to utilize DI in Spring Boot is to use `@Autowired` annotation.

Chapter 3

1.   **ORM** is a technique that allows you to fetch and manipulate data from a database using an object-oriented programming paradigm. JPA provides object-relational mapping for Java developers. Hibernate is a Java-based JPA implementation.

2.   The `entity` class is just a standard Java class that is annotated with the `@Entity` annotation. You have to implement constructors, fields, getters and setters inside the class. The unique ID field(s) are annotated with the `@Id` annotation.

3.   You have to create a new interface that extends the Spring Data `CrudRepository` interface. You define the entity and the type of the id field in the type arguments—for example, `<Car, Long>`.

4.   The `CrudRepository` provides all CRUD operations to your entity. You can create, read, update, and delete your entities using the `CrudRepository`.

5.   You have to create entity classes and link the entities using the `@OneToMany` and `@ManyToOne` annotations.

6.   You can add demo data to your main application class using `CommandLineRunner`.

7.   Define the endpoint for the H2 console in your `application.properties` file and enable it. Then you can access the H2 console by navigating to the defined endpoint with a web browser.

8.   You have to add the MariaDB dependency to the `pom.xml` file and define the database connection settings in the `application.properties` file. Remove the H2 database dependency from the pom.xml file, if you have used that.

Chapter 4

1.   **REST** is an architectural style for creating web services, and it defines a set of constraints.

2.   The easiest way to create a RESTful web service with Spring Boot is to use the Spring Data REST starter package. By default, the Spring Data REST package finds all public repositories and creates automatically RESTful web services for your entities.

3.   You can send a `GET` request to the endpoint of the entity. For example, if you have an entity class called `Car`, the Spring Data REST package creates an endpoint called `/cars` that can be used to fetch all cars.

4.   You can send a `DELETE` request to the endpoint of the individual entity item. For example, `/cars/1` deletes a car with the ID 1.

5. You can send a POST request to the endpoint of the entity. The header must contain the Content-Type field with the value application/json. The new item will be embedded in the request body.

6. You can send a PATCH request to the endpoint of the entity. The header must contain the Content-Type field with the value application/json. The updated item will be embedded in the request body.

7. You have to annotate your repository using the @RepositoryRestResource annotation. The query parameters are annotated using the @Param annotation.

Chapter 5

1. Spring Security provides security services for Java-based web applications.

2. You have to add the Spring Security starter package dependency to your pom.xml file. You can configure Spring Security by creating a security configuration class.

3. **JWT** (short for **JSON Web Token**) is a compact way to implement authentication in modern web applications. The size of the token is small, and so it can be sent in the URL, either in the POST parameter or inside the header.

4. You can use the Java JWT library—that is, the JSON web token library for Java. The authentication service class adds and reads the token. The filter classes handle the login and authentication process.

5. You have to add the Spring Boot test starter package to your pom.xml file. The Spring Boot test starter package provides a lot of nice testing utilities—for example, JUnit, AssertJ, and Mockito. When using the JUnit, the basic test classes are annotated with the @SpringBootTest annotation, and the test methods should start with the @Test annotation.

6. The test cases can be easily executed with the Eclipse IDE by running the test classes (**Run | JUnit test**). The test results can be seen in the JUnit tab.

Chapter 6

1. Node.js is an open source, JavaScript-based, server-side environment. Npm is a package manager for JavaScript.

2. You can find the installation packages and instructions for installing these on multiple operating systems at https://nodejs.org/en/download.

3. **Visual Studio Code (VS Code)** is an open source code editor for multiple programming languages.

4. You can find the installation packages and instructions for installing this on multiple operating systems at `https://code.visualstudio.com`.

5. You can create an app using the `npx create-react-app projectname` command.

6. You can run the app using the `npm start` or `yarn start` command.

7. You can start by modifying the `App.js` file, and when you save the modification, you will see the changes immediately in the web browser.

Chapter 7

1. Components are the basic building blocks of React apps. The React component can be created using a JavaScript function or the ES6 class.

2. The props and state are the input data for rendering the component. They are JavaScript objects, and the component is re-rendered when the props or state change.

3. The data flow goes from the parent component to the child.

4. The components that only have props are called **stateless components**. The components that have both props and a state are called stateful components.

5. JSX is the syntax extension for JavaScript, and it is recommended that you use it with React.

6. Handling events in React is similar to handling DOM element events. The difference in React is that event naming uses the camelCase naming convention—for example, `onClick` or `onSubmit`.

7. We will often want to invoke a JavaScript function that has access to form data after the form submission. Therefore, we have to disable default behavior using the `preventDefault()` function. You can use the input field's `onChange` event handler to save the values from the input field to the state.

Chapter 8

1. A promise is an object that represents the result of an asynchronous operation. The use of promises simplifies the code when performing asynchronous calls.

2. The fetch API provides the `fetch()` method that you can use to make asynchronous network calls using JavaScript.

3. When using the REST API, it is recommended that you use the `useEffect` hook function if the request is sent after the first render.

4. You can access the response data using the promises with the fetch() method. The data from the response is saved to the state and the component is re-rendered when the state changes.

Chapter 9

1. You can find React components from multiple sources—for example, https:// js.coach/ or https://github.com/brillout/awesome-react-components.

2. You can install React components using the npm or yarn package managers. If you are using npm, use the npm install <package_name> command.

3. First, you have to install the *Ag-grid* component. After the installation, you can use the AgGridReact component in your component. You have to define the data and the columns using the AgGridReact component props. The data can be an array of objects.

4. First, you have to install the MUI component library. After the library is installed, you can start to use components. The documentation of the different components can be found at https://mui.com.

5. Routing can be implemented using the React Router component, which can be found at https://github.com/ReactTraining/react-router.

Chapter 10

1. With the mock-up, it is much easier to discuss needs with the client before you start to write any actual code. Changes to the mock up are really easy and quick to make, compared to modifications with real frontend source code.

2. You can modify the security configuration class to allow access to all endpoints without authentication.

Chapter 11

1. First, you have to call the REST API using the fetch() method. Then, you can access the response data using the promises with the fetch() method. The data from the response is saved to the state and the component is re-rendered when the state changes.

2. You have to send a DELETE method request using the fetch() method. The endpoint of the call is the link to the item that you want to delete.

3. You have to send a POST method request to the entity endpoint using the fetch() method. The added item should be embedded in the body. You have to add the Content-Type header with the application/json value.

4. You have to send a PATCH method request using the fetch() method. The endpoint of the call is the link to the item that you want to update. The updated item should be embedded in the body. You have to add the Content-Type header with the application/json value.

5. You can use a third-party React component, such as MUI SnackBar, to show toast messages.

6. You can use a third-party React component, such as Ag-grid export functionality to export data to a CSV file.

Chapter 12

1. MUI is the component library for React, and it implements Google's material design.

2. First, you have to install the MUI library using npm. Then you can start to use components from the library. The documentation of the different components can be found at https://mui.com/.

3. To use icons, you have to install @mui/icons-material package using npm. Then you can use icons with for example, IconButton component.

Chapter 13

1. **Jest** is a test library for JavaScript developed by Facebook.

2. Create a test file using the .test.js extension. Implement your test cases inside the file. You can run the tests using the npm run test command.

3. You can use fireEvent method that React testing library provides.

4. For snapshot testing, you have to install the react-test-render package and import renderer to your test file. Implement your snapshot test cases inside the file and run the tests using the npm run test command.

Chapter 14

1. You have to create a new component that renders input fields for the username and the password. The component also contains a button that calls the /login endpoint when the button is pressed.

2. The call from the login component is made using the `POST` method and a user object is embedded in the body. If the authentication succeeds, the backend sends the token back in the Authorization header.

3. The token can be saved to session storage using the `sessionStorage.setItem()` method.

4. The token has to be included in the request's Authorization header.

Chapter 15

1. You can create an executable JAR file by using the Maven `mvn clean install` command.

2. The easiest way to deploy a Spring Boot application is to push your application source code to GitHub and link your GitHub repository to your app in Heroku.

3. The easiest way to deploy a Spring Boot application is to push your application source code to GitHub and link your GitHub repository to your app in AWS Amplify.

4. Docker is a container platform that makes software development, deployment, and shipping easier. Containers are lightweight and executable software packages that include everything that is needed to run software.

5. The Spring Boot application is just an executable JAR file that can be executed with Java. You can use it to create a Docker container for your Spring Boot application in a similar way to creating one for any Java JAR application.

6. You can pull the latest MariaDB container from the Docker Hub using the Docker `docker pull mariadb:latest` command.

Chapter 16

1. It makes code more readable and easier to maintain. It also makes teamwork much easier because everyone is using the same structure in the coding.

2. It makes code more readable and easier to maintain. The testing of the code is easier.

3. It makes code more readable and easier to maintain. It also makes teamwork much easier because everyone is using the same naming convention in the coding.

Index

Other Books You May Enjoy

If you enjoyed this book, you may be interested in these other books by Packt:

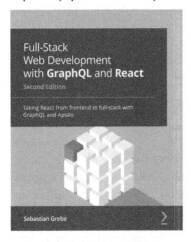

Full-Stack Web Development with GraphQL and React

Sebastian Grebe

ISBN: 978-1-80107-788-0

Build a GraphQL API by implementing models and schemas with Apollo and Sequelize

Set up an Apollo Client and build frontend components using React

Write Reusable React components and use React Hooks

Authenticate and query user data using GraphQL

Use Mocha to write test cases for your full-stack application

Modern API Development with Spring and Spring Boot

Sourabh Sharma

ISBN: 978-1-80056-247-9

- Understand RESTful API development, its design paradigm, and its best practices
- Become well versed in Spring's core components for implementing RESTful web services
- Implement reactive APIs and explore async API development
- Apply Spring Security for authentication using JWT and authorization of requests
- Develop a React-based UI to consume APIs.

Packt is searching for authors like you

If you're interested in becoming an author for Packt, please visit `authors.packtpub.com` and apply today. We have worked with thousands of developers and tech professionals, just like you, to help them share their insight with the global tech community. You can make a general application, apply for a specific hot topic that we are recruiting an author for, or submit your own idea.

Share Your Thoughts

Now you've finished *Full Stack Development with Spring Boot and React*, we'd love to hear your thoughts! Scan the QR code below to go straight to the Amazon review page for this book and share your feedback or leave a review on the site that you purchased it from.

https://www.amazon.in/review/create-review/error?asin=1801816786

Your review is important to us and the tech community and will help us make sure we're delivering excellent quality content.

Made in the USA
Coppell, TX
02 July 2022

aSTIGMAtism In My Soul!

A Black American Males adventure from dead broke to millionaire to dead broke to "white collar crime" incarceration in the United States Federal Bureau of Prisons (The Feds) to back on top!

volume II

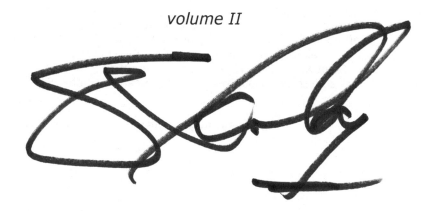